Highpoints

Highpoints

A 3,500-mile walk from John O'Groats to Land's End
via the highest point of every county

VICTORIA MORRIS

HAYLOFT

First published in Great Britain by Hayloft Publishing Ltd, 2020

A CIP catalogue record for this book is available from the British Library

ISBN 978-1-910237-55-7

Designed, printed and bound in the UK and EU

Hayloft policy is to use papers that are natural, renewable and recyclable products and
made from wood grown in sustainable forests. The logging and manufacturing processes
are expected to conform to the environmental regulations of the country of origin.

ClimatePartner.com/12667-2004-1004

This book was printed with the offset of carbon emissions
and support for forest protection in Pará, Brazil

Hayloft Publishing Ltd,
a company registered in England number 4802586
10 Kendal Fell Business Park, Kendal, LA9 5RR (registered office)
L'Ancien Presbytère, 21460 Corsaint, France (editorial office)

Email: books@hayloft.eu
Tel: 07971 352473
www.hayloft.eu

Contents

Prologue	*vii*
The Agony of Trees	1
Blue Remembered Hills	22
The Relocation of Slugs	42
Wrapped Between Borders	67
The Places We Know Well	87
Always Summer, Always Alone	113
Beyond Hope	125
'It *has* been known to rain in Wales'	147
Illegal Freedoms	168
Forgotten Familiarities	190
The Apathy of Trees	208
The Revenge of Slugs	221
Epilogue	251
Acknowledgements	255
Appendix 1: Walking by numbers	257
Appendix 2: Equipment	259
Appendix 3: Itinerary	263
Bibliography	277

No one can know the full value of summer
who has not known it in a land of mountains

John MacCulloch, 1824

Prologue

On the wall of my bedroom hangs an incomplete patchwork map of the British Isles, a ten-year work in progress. This map has its origins in my final year at university, when, having outlasted any natural affinity with my studies, I was spending an increasing proportion of the time walking, attempting to escape the confines of city and mind. My walks grew in length and ambition, to the point where a friend would enquire whether a proposed walk was 'better represented on a road atlas than an Ordnance Survey map,' before agreeing to accompany me. It was perhaps this phrase which inspired me to create the patchwork: a cloth atlas upon which I could track my wanderings in crewel embroidery. I purchased a paper map of the British Isles at ten miles to the inch to use as a template, sent out an appeal to friends and family for scraps of green and brown fabric, and began to sew.

Early adventures in map reading.

My efforts did not go entirely to plan: Cambridgeshire somehow ended up with a coastline; I muddled Greater Manchester and Cheshire, making the former a pleasant green and the latter an inky black; and I never did get round to adding Orkney and Shetland, which were inset on the paper map at a different scale, leaving me at a loss as to what size to make them or where to put them. Yet, by the end of the summer I had assembled something resembling the British mainland, which I could embroider and adorn with ribbons and buttons representing walking routes and favourite hills and places. As my fingers traced and cut and sewed, my mind began to dream of how I might connect these places on foot as well as in stitches. And thus my idea: to walk from John O'Groats to Land's End via the highest point of every county.

Throughout my life, I have looked to the hills for companionship and context. As children, my sister and I would climb the stairs to bed each night and part on the landing: she would turn right, towards the sodium glow of the street; I, left, looking eastward to the Forest of Bowland. I was determined as only a seven-year-old can be to befriend each fell, and would often creep out of bed while the rest of the household slept to trace the soft outlines of the hills against the night sky, or to watch the sunset burn itself out behind them.

Many family weekends were spent in the nearby Lake District. I summited my first Lakeland fell, Silver How, on 12 October 1986, at an age of less than two months – although it was the July of 1992 before I walked to the top of that same hill. One of the few photographs I possess of myself as a young child shows me on the summit of Loughrigg, above Grasmere, my right elbow just about level with the face-plate on the trig point.[1] Red socks rolled above the ankles of chocolate-coloured leather boots proclaim that this ascent was achieved by my own efforts.

Perhaps it is not surprising, then, that from a childhood bounded and defined by hills, I have grown into an adulthood in which I find myself inexorably drawn to the high and wild places.

As children do, I constructed my own reality from the world around me; and, because my home-town was a place where folk-memory still flowed strong, without realising it, I grew up years – if not decades – behind the present. I grew up in an insular town which saw Cumberland sausages and the *Westmorland Gazette* as evidence for the continued existence of Cumberland and Westmorland, and where the destruction of the castle by Oliver Cromwell's army was described with the same vehemence as the town council's proposals for a new housing estate on the site of a derelict oil depot.

---

1 This was the original face-plate; the trig point has since been re-built, with the new face-plate set lower into the column than the original.

Red socks on Loughrigg.

Insularity is a contradictory concept: to insulate is at once to safe-guard and to separate, to protect from bad influences and to keep the good at bay. To grow up in a hidebound northern market town is to live and breathe the bittersweet air of insularity.

Just as the coming of the railways dragged time across the country into conformance, so with the coming of the bus to secondary school I was ripped forwards to join the present day. From the time I caught up with reality, I have been completing a mental farewell tour, realising one by one that my childhood ideals no longer exist, and saying goodbye to them. Westmorland was expunged from the map before I was born. The Three Shires Stone is well and truly in one county. Trains are not pulled by steam-engines.

There came a day, too, when I woke to the realisation that the fells were only a small part of the view from my bedroom window. Out there, too, were the M6 motorway, the West Coast Main Line, the flood embankment and other man-made parts of the landscape that I had previously failed to acknowledge. I felt betrayed that the fells could have cheated me, by looming so large in my mind, yet being so small in the landscape.

In seeking to escape my insular childhood, barely a week after my eighteenth birthday, I left home to attend university in a place as far removed from the hills and high places as it is possible to get within the British Isles: the East Anglian fens.

Living in the south of England for the first time, I came to realise just how much the hills had meant to me, and became aware of a mountain-shaped hole in my life. Naturally, I joined a walking club, and it was here that I met Laurence, who, like me, had realised only after moving south that his soul had remained in the North Pennines of Tynedale, Weardale and Teesdale. As we came to know each other better, Laurence gradually taught me to hold something of the hills inside myself, to sustain myself through the agonisingly horizontal academic terms. Together, we shared memories of mountains climbed and dreams of the wild places waiting to be explored. Together, we delighted in the discovery that legs accustomed to ranging over Lake District fells can cover great swathes of fenland without tiring; and thus we began to find new ways to challenge ourselves: walking fifteen miles in a dead-straight line beside the Old Bedford River, or a non-stop eighty miles, or a plan to connect the highest point of every county…

In some ways, my County Tops walk was the natural combination of my lifelong love of hills and this relatively newly-discovered love of long-distance walking.

In other ways, my walk would be the physical undertaking of my farewell tour. It made perfect sense to me that I should walk between the highest points of the historic counties of Britain, rather than the modern administrative areas defined during the 1970s.[2] I would visit

---

2 For a fuller discussion of what constitutes an 'historic' county, see Appendix I.

Cumberland, Westmorland and other non-existent places, travelling in an outmoded way, shunning the trappings of the modern world. I would, at the same time, perpetuate my childhood fantasies, by seeking freedom amongst the hills I knew intimately, as well as those glimpsed only in my mind's eye.

In the decade that followed my graduation, the rise of Scottish nationalism rekindled debates over our concepts of nationhood and national identity. Then, as the position of the United Kingdom within the European Union was called into question, our island government sought to convince us that we could enjoy both aspects of insularity. But, as Benedict Anderson[3] asserted, nations are imagined communities. At such a time of re-examination and re-definition, it felt strangely appropriate to walk between imagined places and arbitrary objectives within an imagined national community.

Though I began to formulate my long walk whilst still a student, I was approaching thirty before my plans began to coalesce into reality and I had put aside what I considered sufficient savings to fund an eight-month absence from work. Around me, friends were beginning to settle down and start families. Friends with whom I'd tramped through midnight mid-winter mud, or ranged across Scottish moors were becoming teachers, engineers, city workers – in other words, respectable, normal. I watched their fitness slough away as their families grew in size. Camping no longer meant striding over mountains with your life in your rucksack, but the assembly of cavernous multi-roomed tents on formal, serviced campsites.

A further aspect of Anderson's theory is that a nation – like an island – is insular. An imagined nation excludes not only literal outsiders, but also those within the community who cannot readily be accommodated by its imagined national identity. Watching those around me find their societal niches, I found myself excluded, but willingly so, and recoiled against the very notion of being accommodated. I did not want to become respectable, or succumb to the temptations of normality. I realised that it was time to depart, before I, too, became ensnared by the everyday world.

---

3 Benedict Anderson, *Imagined Communities: Reflections on the Origin and Spread of Nationalism* (London: Verso, 1983).

Note

Sketch maps and sub-headings within chapters are intended to provide a sense of where I am within the country; a full itinerary is included in Appendix 3.

The Agony of Trees

Caithness – Sutherland – Ross and Cromarty

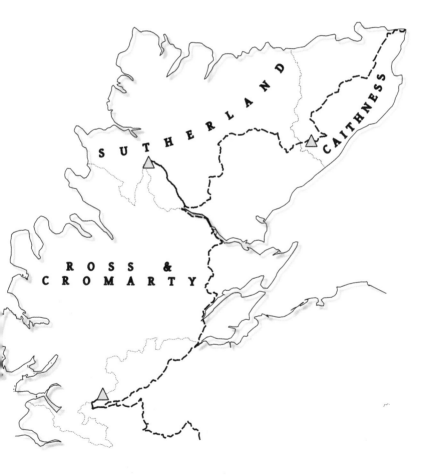

Morven (County Top of Caithness)

John O'Groats to Lairg. 104 miles, 2,490 metres ascent.
Tuesday 7th – Monday 13th March

As I step down from the bus into the deserted car park at John O'Groats, I reflect that – if all goes to plan – it will be seven or eight months before I next travel in a vehicle. I have set myself the challenge of reaching the highest point of every mainland county on foot only, and will not allow myself recourse to any other form of travel, even on rest days. A decade of anticipation, a year of concentrated planning and preparation and an eleven-hour train journey from my Yorkshire home have culminated in my presence here on Scotland's rain-swept northern coast. I am finally ready to begin my long walk. Ready, that is, in a practical sense: the maps for my journey have been dispatched to friends, to be delivered to me along the way, and the contents of my rucksack have been pared down by experience, until I am confident that I am carrying exactly the equipment that I will need.

As for emotional readiness, though, I am completely unprepared. Having never previously walked further than the length of the Pennine Way, I have little idea of whether I am physically capable of covering more than ten times that distance. Nor can I be sure of my resilience in terms of spending the greater part of seven months alone. But the moment of departure is not the time to worry about such things. Instead, I must focus on the immediate first stage of my journey: I have a week to cross the Caithness Flow County and reach the village of Lairg, where I will have my first rest day. I pick up my rucksack: it is time to start walking.

I skirt the shoreline eastwards from John O'Groats, past the Ness of Duncansby, to Duncansby Head, from where David Stevenson's surprisingly squat lighthouse looks out towards its much taller counterpart on Muckle Skerry. The two lighthouses remind me of friends carrying on a conversation from opposite sides of a street; the point at which either could cross over having long since passed, the conversation continues as an indefinite relay, oblivious to the passage of traffic.

Walking back towards the John O'Groats tourist hub, I slip and

Duncansby Head, 7th March 2017.

fall, coating my left side with sphagnum-slime. Perhaps getting covered in mud less than three miles into my walk is not the most auspicious start, but it is also strangely liberating – I can now abandon any pretence of trying to keep clean.

For the rest of the day, I follow minor lanes, on a diagonal heading into Caithness through arable farmland and moorland. Lapwings fluster about, their badly-tuned-radio cries drowning the calls of curlew, skylark and buzzard. I catch a fleeting glimpse of something that might be a wheatear, but it is perhaps too early in the year.

The woodland where I had planned to camp for the night has been felled, so I pitch my tent behind a roadside row of gorse, which proves an excellent windbreak.

Over breakfast the next morning, I realise that I have forgotten to pack any teabags. Not wanting to add caffeine withdrawal to the list of hardships to be endured, I make straight for Watten, where the village shop provides me with a packet of Yorkshire Tea.

It's not only the tea: the landscape, too, reminds me very much of my home county, although flattened out, as though a heavy book has been placed on top of the Yorkshire Dales, squelching the topography out sideways. One difference, however, is the drystone walls constructed from vertical sheets of rock, resembling Norse *skjaldborger*. The size and shape of the sheets suggests slate, although the colour is wrong: pale grey and lichenous. These are Caithness flagstones, a layered formation of limestone, sandstone and mudstone, cleaved sheets of which have been used in construction since prehistoric times.

I make a poor choice of road on leaving Watten. At intervals of between ten and thirty seconds, I am forced to scramble out of the road and balance myself – plus eighteen kilograms of rucksack – on the tussocks of rough grass between the road and a parallel drainage ditch, as a twenty-ton truck thunders up behind me. My map shows a quarry some six miles further along the road; a glance down at the front of my jacket suggests that it might be a cement quarry. I dust myself off as best I can and hope that it doesn't rain any time soon.

'Not too soon' proves to be mid-afternoon.

Rain lashes my tent through the night and harries me to strike camp in the morning. Once I am walking again, the weather races at me from behind: clenchingly cold showers of stinging sleet alternating with the wind-tempered warmth of winter sunshine. Walking generally south, I am grateful to have the wind at my back for most of the day, although the intensity of the sleet showers forces me to keep my waterproofs on and swelter through the sunny intervals.

Several large herds of deer are roaming around, their hooves leaving clean, precise prints in the wet sand wherever they have crossed the track ahead of me. Close to a shooting lodge labelled *The Glutt,* I stop to rest by a stream, and strip my upper body of clothing for a wash. Wary of the rapidly-changing weather, I don't dare to remove my legwear for fear of being caught stark naked in a sleet shower.

Leaving the River Thurso, I traverse the moorland watershed towards Berriedale, passing a prefab shelter – presumably a lunch stop for deer stalkers – containing only a picnic table and a sodden Gideons' New Testament. Once in Berriedale, I cross the river and head back upstream on the southern bank. Morven, my first County Top, lies only a few miles away, although the climb from the col between Morven and Càrn Mòr manages to fit in 400 metres of ascent in less than half a mile: the Cicerone guide to the County Tops describes this climb as 'brutally steep'.[4] I am now walking into the pre-vailing wind, but rock outcrops on Morven's east flank provide some shelter until the final steps to the bitterly cold summit. The name Morven is derived from the Gaelic for big mountain, *mòr-bheinn* (more commonly encountered as *beinn mhòr*, hence Ben More), out of kilter with the Norse names of most of the surrounding hills.

Morven, County Top of Caithness, 9th March 2017.

One down (or should that be 'one up'?) and eighty-nine to go. I descend over Small Mount to camp next to a peaty lochan.

The Scottish Highlands often offer a sense of true wilderness, where it is almost possible to believe that you are somewhere that no-one has ever been before. So, it is something of a surprise on descend-ing at first light over a small summit – nameless on my map – to find it adorned by three cairns. Not only have people been here before, but sufficiently many people have been here to have disagreed over

---

4 Jonny Muir, *The UK's County Tops: 82 Walks to Read the Top of 91 Historic Counties* (Milnthorpe: Cicerone, 2011).

the precise location of the highest point.

Once veined with gold, this part of the Strath of Kildonan witnessed a brief gold rush in the mid-nineteenth century, but I see no traces of the prospectors' activities as I descend through deep bog to emerge onto the A897 close to Baile an Or, the 'Town of Gold'. For the rest of the day, my route is simply to follow the River Helmsdale upstream, the easy navigation welcome in the persistent rain. I seek temporary refuge on Kinbrace railway station and retrieve a weather forecast on my smartphone: apparently it isn't raining at the moment, but heavy rain is due to begin later in the afternoon. Although this is only day four, I am already feeling sufficiently under-nourished to begin to daydream of holding up the buffet trolley on a passing train. But there are two more days' walking between Kinbrace and the first shop at which I can replenish my food supplies.

Soggily, I press on to pitch my tent upon the southern shore of Loch Badanloch.

Wilfully ignoring the sunrise, I linger in my sleeping bag for an extra hour to let the rain abate. The air is thick with the musky scent of deer. Two stags pose for me atop a grassy hillock: they would make perfect photographic targets if I had my camera to hand, but it is packed in my rucksack for protection from the elements. I am very much a beginner when it comes to photography and still have a tendency to confuse the shutter with the 'off' button.

The sun prevails over the remaining trails of rain by late morning, and, with it, spring arrives. The gorse is just beginning to bloom around the shores of Loch Choire and bullfrogs are creaking and groaning in the drainage ditch alongside the track. At the loch inflow, satisfied that the clouds pose no imminent threat, I spread my damp belongings out to dry on the sandy beach, then strip off and splash myself clean in the loch. I have nothing to dry myself with except my sleeping bag liner (by this point, neither particularly clean nor dry itself) and re-dress in the same sweaty, grimy clothes, but I feel nonetheless much refreshed.

Crossing the head of the loch by a rickety suspension bridge, I climb into a side glen, aiming to cross a pass that will lead me down to Lairg the next day. The pass lies at 450 metres. How perspectives change: in England, 450 metres would constitute a hill; in Scotland, it is a pass between two much higher hills, and those dwarfed by the Ben Klibreck Munros[5] on the northern side of the glen. The track comes to an abrupt conclusion at a new deer fence. I trail the outside of the fence for a mile or so, but reluctantly conclude that I will need to climb over it to access the higher slopes beyond. One of the problems of climbing deer fences is that you almost inevitably need to climb a second one, higher up the hillside. However, the moment of sitting astride the top of the fence, as you steady yourself before swinging your second leg over the wire, all the while acutely aware of the weight of the rucksack on your back, is a marvellous vantage point; I am rewarded with views back towards snow-capped Ben Klibreck set against a rich blue sky.

Continuing my ascent alongside a burn, I come across a reassuring sign that someone else has walked this route: a drinks flask, of the tough plastic, wide-mouthed, screw-top variety. I consider adopting the flask, and rinse it in the burn to remove some of the peat. The liquid inside appears a little frothy, and there is something resembling a mermaid's purse suspended in it. I tap on the plastic. The Thing inside winks at me. I decide the flask is probably best left where I found it.

At the top of the pass, I pause to take a compass bearing to find my way through a flattish area of bog and peat hags – I don't want to descend accidentally into the wrong glen. As soon as I start walking on my bearing I notice another sign of previous walkers: a pair of expensive-looking winter mountaineering gloves, darned to the ground by this year's star moss forcing through the cuffs.

That night, I dream that I live in a three-storey house and that the rain pours in through the roof, penetrating all the floors. In the morning, everything is sodden – I think from condensation or low cloud rather than overnight rain – one of the perils of camping next to the burn.

I descend through bog until the dry, sweet smell of sheep heralds the start of a farm track. When the sun makes a fleeting appearance,

---

5 A 'Munro' is a Scottish mountain that exceeds a height of 3,000 feet.

I stop at a railed bridge and hang everything up to dry. Suddenly the snow-covered mountains of Sutherland appear beyond the dark green forest, like the ramparts of the Himalaya.

It is raining again before I reach Lairg. I collapse into the Pier café and consume an enormous ploughman's lunch – huge wedges of cheese, thick slices of ham and a large salad including grapes, peppers and pineapple – to make up for the absence of protein, fruit and vegetables from my diet for the past week.

Lairg has: a café (closed Monday); a fish-and-chip shop (closed Sunday and Monday); a visitor centre (closed until April); and a Post Office (closed) – Monday is evidently not the best day of the week to have chosen for my first rest. But – if the road signs are to be believed – Lairg does appear to have *two* Goods Vehicle Testing Stations.

In the evening of my day of rest, I sit on a bench in Church Hill woodland overlooking the loch and am engaged in a long and rambling conversation by a couple (Andrea, I think, and Gordon; she fifty-nine, he seventy-three) who have a croft between Helmsdale and Brora. Gordon's accent is distinctively indecipherable enough for me to be able to diagnose it as Glaswegian, so Andrea acts as translator. It is little more than a week since I left home, yet already I find that I am losing the art of dialogue. I scoop up handfuls of words and sift them through my fingers, hoping to shake them into order.

Lairg is the end of the beginning of my walk. Having survived this far, I can allow myself to look further ahead. I need to make a foray out to the west to climb my next County Top before resuming a southerly trajectory towards the Black Isle, where my husband, Laurence, will pay me a visit.

Ben More Assynt (County Top of Sutherland)

Lairg to Conon Bridge. 88 miles, 2,630 metres ascent.
Tuesday 14th – Sunday 19th March

A pair of white-throated divers are bobbing about on the loch as I leave Lairg. I decide that this augurs well for the next leg of my journey; it's easy to comprehend how common occurrences become omens when you are feeling in need of reassurance.

Near Rosehall, a road sign shows eight miles to Lairg. I have walked more than a third of the day's distance without a break: the hotel breakfast of kippers is fuelling me well. During a Carlisle-to-Alnwick practice expedition, days on which I was able to purchase fresh food were noticeably easier than those on which I was restricted to the rations I carried. With hindsight, I realise that my exhaustion on walking into Lairg – needing to stop every hour or so – was probably in large part a consequence of my minimal rations.

Achness Falls are an explosion of emulsified sound and water. The power of the water is palpable, as though the River Cassley is ripping apart the rock strata as it surges towards the Kyle of Sutherland. It saddens me to think that the modern experience-surrogate of the internet can deceive us into thinking that we have 'seen' the waterfall, without ever having stood here to breathe the spray-soaked air or hear the thunder of the water competing with the roar of the wind.

Glen Cassley, too, is beautiful beyond words. The contorted birches along the river bank, scaly grey with lichen, still bare of buds, writhe in the agony of the wind. I watch as a yellowhammer tries again and again to land on a wire fence, before finally yielding and letting the wind carry it where it will. I ache with longing for this place, knowing that I will almost certainly never return.

There is a soft moss trod along the river bank, clearly well-used by fishermen, which I follow to rest my feet from the hard tarmac of the road. A man driving a truckload of chocolate spaniels pulls over to ask where I'm walking to. I tell him that I hope to climb Ben More Assynt tomorrow. "Aye," he nods, "you'll be well past the trees by then." Something about his intonation is concerning – it's the tone of voice used to implicitly suffix the word 'scene' with 'of the crime'. Is there something I should know about the trees in Glen Cassley?

At noon precisely the weather turns vicious, a fierce hailstorm sweeping in without warning. I struggle into my waterproof trousers and continue, head down, trying to walk in a straight line whilst looking away from the hail rather than at the road ahead. When eventually the hail abates, Ben More Assynt has appeared, mirage-like, at the head of the glen. Although the peak is snow-covered, I can make out dark patches of rock on the higher slopes, so hopefully my lack of winter mountaineering equipment will not be a problem.

After passing the ruined croft at Dalnaclave, I clamber though a fence-gap into an area of pine trees, thinking to camp somewhere sheltered. Campsite criteria: 1) shelter; 2) dry. The woodland is mostly flooded. I blunder around, crashing through ground vegetation and ducking under fallen trunks until I stumble upon what seems to be a suitably dry island. That is, until I remember: 3) I must be able to find my tent again after climbing Ben More Assynt. I abandon the idea of camping in the woodland and instead pitch my tent a little further up the glen, right next to the track, where I will definitely be able to find it.

Ben More Assynt: the name has the same origin as Morven, with a geographical suffix to disambiguate it from the numerous other Ben Mores. I have climbed this mountain before, following the conventional route from Inchnadamph over the neighbouring peak of Conival. My arrival from the direction of Caithness, however, now forces me to approach the rarely-climbed east flank.

The mountain proves to be one of the hardest winter ascents that I've ever undertaken, the ten-mile round trip taking over five hours. The challenge is not technical – I have climbed far more technically demanding peaks in the Alps and Scandinavia – but mental. When you are walking with others, decisions can be made by consensus, and reassurance sought if needed: *Do you think I should put my waterproofs on before we enter the cloud, or will I overheat? Do you think crampons would make that snowfield easier? Is this safe? Is it time we turned back?*

When you are walking alone, all of the mental pressure of these decisions falls on you and you alone. Today in particular, alone on a winter ascent without proper winter equipment, I struggle to find the courage to make decisions and to feel confident in my choices. The American climber Royal Robbins once described mountains as being "a battleground between a man's weaknesses and his strength, be-tween his pride and his humbleness."[6] Am I too proud, forcing myself to climb, against my better judgement of the weather conditions – or too humble, questioning my ability to keep myself safe?

The wind rages – I estimate sixty miles per hour, gusting stronger. Within a scant hundred yards of leaving my tent, it is all that I can do to keep my head down and force myself into the wind, step by laboured step. The ridge cradling the north rim of Coire Rèidh is snow-covered above an altitude of 700 metres. When planning my expedition, I had decided not to bring ice axe and crampons for the simple reason that I didn't think I was capable of carrying them. In-stead, I have arranged for Laurence to deliver my winter equipment to Conon Bridge, in the hope that after two weeks of walking I will have become sufficiently accustomed to the weight of my rucksack to add a couple of extra kilograms of ironmongery to it. For now, I have a pair of lightweight 'spider' crampons: plastic plates with metal studs a little like those on football boots. I strap these to the soles of my boots, select a shard of tapered rock about eight inches long to use as a substitute ice axe and continue to climb. The spider crampons keep sliding round to the sides of my boots, and prove worse than useless on mixed ground. I remove them when the ridge becomes rockier, vowing only ever to use true crampons after this expedition.

Hail stings my face, despite my best efforts to keep my hood pulled down low. Movement becomes increasingly difficult, and I am forced to move on hands and knees on more exposed sections of the ridge. Had I been cold, tired, or short of daylight, now would be the time to turn back. But I can sense from the changing angle of the wind that the ridge is curving southwards, meaning that I am close to the summit, so continue. I crawl the final yards to twin summit-cairns atop an outcrop of shattered coarse-grained quartzite. Four faint paths approach from the west, where the very beginning of the ridge to-wards Conival is dimly visible through the cloud.

Overnight, the weather slumbers too, but barely a second after the sun levers itself out from behind the ridge, I hear the wind resume for

---

6 Royal Robbins, 'Foreword', *Mirrors in the Cliffs,* Jim Perrin (ed.) (London: Diadem, 1983), pp.13-15. Unbeknown to me, Royal Robbins had died just the day before my ascent of Ben More Assynt, at the age of 82.

another day, screeching like old and badly-oiled heavy machinery. I am herded out of Glen Cassley by the weather, which pelts me with hail and lashes me with wind-tongues. On the north-eastern side of the glen stand Beinn Sgreamhaidh and Beinn Sgeireach. The Gaelic names mean 'loathsome hill' and, I think, 'shelved hill' (presumably on account of its shape), but in the current stormy conditions I can't help but think of them as Beinn Screamy and Beinn Screechy. This is the wild land, marked on sketches by the sixteenth-century cartographer Timothy Pont with the words EXTREEM WILDERNESS.

After I pass Rosehall for a second time, the weather relents, permitting brief spells of warming sunshine to revive me between the hailstorms. During one such lull, I stand and watch a quiver of goldfinches and another white-throated diver, flying as though straining to elongate itself.

Having completed my westward foray to reach Ben More Assynt, I can resume my southward progress and have the wind behind me once more. I lurk in the waiting-shelter at Culrain station to let another squall pass. I am tempted to spend the night here, but am unsure how ScotRail would react if I were to be spotted from one of the evening trains. Instead, I camp in a patch of rather damp roadside scrub.

Winter descends at least 300 metres during the night, snow-dusting the surrounding hills. After only an hour's walking, I stop in Ardgay for a second breakfast at the Highland Stores. A bacon and egg roll: that's protein covered. I also purchase a small apple and a packet of chocolate raisins, wondering if the latter counts as one of my 'five a day'. I am getting very little in the way of fruit and vegetables – perhaps I should count the brown sauce on my roll? Jock has also called into the stores for a cuppa part-way through the morning paper round. Later, he cycles past me, having by now resumed his deliveries. He asks after my destination. Unsure of any place names close to my intended campsite, I fudge my response: "Halfway to Conon Bridge today, and then the rest of the way tomorrow."

"You must be tough," Jock responds, "it's going to be a cold night."

Although I could follow the coastline to reach the Black Isle, I prefer to keep away from the settlements strung along the shore road and to travel instead through the high ground a little way inland. I leave the road to head back into the hills at Wester Fearn. Of two possible tracks, one has the appearance of a private driveway and the other is defended by three large black bulls. Although I sometimes find it difficult to assess the access rights along Scottish tracks – unless helpfully signposted *ceum* by the Scottish Rights of Way and Access Society – on this occasion I have no qualms about walking up the driveway, private or otherwise.

Climbing above the snowline, I pass a rock which resembles a tombstone or memorial marker. The inscription is barely legible, but I can just make out a name – Alexander Donaldson – and the words 'killed by lightning'. There is a saying about lightning never striking twice: is that people or places? I decide not to linger.

Tracing a faint track can often be made easier by snow, which accentuates the narrow stripe of exposed ground threading through the heather; the Scots word is *snaw-rink*. Once compacted by footsteps, the snow lingers longer than the looser, more powdery snow dusting the surrounding vegetation. I am firmly of the opinion that following a track, however boggy and indistinct, is easier than walking cross-country on a bearing over blanket bog or heather moorland. This opinion is reinforced when I lose the path at the top of the pass; the descent takes just as long as the ascent, is doubly arduous, and I come down into Strath Rusdale in quite the wrong place.

My intention had been to descend Strath Rusdale, cross the Black Water and the River Averon, and camp on the hillside on the far bank. Crossing the first river is easy enough, but the bridge over the Averon marked on my map is simply not there. The river is fast-flowing, and, I estimate, up to eight metres wide – not something I could hope to ford. I force my way upstream, pushing through young alder, broom and gorse, and at one point needing to descend a steep bluff, clinging on to a wire fence for balance, until I reach a bridge at a place where there definitely isn't one on the map.

I am ready to camp: I have been walking for eight hours and am once more thoroughly soaked and exhausted – but a sign informs me that all rights of access are currently suspended owing to wind farm construction. It being after 4.00pm on a Friday, and snowing heavily, I decided to ignore the sign, pitch my sodden tent and collapse into it.

The temperature plummets and I get very little sleep, turning frequently to try to warm up different parts of my body. In the morning, when I remove the tent pegs, the tent stays up: the guylines have frozen to the ground. I prize them free as gently as possible to avoid snapping the ice-bound elastic ties. For the first couple of hours, I want to keep stopping to photograph the snow-covered hills, but my fingers quickly become painfully cold whenever I remove my mittens to operate the camera. I stamp my feet as I walk in an effort to warm them.

I meet Laurence for a late lunch in Dingwall. He has just walked the Corrieyairack Pass through deep powder snow, so we have a very British conversation about weather conditions. Later, Laurence drives to Conon Bridge, while I walk in borrowed dry shoes. A police car whizzes round the Maryburgh roundabout just as a flock of geese passes overhead, the sounds of the two sirens swirling together to create an unearthly wail.

The component pieces of a pair of ball-point pens are lurking in the bottom of my rucksack. I reassemble them and wrap plasters around the barrels to prevent them from becoming unscrewed again.

Having replenished my food supplies and added ice axe and crampons, I find that my pack now feels worryingly heavy. I would like to add an extra layer of clothing, as the forecast for Glen Affric includes a rather concerning −8°C, but am unsure whether I will be able to cope with the weight. I decide that if my pack does prove unmanageable I can leave some equipment behind in the Camban bothy.

Càrn Eighe (County Top of Ross and Cromarty)
Conon Bridge to Fort Augustus. 87 miles, 3,740 metres ascent.
Monday 20th – Friday 24th March

Back on the road again. Laurence loads my rucksack into the van and disappears off to climb in the mountains above Loch Mullardoch, leaving me with just a day-sack and an arrangement to meet later in the day in Cannich, a village towards the southern end of Strathglass at the confluence of the Affric and Cannich rivers.

My route is just short of twenty-four miles, entirely on roads, and the weather is sufficiently unpleasant for two drivers to stop to offer me a lift. Views of snow-capped ridges in Glen Monar bring to mind an Easter expedition about three years previously, when I walked eastwards from Achnashellach in a three-day blizzard, carrying my full rucksack along the tops of the mountains. When I alighted from the train in the dark at the start of the trek, a fellow passenger went to great lengths to explain where he lived, repeating that if anything went wrong I was to retreat and call at his house for assistance. I could tell he was very concerned about a lone walker heading off into a blizzard, but I did my best to reassure him that I was well-equipped. Perhaps over-equipped, as with the weight of the bag I sprained an ankle, not feeling the injury in the cold – but as soon as I descended to Struy and thawed out, I realised that I had to abandon my plans. I limped slowly along the road to Cannich, caught a bus to Inverness and came home.

Today, I arrive in Cannich in much better shape. A little footsore, but I have covered the twenty-four miles in under six hours, much to Laurence's surprise. We let another hail-squall pass over cups of coffee in the Bog Cotton Café, before he returns the large rucksack to my custody and sets off on the long drive back to Yorkshire. I drag myself and my rucksack up the steep incline out of the village, until the roadside scrub becomes dense enough to conceal a tent.

At 2.00am, I am woken by an immense silence. I can no longer hear the rain hammering on my tent, or the wind tearing through the trees. In the morning, I find the tent trying to smother me, sagging against my face under the weight of new-fallen snow.

There is something about the way that snow muffles some noises, yet accentuates others, that kindles loneliness. The only sounds are the creak of snow under my feet and the gurgle of far-away freshet burns. My footprints are the first marks upon the pristine path and I feel utterly alone.

Perhaps I tempted fate when writing yesterday's diary: the snow works itself up into a true blizzard, flurrying thickly into my face. An ice-crust forms down the front of my jacket, over my hood and on the top of my rucksack. I am unsure whether to keep brushing it off before it melts and soaks through my clothes, or whether I will get less wet if I let it build up to form some sort of protective layer.

My sense of isolation is heightened by Laurence's recent departure. I find some comfort in a set of footprints that converge on my trail, although this is tempered by anxiety that my unknown companion will turn off onto a different track, leaving me even more alone than before. Whenever the path passes through surface water or slush, I feel a physical sense of relief to find the footprints continuing in the next patch of fresh snow.

Should I camp, which would make my route shorter, or press on to the Camban bothy? With visibility limited to about fifty metres, I am not confident of being able to find the bothy. But, when I stop walking for even a few seconds, my fingers begin to scream with pain in the freezing air. I walk on.

Glen Affric Youth Hostel is closed until spring, so I haven't considered it as a possible accommodation option – but a notice in the front window informs me that one of the dormitories has been left unlocked as a winter refuge. The room contains five metal bunkbeds – no mattresses – and a couple of chairs; it will be very cold, but at least dry.

The evening mellows into perfection. I lie on my front in my sleeping bag and watch as the clouds lift above the summits, becoming a saturated rose-pink against the pale blue beyond. The sun sinks behind the mountains, gradually dragging the colour out of the air until clouds and sky meld into the same soft grey.

Inside my sleeping bag, I'm wearing every item of clothing that I have with me, even my waterproofs, and my feet are wrapped in my balaclava. My hands are so cold that I can barely grasp a pen to write my diary.

Given the recent heavy snowfall, my preferred route to Càrn

Loch Affric, 23rd March 2017.

Eighe, which ascends via a north-facing corrie where the avalanche risk will be greatest, is out of the question. The only sensible option seems to be a track leading up to a bealach at 850 metres, followed by a couple of miles along the ridge.

The snow is powdery – too powdery for crampons to be of any use. In the glen it is only ankle-deep, but by the time I have wallowed my way up to the bealach I am sinking to my thighs with every step. I make very slow progress and begin to worry about whether I have enough daylight to complete the climb.

On the ridge, I am scoured by spindrift. The visibility drops to between five and ten metres, barely enough for me to see my way along the ridge. Should I continue? If I do not, I must endure another freezing night in the unheated dormitory, then repeat the ascent tomorrow – with less food available to me. I decide to continue, but to turn back if I have not reached the summit by 2.00pm. I stagger onwards, soon needing crampons to cross verglaced rocks.

There are two ruined structures on the summit of Màm Sodhail, one a tower constructed by surveyors of the Ordnance Survey who occupied the summit for a month in 1848 during the primary triangulation of Scotland. I am told that there is a visitors book inside the tower, but in the current weather I am not going to attempt to scale the walls to find out. Càrn Eighe is Màm Sodhail's twin; a similarly angular shape, and only two metres higher. Although it is tempting in today's tempest to interpret *Eighe* as a derivation of the Gaelic for ice, it is more plausible that it means 'file shaped' in reference to the mountain's distinctive profile.

Shortly after noon, I reach the summit, an island amidst an angry sea, breakers frozen into cornices. Without snow-goggles, my eyes are beginning to play tricks on me, and there is a blood-red tinge at the rim of my vision. I experiment with a technique of shutting each eye in turn, but desist after my left eye freezes shut; un-gumming it with ice-crusted mittens is far from easy.

On the return journey, I encounter the outlines of my own footsteps, snow-filled in the short time that has elapsed since I trod them. All that remains from the bealach is to stagger down through the powder snow. Nearing the glen, I stop to refill my water bottle – and discover that I no longer have it. I leave my pack by the burn and stomp half a mile back up through the powder snow until I find my bottle lying in a snowdrift, where it must have tumbled from my bag. By the time I have descended back down to the glen for a second time, the hillside looks as though a large party of people – or possibly elephants – has climbed the mountain by this route.

"Bloody hell, it's freezing in here."

Mike arrives at the Youth Hostel as the last of the light is fading. He's a Munro-bagger, here to 'tidy up' some of his unclimbed mountains. Our evening's conversation ranges from the Cuillin to Chomolungma. In the morning, as he attempts to articulate just how cold it is, Mike's vocabulary blossoms to match the skies outside.

Glen Affric is beyond compare. Today inhabits that tiny sliver of perfection between the end of the blizzard and the start of the thaw, when sunlight shatters the still air and colours become implausibly, beautifully bright. Càrn Eighe is hard to identify amongst the groping ridges on the northern side of the glen, but I have a clear view through Fionngleann to the Five Sisters of Kintail, and can make out the pass of An Caorann Mòr which Mike traversed to reach Affric. My own route out of the glen will be to the west, crossing lower-lying hills to reach Fort Augustus.

The snow-silence persists. When I stand still, I can hear only the rush of allt-water and the occasional trill of birdsong, too faint for me to recognise the species. When I walk, I feel as though I am transgressing the valley's vow of silence, despoiling the immaculate whiteness with my trampling muddy boot-prints.

Camping at Loch na Beinne Baine, 23rd March 2017.

The temperature soars, to a point where heat-stroke is a definite possibility – and yet only yesterday I was worried about snow-blindness. I open a packet of liquorice and suck each lozenge with a mitten-full of snow. The numbing chill of the grainy flakes accentuates the sweet aniseed flavour, and, I hope, prevents me from overheating.

I camp next to Loch na Beinne Baine, high on the ridge separating the Affric and Moriston glens. A causeway of sunlight reaches out across the loch to the low hills beyond.

How I envy the power lines. They march purposefully, powerfully, climbing ridges in two or three strides, stepping neatly across rivers and forests. From Loch na Beinne Baine, I have two ridges to traverse: the first to complete the crossing from Glen Affric to Glen Moriston, the second the old military road to Fort Augustus. Both are deep with powder-snow, mostly to mid-calf, but drifting deeper. Each step is like clambering into a bathtub without knowing how deep it is.

The landscape aches past. I am continually revising my objectives: I will stop for a break when I'm abreast of that outcrop; when I reach the track junction before the outcrop; when I think I'm nearly at the track junction; whenever I next see a snow-free rock that I can rest on. All the while, the power lines stride alongside. They will reach Fort Augustus many hours ahead of me.

Introspection: Resilience

Looking back, perhaps I should have been surprised at, or at least consciously satisfied with, my physical resilience to so many consecutive days of walking, with such a heavy load to carry over rough terrain. But at the time I accepted this almost inappreciatively, as though there had never been any uncertainly about my physical fitness and ability to succeed. Given that my first attempt at the Pennine Way had terminated in a bus shelter in Earby – a long way from the end of the National Trail, whichever your direction of travel – and, moreover, had been followed by three frustrating months of gradually learning to walk again, this was undeniably an unwise premise. However, in the years since this inglorious failure, I have come to a better understanding, and acceptance, of my own limitations.

The challenge at the outset of my long walk lay more in the weather than the walking: staying warm through the long hours of darkness proved far more difficult than covering twenty miles during the day. Thoreau endorses the sentiments of many writers, both before and since, when he observes that, "Living much out of doors, in the sun and wind, will no doubt produce a certain roughness of character."[7] By the time I reached Conon Bridge, if not before, I found myself comfortable in this roughness; notwithstanding the challenge of my walk, at no point did I find myself wishing that I were elsewhere. Even in Glen Affric, shivering through the darkness, with my feet stuffed into my balaclava and my fists clenched tight under my armpits, I was aware of how truly alive I felt and how fortunate I was to be able to be there, so far removed from the everyday world.

---

7 Henry David Thoreau, 'Walking', *Atlantic Monthly,* IX, no. LVI (1862), pp. 657-74.

Blue Remembered Hills

Nairnshire – Morayshire – Kincardineshire – Angus – Aberdeenshire – Banffshire

Carn Glas-choire (County Top of Nairnshire) and Carn a'Ghille Chearr (County Top of Morayshire)

Fort Augustus to Tomintoul. 78 miles, 2,870 metres ascent.
Saturday 25th – Thursday 30th March

I spend my rest day people-watching. My hostel dormitory hosts all the usual suspects: two snorers, one sleep-talker and someone in possession of two suitcases containing items which sound like they are wrapped in cellophane and which urgently require re-packing in the middle of the night. I make a mental note to acquire some better earplugs when the opportunity arises.

A coach party of American high-school students arrives. Thirty-seven suitcases are trundled into the hostel reception. Thirty-seven pairs of feet shuffle awkwardly as the warden provides information about meal times and fire evacuation procedures. Then, at the mention of the word 'wi-fi', thirty-seven pairs of ears prick up and there is a scramble of activity as thirty-seven re-animated teenagers try to get online simultaneously.

Other guests include a 'Wild and Sexy Haggis Tour', who are being bussed to the Isle of Skye for the day. I wonder how they can possibly hope to experience Skye in so little time. The following morning, listening to the members of the Haggis Tour comparing *Pokémon Go!* scores over breakfast, I realise that they have appreciated even less of Skye than I had anticipated.

⚠

Now my journey resumes. From the Great Glen, I must continue west, across the Monadhliath plateau, to reach the Cairngorms. Though Laurence's recent journey has tempted me to follow the Corrieyairack Pass through the Monadhliath, this would lead me too far south of my intended route. Instead, I will traverse the mountains by connecting two remote glens which extend into the plateau from west and east.

Walking pace is just the right pace for such a beautiful day. I can admire each tree individually, listen to the croaking of frogs and toads, watch a dipper skim upstream. I don't immediately recognise the shrill *kleep* until I see the black and white shapes: oystercatchers come inland to breed. I pause frequently to douse my t-shirt and headscarf in the burns that run down the hillside and relish the trickle of icy water down the back of my neck.

A red squirrel materialises on the wall to the right of the road. It runs along the crest of the wall and makes an impossible leap to fasten itself to a tree, which it then scurries up. Moments later, another repeats the acrobatic feat in the opposite direction.

The lousing snow reveals subtle changes in the landscape that mark this as the Monadhliath: the hills become smoother, rounded, the boulders grittier, the heather more red than purple. Glen Markie climbs steadily yet gently towards an arrow of blue sky indicating the head of the pass. The terrain beyond is hidden from view, giving me an unsettling feeling that I am walking towards an abyss, that the watershed is also the threshold of the end of everything.

The top of the pass is not a threshold but a mirror. I step through the glass and descend into a reflection of my ascent, towards the River Findhorn.

Coignafearn Lodge has the appearance of a doll's house, with its pale pink rendering and slate-grey roof. Next to it stands a pair of fuzzy-felt trees and the surrounding hills are coated with model-railway flock. The interior is furnished like a doll's house too – I glimpse chandeliers and chintzy, period furniture as I pass – and I feel out-of-scale with my surroundings, as though I have supped from Alice Liddell's potions.

A mumpish toad is waiting for me on the tarmac road. I try to suggest gently that, given the evidence left by his erstwhile friends and family, this is not a safe place for a toad to be sitting. He politely ignores me. Maybe he doesn't understand my Sassenach accent, or perhaps he simply needs some respite from the raucous copulation being carried on in the roadside ditches. I meet several more amphibians in the road over the next mile and realise that if I stop to try to give each one an individual lesson in road safety then I will never reach tonight's campsite. A few minutes later, the bin lorry trundles past me on its way to Coignafearn.

A patch of moorland is spouting smoke. Several small fires are creeping across the ground, creating the impression of geothermal springs. A man observing the fires' progress from his Land Rover informs me that they're "tidying up the old stuff," like the heather-burning I am familiar with on Pennine moors.

By now I have settled into a rhythm, the feeling of safety in my own tight little world depending upon the ritual and routine of camp craft. At the same time, concepts from the workaday world – words like 'yesterday' and 'tomorrow' – are becoming hazy.

At the end of each day's walk, I pitch my tent and empty my belongings into it. Wet and dry equipment are stowed at opposite ends, and my cooking pot, mug, gas cylinder and water bottles go into the narrow space between inner and outer tent. I find a burn or pool from which to collect two litres of water before I clamber into the tent, sitting in the centre between my wet and dry gear. Chlorine water-purification tablets go into the water bottles, and I make sure to check my watch so that I know when the allotted half-hour has passed and the water is safe to drink.

When tea-time (which can be any time from 5pm onwards) arrives, I boil a pot of water, using half for my food and the remainder for a mug of tea. After eating, I read, write my diary, or study my maps.

When the air begins to chill, I spread my rucksack at the lower (or wet) end of the tent, to form the lower third of my sleeping mat, then inflate my air mattress for the upper two-thirds of my body. There is now not enough headroom for me to sit upright, so I must lie down – but it is wonderful to be able to stretch my legs and flex my ankles. Into my sleeping bag with me come spare clothes and anything that needs to dry or be kept warm overnight; the gas cylinder is wrapped in my balaclava, to avoid the burn of cold metal on bare skin. My 'pillow' is either my bag of spare clothes, or my rolled-up jacket. My torch is in the zipped pocket of my fleece so that I know where to find it in the dark.

I wake as the sky begins to grow light, but try to catch chunks of sleep until 7am, or a little before. The first thing I do when it is time to rise is to reach out of my sleeping bag and unscrew the valve on my air mattress. The weight of my body forces the air out of the mattress and thus buys me enough headroom to sit up. I pack the sleeping bag away and stow it in my rucksack, followed by my bag of spare clothes and rolled-up mattress.

By now it is 7.10 or 7.15am. I boil a pot of water. Half goes into my mug with the contents of a sachet of porridge or a couple of

Weetabix and a little powdered milk. I drop a teabag into the remaining water and wrap the cooking pot in my fleece or balaclava; the tea brews while I eat my porridge and peruse the day's maps.

After breakfast, I clean my teeth and pack the remainder of my belongings into the rucksack. By 7.45am I am ready to strike the tent. I shake as much snow/frost/moisture off the flysheet as I can, before rolling it up and sliding it down the inside of the rucksack.

The four miles from my campsite near Slochd Summit to Carn Glas-choire, the County Top of Nairnshire, take almost two hours. The ground is rough, heathery, trackless, and the soles of my boots have worn so smooth that I slip on patches of soft star-moss.

When I reach the top of the ridge, the blue, snow-covered Cairngorms rise up behind the glacier of cloud rolling out from Glen Feshie. I am so accustomed to the feeling of being in the midst of the Cairngorms, aware of their immensity around me, that it is quite strange to see them holding themselves aloof, asserting their identity in isolation. In my preoccupation with the Cairngorms, I walk myself into a dead end of peat hags, from which it takes a good fifteen minutes to extricate myself. It occurs to me that anyone undertaking a glacier climb should practise in peat hags, as the navigation skills are very much the same as those required when one is crossing a crevasse field: *if I pass that one on the left, there's a clear area ahead, but I must be careful not to get stuck in that dead end over there; I could probably jump that one but I'm not sure how stable the landing ground looks.*

Later in the day, I walk through Grantown-on-Spey into the Anagach Woods. The woods here are an important stronghold of the capercaillie, which feed on the needles of the Scots pine, but – like bunkhouses – the birds don't open for business until April.

The chapel clock at Cromdale strikes 4pm as I cross the Spey towards it, and by 5.30pm I am snug within my sleeping bag once more.

Low clouds sink past the Cromdale Hills as the air cools overnight, but I succeed in striking camp before they descend as far as my campsite, ensuring that my tent is merely damp, rather than sodden, when I pack it away. I climb onto the ridge, then turn north towards Carn a'Ghille Chearr – *hill of the wronged boy* – the County Top of Morayshire, sitting hunched and petulant in the drifting cloud. Carn a'Ghille Chearr is not in fact the highest point in the Cromdale

Carn Glas-choire, County Top of Nairnshire, 28th March 2017.

Hills: the rich blue pyramid of Creagan a'Chaise, at the southern end of the ridge, rises to 722 metres, but the absolute summits of the two hills lie on opposite sides of the Morayshire-Kincardineshire boundary which has been strung along the crest of the ridge.

I find a particular joy in being the first person out on the hills in the early morning. It is a feeling of possession – but of the hills possessing me, not the other way around – and yet also a feeling of freedom. The presence of others distracts from the vastness of the hills; only when alone can you absorb and become absorbed into your surroundings. Colin Fletcher, who in 1963 became the first person to walk the length of the Grand Canyon National Park, encapsulates perfectly this response to solitude, describing how the companion-less walker will "not grow lonely [but] pass over instead into an aloneness that leaves you free and content."[8]

An invisible magician plucks white hares out of the heather. Still in winter clothing, the hares are presumably as disconcerted as I am

---

8 Colin Fletcher, *The Thousand Mile Summer* (New York: Vintage, 1987).

by the abrupt change in the weather.

Reaching Tomintoul, I make a pilgrimage to Torrans, where the distinguished diplomat and mountaineer Sir Edward Peck lived in retirement. Some years ago, Laurence and I spent a week walking in the Cairngorms in the company of one of Peck's grandchildren, David, and his wife, Helen, good friends from our time at university. Both have an insatiable curiosity about the world around them, although while Helen prefers to learn by reading about things, David has more magpie-like tendencies. I will never forget the look on Helen's face when, returning from a walk in the mountains above Glen Shee, Laurence, David and I proudly emptied all of the fascinating things we'd found out of our rucksacks and onto the kitchen table. Several rusted metal cogs from broken fence-posts now adorn the planting troughs in our back yard, but I am unsure whether David will have been permitted to retain his Cairngorm treasures.

Mount Battock (County Top of Kincardineshire)

Tomintoul to Glen Doll. 72 miles, 3,030 metres ascent.
Friday 31st March – Monday 3rd April

Four counties converge on the Cairngorm mountains; to reach the highest points of each of them, I will need to cross the region twice, although Ben Macdui helpfully straddles a county boundary and is considered the highest point of the counties on either side. My first crossing follows an L-shaped pass, ascending from Tomintoul alongside the River Avon[9] and the Builg Burn to Loch Builg, then descending Glen Gairn towards Ballater. This is an easy route, rising to only 500 metres at the watershed, with good estate tracks for much of the way – quite a contrast to my higher, wilder crossing of the Monadhliath.

A thin, silvery rain is falling, but I resist the temptation to put my hood up, perceiving this as a declaration of opposition to the weather, which would turn my walk into the clichéd battle against the

---

9 Pronounced 'A'an', the name Avon derives from the Gaelic *abhainn* (river),
which has the same etymological root as the Welsh *afon*.

elements. Where possible, I prefer to stay respectfully on the same side as the weather, to feel a part of it rather than trying to shut it out. Water does no more than get you soaking,[10] as Bridget St John observes.

In Glen Gairn, the reddish-pink of exposed granite amongst the darker shades of heather imbues the glowering weather with a dusky pink warmth, a colouration which is also reflected in the Gaelic name for the area: *Am Monadh Ruadh*, the red mountains. Vibrantly inconsistent, the 'gorm' of Cairngorm means 'blue', but this English toponym is in truth an extension of the name of one of the range's highest peaks. And, as Housman reminds us, remembered hills are forever blue.[11]

Cooking my evening meal, I drop my socks into my mug of tea. Should I be more concerned about having wet socks, or about the health hazard posed by drinking the tea?

My boots, like my socks, are in a bad way. Numerous writers have commented on the relationship between walkers and their walking boots, the acquisition of new boots being a 'rite of passage,'[12] a memory milestone, enabling walks to be precisely located in the chronological sequence of successive pairs of footwear. A hazy memory of the Wessex Ridgeway can be precisely located in the spring of 2004 because I was wearing a pair of my father's old gardening boots. I went through a phase of shunning leather boots in favour of wellies soon after I turned twenty-five.

When planning my walk, I had little idea of how many pairs of boots I would need, and somewhat arbitrarily settled upon a figure of four: one pair of sturdy winter boots to set off in, then three pairs of lighter summer footwear to be left with Laurence for delivery as and when needed. My winter boots have been deteriorating rapidly since Fort Augustus, and by the time I reach Ballater the soles are paper-thin. To make matters worse, I have disproportionately worn away the outer edge of the heels, so that my feet walk on a slant even when

---

10 Bridget St John, 'To B without a Hitch' *Ask Me No Questions* (Dandelion, 1967).

11 Alfred Edward Houseman, *A Shropshire Lad* (London: K. Paul, Trench, Trübner, 1896).

12 Stuart Maconie, *Never Mind the Quantocks* (Newton Abbot: David & Charles, 2012).

the ground is level. But the weather is still definitively winter, and none of my reserve shoes are compatible with crampons: I need new winter boots urgently.

Fortunately, Ballater has an excellent outdoor equipment shop. Despite the fact that my feet are an ungainly size nine, the shop is able to furnish me with a pair of garishly bright red trekking boots. Feeling equipped to trek to Everest Basecamp rather than round the

Mount Battock, County Top of Kincardineshire, 2nd April 2017.

Cairngorms, I am ready to continue, and stride confidently off eastwards along a disused railway line.

In the forest of Tanar, I sleep and wake to the barking of deer.

The Firmounth drove road connects Glen Tanar with Glen Esk. A carved stone, commissioned in the mid-nineteenth century by the then owner of the Glen Tanar estate, falsely commemorates the passage of Edward I along the Firmounth in the years 1296 and 1303, falsely followed by the Marquis of Montrose in 1645. My travel on the Firmounth is genuine only as far as the summits of Gannoch and Tampie, after which I turn east along the ridgeline towards Mount

Battock, most easterly Corbett,[13] as well as County Top of Kincardi-neshire. The 'Mount' of Mount Battock derives from *Mounth*, a name once applied to the east-west ridge stretching from the Aberdeenshire coastal plain to the edge of Rannoch Moor, and which forms a com-ponent of many toponyms in the locality. The chevrons of snow on nearby Mount Keen have the appearance of direction signs.

Scenting long-distance walker, a large German Shepherd comes bounding downhill towards me. Some distance behind it, a man on a bicycle is definitely not in control. Muzzle notwithstanding, the dog does its best to eat me while the owner dismounts, carefully lays down his bicycle, removes rucksack and helmet, and strolls over to recap-ture his hound.

That night, I camp on a gravel bar in the braided channel of the North Esk river. Despite the proximity of running water, this is the first morning when neither my tent nor my sleeping bag is damp. The weather requires reparation and dollops thick muggy cloud onto the ridge I need to cross to reach Glen Clova. I soon lose the track and bubble around inside the coarse poetry of the Scots hill-names: Shank of Inchgrundle, Wester Skuiley, Benty Roads, Boustie Ley – names that feel as though they belong in the Borders rather than the High-lands.

A break in the clouds allows a brief glimpse of the far side of the glen, mottled blue-green, like the marbled endpapers of a leather-bound book, before I plunge downhill to Clova. A team of volunteers are shoring up the footpath on the west rim of Loch Brandy. The sec-tions they have completed are tidily stepped, but the lower half of the slope is an obstacle course of rocks queueing to be admitted to the newly-constructed path. My only previous visit to Glen Clova came to a premature and inglorious conclusion in the Accident and Emer-gency Department of Ninewells Hospital, Dundee, following a mishap with a camping stove. Keen to avoid a similar performance, I step carefully around the helicopter lifting bags that are spewing their contents about the hillside.

Down in the glen, I am led astray by a sign which directs 'muddy

---

13 A 'Corbett' is a Scottish mountain with a height of between 2,500 and 3,000 feet which is separated by a drop of at least 500 feet from surrounding high ground.

boots and four-legged friends' into the bar of the Glen Clova Hotel. A father and two young children are celebrating having climbed All The Way To Loch Brandy. Robert pauses mid-mouthful to scrutinise the new arrival in the room.

"Who's she? She looks funny."

I try to explain the concept of long-distance walking to a four-year-old, but, since I cannot possibly have walked as far as All The Way To Loch Brandy, Robert soon loses interest.

River Esk, 2nd April 2017.

From Clova, I continue up the glen to take Jock's Road. This high-level route linking Glen Clova with Braemar became Scotland's first designated Right of Way in 1888, following a lengthy lawsuit which bankrupted both the local landowner and the Scottish Rights of Way and Recreation Society. It has been suggested that John (Jock) Winter, who testified in the court case, also lent his name to the route, but in truth the appellation pre-dates the legal action.

Glas Maol (County Top of Angus) and Ben Macdui (County Top of Aberdeenshire and Banffshire)

Glen Doll to Glen Nevis. 118 miles, 4,130 metres ascent.
Tuesday 4th – Monday 10th April

Jock's Road climbs past Davy's Bourach shelter, with its incongruous post-box door, and out onto the rocky plateau. In the glen, the wind is strong enough to splay my tent onto the ground; on the plateau it is biting, steel-edged: into my heart on air that kills.[14] I pull on all of my spare layers and my balaclava before plunging through the chill, over Tolmount and Cairn of Claise, to Glas Maol, the second of my Cairngorm County Tops.

The granite tors and over-deep glens of the Cairngorms imbue me with a sense of imposing, spacious solitude. This is a feeling that I have experienced in only one other, somewhat implausible, location: the industrial estate adjacent to where I work, which has evolved over the past half-century on the site of an old munitions factory. The commonality is a landscape of grand and shattered history, devoid of people, apart from the fleeting glimpse of a solitary figure toiling up a distant spur, or ducking out of sight behind a prefab warehouse. In the Cairngorms, you are transported back to the early Holocene; on the industrial estate, to the post-war years, but the effect is oddly the same: both are places where you are a visitor from the future. For me, this is the opposite of that sense of being a forward-cast which amplifies my loneliness, and means that these are places where it is safe to be alone.

This sentiment is not uniquely mine. In Cecil Day Lewis' verse-play *Noah and the Waters*, we are reminded that "Before / Man set a value on his thoughts or made a prison for fear, / These hills were grown up."[15] The hills themselves speak directly to us. "Stand with us here," they appeal, and "feel underfoot the linked vertebrae of your land."

Stand *with us* – not alone.

In the long weeks between escapes to the Highlands, I run instead to the industrial estate as my refuge of calm.

---

14 Alfred Edward Houseman, *A Shropshire Lad* (London: K. Paul, Trench, Trübner, 1896).

15 Cecil Day-Lewis, *Noah and the Waters* (London: L. & V. Woolf, 1936).

33

My parents are up in Scotland for the school Easter holidays and are keen to act as my support team over the next two weeks. My mother is laden with good intentions and tasty treats; I try to emphasise that 'just a few little extra somethings' add up to an unbearably heavy bag. Individual pots of porridge for breakfast might sound like a wonderful idea, but stack up a week's supply and they take up more space in my rucksack than does my tent.

In Braemar Mountain Sports, I find a waterproof jacket identical to the one I'm currently wearing, but without the holes on the shoulders where my rucksack has rubbed through the fabric. I decide to purchase it, but to give it to my parents to keep in reserve for later in the trip.

"What are you up to today, then?" the shop assistant asks when I take the jacket to the till. Presumably this is a routine friendly question asked of all customers.

"Er... nothing."

Feeling that I should explain the disparity between my expensive purchase and my stated lack of active ambitions, I elaborate: "I'm doing a long-distance walk, and this is my day off."

"Where did you start?"

"John O'Groats, so you can probably guess where I'm heading."

"That's unusual – don't most people cycle it?"

"Probably, but I'm not doing it by the usual route. I'm going via the highest point of every county."

By now, the shop assistant appears genuinely interested. He enquires about mileage, equipment and whether anyone has done this before. Only my diet seems to fail to impress him.

"You'll get scurvy!" he warns me, before turning to serve the next customer.

Back in the Youth Hostel in the evening, I meet a group of walkers who are trying to find their dormitory. Youth Hostels never cease to amaze me with the way they contrive to conceal Escher-esque staircases within outwardly conventional buildings. One flight of stairs is never sufficient: you have to go up some steps, round a corner, up a bit more, along a corridor, down again, along another corridor... staircases may even be required to reach rooms on the ground floor. I hear a cry of jubilation when one of the party discovers that the correct way to the male dormitory is to follow signs to the ladies' washroom on the top floor.

"We're on the summit plateau!"

The next morning, I meet my parents again at the Linn of Dee, where the River Dee tumbles out of the mountains through a narrow, rocky gorge. We walk together into the true heart of the Cairngorms. Blue tits question us from the branches of the Caledonian pinewood, and we squint at silhouettes soaring high above us, hoping in vain for an eagle. A lizard flashes beside the path, and is gone.

So blue when viewed from a distance, the mountains around us are aflame with tongues of autumn: the chocolate-mahogany of heather glowing on hillsides of medallion gold; the deep green of the gnarled Scots pine; the granite-speckled charcoal peat-bog. As though to atone for letting the blue escape, the mountains have trapped every other shade in the splintered spectrum.

At Luibeg Bridge, we part. My parents return along the glen to climb Creag Bhalg. I pitch my tent and then continue to Ben Macdui. Despite its height, Ben Macdui is by far the easiest of the County Tops that I have climbed so far – a combination of the fair weather

Ptarmigan, Ben Macdui, 6th April 2017.

and the fact that I am following a good path from a glen which has already ascended to 600 metres. The final hundred metres to the summit are cloud-shrouded, but from the speckled nose of Sròn Riach lower down the ridge I have wide views over the southern Cairngorms and back towards Glas Maol.

Mindful of the approach of dusk, I do not linger long enough to listen for the footsteps of *Am Fear Mòr Liath*, the legendary Big Grey Man of Ben Macdui. Instead, I descend to my burn-side campsite and watch the sky smouldering until the shadow of Carn a'Mhaim creeps out to smother the world.

The Lairig Ghru is veiled with rainbows as I climb past Corrour Bothy towards the Pools of Dee. The hills are empty of people – until I reach the Rothiemurchus Forest and emerge out of my reverie onto the purple cycle route. Suddenly, cyclists of all abilities and stabilities are everywhere. The same family dynamic is repeated over and over again in each group that passes me. Dad leads the way, cycling confidently on a rugged-looking all-terrain bicycle, oblivious to whatever Mum is trying to communicate as her somewhat older wicker-basketed contraption jolts over the rough gravel. A straggle of children

Entering the Lairig Ghru, 7th April 2017.

follow in their wake like mechanical ducklings. Anyone over the age of seven is cumbered with a full-size bicycle, regardless of whether this puts the ground – or the pedals – out of reach, while the youngest have tiny-wheeled toy bikes and mumble "Mum, Mum" as they struggle to keep the rest of the family within tear-blurred sight.

Having completed my south-to-north crossing of the Cairngorms, I turn southwards again and follow the Spey upstream through the Insh marshes. The name is a familiar motif from my childhood, when appeals from environmental charities would arrive through the letterbox on a seemingly daily basis. *Save the Insh Marshes! Save the Ouse Washes! Save the Winks Meadows!* To be worth campaigning for, reserves were evidently required to have names conforming to the three-syllable pattern: long short-short.

I leave the glen of the Spey at Loch Ericht, from where I can walk through the Ben Alder hills and then cross Rannoch Moor to reach Ben Nevis, the highest of the County Tops. The loch stretches further than I can see. A light breeze is sandpapering the surface of the water. Layered ridges reach down towards the loch shore, fragmenting the simple colour blue into infinitesimal, unnameable shades. I have continued long past the point where my schedule tells me to stop walking for the day, but I recoil as I brush against the fringes of the populous world in Kingussie, Newtonmore, Dalwhinnie, and am lured on by the perfect weather into the wide wildness of the Ben Alder hills.

I can sense a change in the seasons. No longer are frogs gargling in the drainage channels, and bright clumps of *primula vulgaris* are flowering like fields of stars on the banks between the loch and the plantations above. Mountain-bikers in twos and threes are freewheeling back towards civilisation after a long day in the hills. I'm going against the flow, walking into the hills as others are leaving. By the time I pitch my tent on the shores of Loch Pattack, I am alone once more.

The sun sinks neatly into a cleft between two hills on the far side of the loch. With the fall of darkness the sound of the birds around me changes. The plangent call of the snipe sounds like a sheep bleating inside a drainpipe, and there is another call that I don't recognise, like a flock of wet sponges rubbing back and forth across a window pane.

Next day marks the end of the good weather, but not yet the start of the bad: a day of transition. I start walking at first light. When I pass Culra bothy,

BOTHY CLOSED ASBESTOS

is daubed on the front wall. The inhabitants of the tent encampment outside are just beginning to stir. Most tents have a pile of bicycles beside them.

Bealach Dubh lives up to its name, catching the clouds and clasping them at the top of the pass. I descend Uisge Labhair, then follow the southern shore of Loch Ossian through snarls of shocking pink rhododendron.

Although I reach Loch Ossian Youth Hostel by early afternoon, I decide to stop here for the night: the hostel has personal associations for me as the place from where I climbed my first Munro, Beinn na Lap, with Laurence, almost exactly ten years ago. In the intervening decade, a hydroelectric plant at the far end of the loch has brought electricity to the hostel. This means hot showers and a fridge where, ten years ago, there was a paper notice:

THE FRIDGE IS UPSTAIRS
IN THE TELEVISION LOUNGE[16]

The toilets, however, are still of the compost variety.

The warden, Jan, is wonderfully calm and relaxed, although she seems somewhat hazy about who has checked in under which name, and invites us to haphazardly decorate a selection of booking forms with incompatible signatures.

The situation is complicated by the fact that people keep trooping in from Rannoch Moor. Alasdair and his mother Rachel are the first arrivals, on the lunchtime train from Glasgow. Rebecca has cycled all the way from Edinburgh on a bicycle that looks like it would have preferred to stay within the city limits. A teacher from the Isle of Skye cycles in, too, but his friend – a larger man, with 'The fat man at the back' emblazoned on the rear of his cycling shorts – has been pushing his bike since the tyre split. A young man with an enormous rucksack has dropped out of an expedition because of a knee injury. At half

---

16 The hostel is a single-storey building. When I mention the notice to Jan, she says, "Yes, that was Nick's sense of humour," recalling the warden of a decade previously.

Sunset from Loch Pattack, 8th April 2017.

past ten, a family of four appears out of the inky darkness.

One of the things that I love about Loch Ossian Youth Hostel is that with just two dormitories, and no mobile phone reception, everyone stays in the single communal room until bedtime, chatting and swapping anecdotes. Alasdair initiates a game of Munro Top Trumps. The pack of cards is labelled 'volume one'. In it are represented most of the more famous Munros, so presumably volume two will contain all those monotonous, muddy Munros that few people climb twice.

As dusk falls, a stag and hind come right to the front door of the hostel and show too close an interest in Rebecca's bike. "You know what," says Jan, abandoning all pretence of knowing who's who, "if there's a fire, I'm just going to go into each dormitory and yell 'FIRE!'"

We shuffle out of the hostel into the lonely morning, blinking up at the ghost sun through thinning scuds of cloud. Reluctant to leave the companionship engendered by our isolation, we equivocate over leave-taking and luck-wishing, until we risk being left behind by our individual itineraries. I am the first to depart, shortly followed by the teacher and Fat-Man-At-The-Back, who need to catch an early train to Fort William and a bicycle repair shop.

I follow the old *Road to the Isles* route as far as Loch Treig, then slip quietly into the glen of the Abhainn Rath, which sidles up between the Mamores and the Grey Corries to the Tom an Eite pass and the headwaters of Nevis. I know the route well and don't need to check the map other than to gauge my progress. The mountains shelter me from the worst of the weather and for most of the day there are merely soft clouds and a simple blue sky, with only a brief shower as the path hesitates through the bog at Tom an Eite. Even Ben Nevis is cloud-free.

Two cyclists are pedalling up the road in Glen Nevis: it's Fat-Man-At-The-Back and the teacher, both bicycles now returned to full working order. I sense their struggle to account for my untimely appearance before they grudgingly concede that maybe I have made it all the way through from Loch Ossian, on foot, by 3pm.

The Mamores and the Grey Corries from Loch Ossian, 10th April 2017.

Introspection: Time

It might seem incongruous that I chose to name a chapter of my writing about the Scottish Highlands with a line from Housman's poem A Shropshire Lad,[17] *rather than reserving this line until I had actually reached Shropshire. But the blue remembered hills speak more to me of Scotland – and the Cairngorm plateau in particular – than of the Welsh marches, not only because of the 'gorm' of Cairngorm, but also because of the element of temporality within* A Shropshire Lad, *when Housman writes of the "standing hills, long to remain."*

My walk through the Cairngorms, amongst mountains sculpted from granite laid down more than 400 million years ago, led me to a new understanding of my relationship not with people, but with landscape.

As a child, cast as a time-traveller, an interloper from the past, I found myself uncomprehending of, incomprehensible to, the inhabitants of the present. But the landscape has travelled from an even further distant past than myself. My own temporal unconformity is foreshortened by comparison with a geological time-scale, any sense of identity becoming pale and diffuse until it can be absorbed into the land itself. I am not alone – I am part of the hills, and there I am safe.

Perhaps this is why concepts such as 'yesterday' and 'tomorrow' become increasingly irrelevant, almost meaningless, with time spent on moors or mountains. Though I risk being accused of quoting another poet out of her geographical context, I am reminded of the 'time beyond time' of the Lakeland poet Margaret Cropper: the time that cannot be described within the constrained vocabulary of our own narrow present, the time "… up there, where the hills are deep in snow, that is eternity: / That is out of all reckoning and telling."[18]

---

17 Alfred Edward Houseman, *A Shropshire Lad* (London: K. Paul, Trench, Trübner, 1896).
18 Margaret Cropper, 'Up There', *Collected Poems* (Kendal, Cumbria: Titus Wilson, 1958).

The Relocation of Slugs

Inverness-shire – Argyllshire – Perthshire –
Dunbartonshire – Stirlingshire – Renfrewshire –
Clackmannanshire – Kinross-shire – Fife – West Lothian

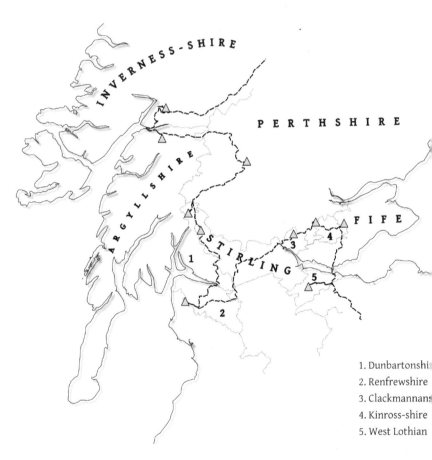

1. Dunbartonshi
2. Renfrewshire
3. Clackmannan
4. Kinross-shire
5. West Lothian

Ben Nevis (County Top of Inverness-shire) and Bidean nam Bian (County Top of Argyllshire)

Glen Nevis to Glen Coe. 40 miles, 3,650 metres ascent.
Tuesday 11th – Friday 14th April

The first time I climbed Ben Nevis, it was as an afternoon extension to an already fairly lengthy walk.

Laurence and I were staying at Glen Nevis Youth Hostel with a group of friends, as a brief addendum to a climbing trip on Skye. Our planned walk was to climb Aonach Mòr and Aonach Beag, two Munros which form the ridge to the east of the Ben Nevis range – the *Mòr* in this case being slightly smaller than the *Beag* – ascending from Steall meadow, alongside Allt Coire Giubhsachan. The weather was kind, the ascent not unduly arduous, and we were hill-fit from our time on Skye, so by mid-day we had visited both summits and returned to the bealach at the head of Coire Giubhsachan – whereupon we realised just how close we were to Càrn Mòr Dearg and its celebrated arête. It would have been inconceivable to let such an opportunity slip by.

The descent from Ben Nevis back to the Youth Hostel was a seemingly never-ending series of switchbacks. The consensus amongst the group at the time was that our route of ascent had been far more enjoyable and that anyone choosing to climb Ben Nevis by the 'tourist route' would be in danger of coming away with the impression of hill-walking as a tedious and unrewarding activity.

Be that as it may, with 500 miles behind me and nearly 3,000 still to go, I am willing to endure the tedium.

Helen, wife of Edward Peck's grandson, and one of the few people I know who consider tackling Ben Nevis in winter conditions to be a good idea, arrives on the sleeper train. 'Sleeper' is something of a misnomer, since seated passengers were required to change carriages in Edinburgh, and the Fort-William-bound carriage had neither heating, nor lighting, nor toilet facilities. Nevertheless, by 10.30am I am dragging her up the tedious tourist route into louring storm-clouds and sheeting rain.

The name Ben Nevis (or *Beinn Nibheis* in its Gaelic form) is variously interpreted as meaning either 'mountain with its head in the clouds'[19] or 'venomous mountain'. Yesterday it was neither; today it is both. Appalling though the weather is, the forecast for tomorrow is even worse: plummeting temperatures will convert today's traipsome slush into a potentially far more dangerous covering of ice on the upper half of the mountain. Better to be climbing when the conditions are merely unpleasant rather than actively unsafe.

Above 1,000 metres we find ourselves wallowing in rotten snow. We do not need the ice axes and crampons that we are carrying, but kick steps to gain purchase for our boots. It is too cold to linger anywhere on the mountain, so we simply touch the summit cairn, then turn and begin the return trudge.9Back at the Youth Hostel, we strip off outer layers of clothing and try to find space for them in the drying

Observatory on the summit of Ben Nevis, County Top of Inverness-shire, 11th April 2017.

19 Statistically speaking, Ben Nevis spends more than half the year with its head in the clougs, and receives at least twice the annual rainfall of Fort William. Indeed, meteorological observations carried out on the mountain between 1883 and 1904 recorded a fog-shrouded summit for 80% of November-January.

room. Bedraggled jackets and waterproof trousers drip from high clothes lines. Rucksacks trail straps and buckles into the warm puddle seeping towards the door. The impossibly humid air is dank and close with the loamy, canvas aroma peculiar to sodden outdoor equipment. "It's like a rainforest in there," the warden laughs as she emerges from the canopy of coats.

Prolonged exposure to the cold has caused my thumb to split. I try to soothe the throbbing fissure with margarine from the 'free food' shelf in the self-catering kitchen, but it's clear that I need a more effective emollient. Helen and I walk into Fort William in search of Vaseline, then meet my parents in a café that has been a favourite of Laurence's and mine since we first sampled their tuna and mango chutney toasties.

My parents treat the next leg of the expedition like a relay baton. My mother accompanies us as we leave Glen Nevis, against the flow of north-bound walkers nearing the end of the West Highland Way in varying stages of soggy disintegration. Over the weeks until I reach Glasgow and next see Laurence I will shadow the route of this long-distance trail, branching out east and west to reach County Tops.

We ford the Allt na Lairige Mòire and climb on a low rising traverse of Mam na Guilainn. Custody of the baton is then passed to my father, who escorts us around Loch Leven to Glen Coe village. The relay culminates in a celebratory meal at the Clachaig Inn. Later in the evening we retire to our tents and fall asleep to the sweet smell of woodsmoke and the sound of children playing in the river as the campsite begins to fill up for the Easter weekend.

Helen's sleepless night on the sleeper train has caught up with her: our pace gets slower and slower as we ascend Coire nan Lochan. When, just below the snow-line, the arms of the corrie curve away into cloud, she decides to abandon the ascent and wait for me while I summit my next County Top alone. Mindful that Helen will be waiting for me on a cold mountainside, I do this as quickly as I can, but I need to climb over Stob Coire nan Lochan to reach a narrow, exposed ridge linking it to Bidean nam Bian, 'pinnacle of the hills', then reprise the first mountain on the return. I use crampons for extra security on the ridge, although on both summits the snow is little more than a powdery dusting on rocky ground.

I return to the corrie to find Helen busy dispensing well-meant advice in an unfortunately upper-class English accent to groups of evidently battle-hardened Scottish walkers.

The west face of Aonach Dubh, Glencoe, 14th April 2017.

Helen: I wouldn't go on up there if I were you – the conditions look pretty nasty.

Innocent Member Of The Public: What are you doing up here on your own?

Helen: Waiting for a friend.

IMOTP: Where's your friend?

Helen: She's gone on up there.

I consider introducing Helen to the term Sassenach, but think better of it. We descend, leaving a trail of newly-converted supporters of Scottish independence in our wake.

Ben Lawers (County Top of Perthshire)

Glen Coe to Killin. 58 miles, 2,540 metres ascent.
Saturday 15th – Tuesday 18th April

Recurring phrases in Helen's chatter suggest a certain lack of optimism: *I think we're going to get very wet. It all depends on whether the track's underwater. Rannoch Moor looked flooded from the train. If only we had a raft with us.* Yet despite Helen's forebodings, there are definite signs of spring: tadpoles are scooting about in the underwater sections of track and daffodils are nodding to themselves on the shores of the 'flood', which usually goes by the name of Loch Laidon.

The weather is generally improving, and the showers become lighter and less frequent the further east we walk. From the limitless sky-filled eternity of Rannoch Moor there are exquisite views back towards snow-dusted Glen Coe, with Buachaille Etive Mòr adopting its classic picture-postcard stance in the foreground.

The weather forecast has predicted an 'envelope of snow' – an incongruous choice of metaphor, and one which conjures some interesting mental images. In Glen Rannoch, though, the air lacks the soft clarity that presages wintry weather. We trudge through fretful drizzle, sombre skies dampening our conversation. The moor appears today, as it did to James Robertson in the year 1771, a "forsaken waste."[20] Robertson crossed Rannoch Moor on his way from Glen Nevis to Killin, just as Helen and I are doing. But, whereas I have a known and definite aim, Robertson was perhaps unaware of his own 'first', having some few days previously made the earliest recorded ascent of Ben Nevis. Though Robertson recorded in his journal that Ben Nevis "is reckoned the highest mountain in Britain,"[21] this claim was not put beyond doubt until 1847, when the Ordnance Survey were able to confirm the height of Ben Macdui as being less than that of Ben Nevis. Robertson is also credited with the first ascent of Morven, the first of my County Tops and now more than a month ago.

---

20 Cited in D. M. Henderson and J. H. Dickson (eds.) *A Naturalist in the Highlands: James Robertson, His Life and Travels in Scotland, 1762-1771.* (Edinburgh: Scottish Academic Press, 1994).
21 *Ibid.*

In the lazy air of evening, we camp next to the Allt Baile a'Mhuilinn in the pass connecting Glen Lyon with Loch Tay. We brew tea, share a packet of white chocolate eggs to celebrate Easter and watch as the last of the daylight leaches away.

With the onset of darkness, the mountains surrounding our campsite resolve into solid, familiar adversaries. I feel I know them with taut intimacy, having once descended Ben Lawers at twilight, crossed the pass where Helen and I now camp, and climbed up into the night cloaking the Tarmachan ridge. The air had thickened with fog, rendering my torch useless. I had sensed my way forwards, navigating with every sense but sight, feeling the fog caress my face, hearing the shape of the ridge in the sound of the wind, tasting the location of the cliffs of Cam Chreag in the temperature of the air. The experience was delectable, visceral. By the time I had pitched my tent at midnight, I felt an immeasurable knowledge of these mountains running deep within me.

I wake from my reverie to find that there are more mundane, molluscine matters to be dealt with. There are slugs in our tents, slugs in our boots, slugs in our cooking pots, slugs in our mugs. Small greyish-green slugs that stick to your fingers when you try to pick them up or flick them away. A larger specimen slicking up the inner wall of my tent distracts me from my lighted stove.

"Oh f**k!"

"Are you OK?" Helen calls across from the neighbouring tent.

"Yes, but I've just melted a huge hole in my tent." I have let the wall of the tent billow too close to the intense heat of the stove, and the nylon fabric has shrivelled, leaving a hole the width of a handspan.

We pack up our belongings and continue through the pass until we reach the start of the path to Ben Lawers, the County Top of Perthshire. We will need to descend the mountain by the same route, so pitch my tent at the side of the track – presumably releasing a colony of disorientated slugs – and stash our camping equipment in it.

It has snowed again overnight, and there is a covering of powder-snow down to about 700 metres. As far as Beinn Ghlas the powder is thin and barely conceals the path, but it deepens for the final mile towards Ben Lawers. Just before the summit, arcs of aureate light rip the clouds apart, revealing a wide unfinished canvas of sparkling whiteness. The sun beats down from the newly-empty blue infinity, and its reflection beats back up: the temperature soars.

Back at our gear stash by early afternoon, we press on, following the main road towards Killin. For Helen, this is the end of the adventure; she is to return home by train from nearby Crianlarich. I dive into the outdoor shop a few minutes before closing time, where a bemused shop assistant sells me a midge-net a good couple of months before the arrival of the first midge of the year: I intend to glue it over the hole in my tent.

I buy a newspaper when the village newsagent opens the next morning, but within an hour Theresa May has rendered it obsolete by calling a general election – although I do not learn this until later in the day, watching televised news in the Killin Hotel.

A notice-board outside the McLaren Hall informs me that it is the second-largest village hall – of its type – in Perthshire. Is Killin intent on damning itself with faint praise?

Ben Lawers, County Top of Perthshire, 17th April 2017.

Ben Vorlich (County Top of Dunbartonshire) and Ben Lomond (County Top of Stirlingshire)

Killin to Dumbarton. 73 miles, 3,650 metres ascent.
Wednesday 19th – Saturday 22nd April

With the mingled after-taste of cooked breakfast and civilisation in my mouth, I am back on the road, walking west towards Crianlarich. Buds are just beginning to open on horse chestnut, birch and alder. A pair of herons are ruminating in the shallows of the River Dochart, but take flight as I approach.

Low cloud is shrouding the mountains. It feels slightly unreal to be walking along Glen Dochart when the weather has expunged the high ground from the landscape. Though I cannot see the mountains around me, I am certain that I have walked most of today's route before. When a student in Glasgow, I would make a weekly pilgrimage up the West Highland Line, to climb anything and everything within a day's travel from a railway station, and would often walk sections of the West Highland Way between stations to while away the time before the return train to Glasgow.

In Crianlarich, my legs take charge and walk themselves to the tearoom on the station platform, ignoring the admonishment from my head that I've already had a cooked breakfast and a late start. I buy a cup of coffee and am doubly rewarded: when the Fort William train pulls in to await the Oban train for re-coupling, Jan, the Loch Ossian Youth Hostel warden appears in the tearoom, having just summarised my last ten days' walking with a short hop on the train. We chat for the allotted seven minutes before her train is due to re-commence its journey, and Jan asks me to send her a copy of this diary.

I re-join the West Highland Way contraflow as I continue southwards from Crianlarich, against a steady stream of heavily-laden hikers. The hills here have a softer texture than those further north, perhaps because there is less heather, more deer grass and bracken. Leaving the West Highland Way at Beinglass, I climb steeply alongside a string of pylons into Strath Dubh Uisge to camp below Stob an Flithich. New bracken stands erect like wax candles, the furled tips giving it the appearance of melting. In another week or so the bracken will render this climb much more difficult.

Nobody ever climbs Ben Vorlich from the north – there's no path, the ground is tussocky and uneven and the gradient is unrelentingly steep. This is my third or fourth ascent of the mountain. The weather has been atrocious on all previous occasions, and today conforms to the pattern. Despite wearing full waterproofs, I can feel rainwater running down my legs and into my boots. I don't think my waterproofs are leaking; they just can't keep the cloud out. There is, however, a sizeable hole on the right shoulder of my jacket, where the rucksack strap has rubbed through.

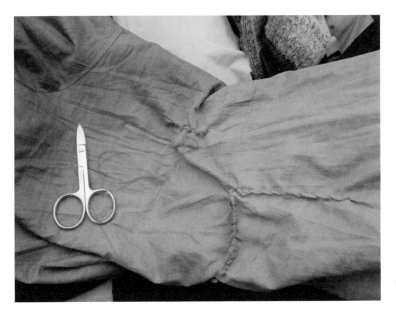

Running repairs.

I inwardly curse whoever decided to put Ben Vorlich and Ben Lomond on opposite sides of the loch: when I have descended Ben Vorlich and packed up my tent, I have to walk in a long distended arc round the north end of Loch Lomond to regain the West Highland Way. For walkers heading north, I might well be the only person they encounter all day, and everybody I meet wants to know whether I've realised that I'm walking in the 'wrong' direction.

A short distance before Inversnaid, I climb high onto the hillside to re-pitch my tent. Sound travels uncannily across the open water: I can hear roadworks on the A82, and a German-language commentary on one of the tourist cruise-boats is so clear that I can make out a lot of what is being said, despite my shoddy knowledge of the language.

Hydroelectric pipes are strung on the opposite hill-slope like strings on the neck of a guitar. Their wire-like appearance serves as a useful reminder: I unpick some of my midge-net and tease out a length of cotton to sew up the hole in my jacket, then glue a patch of net over the repair.

As with Ben Vorlich, I climb Ben Lomond on its obscure northern flank. I gain a little height on a track leading away from the lochside at Cailness, lagger through bog and knee-deep deer grass to a bealach at 500 metres, then struggle up the ridge to a point just west of the summit. I make very slow progress, the wind and the weight of my rucksack sapping what little energy remains in my bone-weary body. One of the first Scottish tourist guidebooks, written in 1792, asserted that Ben Lomond could be ascended from the north "in perfect safety," though it was "steep and rugged."[22] I find myself more in agreement with William Burrell, who had made the first recorded ascent of the mountain some years previously and evidently found it no small challenge:

> The way to [the summit] is very irksome and in some places so steep that we were obliged to crawl on hands and knees... In several parts we sunk up to our knees in mire.[23]

The air seethes with the smells of wild garlic and wild goat – quite a heady mix in high humidity – and boils with the power of the wind. Gusts from conflicting currents slam into each other when they collide around rock outcrops, creating a resounding sub-sonic ache somewhere deep in my skull.

I reach the summit by late morning, but do not linger and head straight down the opposite side of the mountain, now on an obvious track. In the shelter of the Ptarmigan ridge, the wind dies. The rain begins a soft diminuendo as I descend, until I reach Rowardennan in limpid spring sunshine. I know I have been ready to announce the ar-

---

22 Charles Ross, *Travellers' Guide to Loch Lomond* (Paisley, 1792).

23 John Dunbar (ed.) *Sir William Burrell's Northern Tour, 1758.* Sources in Local History, No. 6 (East Linton: Tuckwell Press, 1997).

Loch Lomond, with Ben Vorlich (left) and Ben Lomond (right)
22nd April 2017.

rival of spring many times already on my meandering journey, but this time it feels genuine. The woodland is green and vital: delicate leaves are budding on birch, ash and alder; wood sorrel and primrose are flowering; there are even the first signs of bluebells. I must look out of place walking through the midst of this unabated spring with an ice axe strapped to my pack.

Ben Lomond is the last Munro of my walk. The hills will be smaller now, until I reach the Lake District and Wales. Looking at the weather forecast, it seems that I have descended to the lowlands just in time – and perhaps my predictions of spring are still somewhat premature:

All mountain areas of Britain from Sunday 23rd April 2017:

An abrupt change on Monday as very cold air spreads southwards. Winds persisting northerly, intermittently near gale force, will bring some very low freezing levels. Snow and hail showers, even on some lower slopes as summit temperatures drop as low as, if not lower, than at any time this winter.

I spend the night in a bunkhouse in Balmaha. The sound of snoring rumbles up through the floor from a group of German West Highland Way walkers in the dormitory below. Presumably operating on continental time, the Germans get up at 5.30am and begin clattering around the kitchen. I give up on sleep at 6.00am, and creep downstairs, to find that one of the party has dragged his mattress out into the corridor in an effort to escape the snoring.

The River Clyde, 22nd April 2017.

Crossing the Kilpatrick Hills, I divert a short distance to visit Duncolm, the highest point within the modern unitary authority of West Dunbartonshire. After the steep ascent of Ben Lomond I relish being able to stomp over the tussocky moorland, through patches of gold-and-green marsh marigold. I sit on the summit Duncolm looking back towards Loch Lomond, and watch the shifting patterns of cloud-shadows.

I descend towards Dumbarton, where Laurence is waiting at the Travelodge. Reaching the A82, I wait for a gap in the traffic and sprint to the central reservation. After ten minutes marooned between the lanes of speeding cars, I choose a gap that isn't really big enough, wave my arms around wildly in the hope that this will indicate to drivers that I am about to do something stupid, then dash across the final two lanes.

Hill of Stake (County Top of Renfrewshire)

Dumbarton to Stirling. 90 miles, 2,750 metres ascent.
Sunday 23rd – Thursday 27th April

Laurence returns to Yorkshire, taking with him my ice axe, crampons, bivvy bag and balaclava, and leaving me with a gratifyingly lighter load.

The next leg of my journey will be a meandering course through the central belt of Scotland, by way of Glasgow, Stirling and Edinburgh, until I reach the Lammermuir hills and the Cheviots at the eastern extent of the Southern Uplands. I cross the Erskine Bridge and step out into a new landscape, of arable farmland and gorse scrub, of gently rolling hills and lethargic burns, of ravens and buzzards. A recently-opened path links Ladymuir Plantation and Muirshiel Country Park. The plantation is closed for felling – but there is no forestry work on Sundays. Amongst the dense Sitka spruces, I find the most perfect solitude I think I could achieve now that I have left the Highlands. Safely secluded, I sleep for twelve hours, letting the exhaustion of Ben Vorlich and Ben Lomond seep away.

A track leads to a barytes (barium sulphate) mine. The word 'barytes' is derived from the Greek *barus*, meaning heavy; barytes is four and a half times denser than water. Historically, it has been used as a white pigment in paper, porcelain and paint, and as a lubricant (the India tyre factory at Inchinnan used barytes to assist with the removal of tyres from their moulds). Prior to the sinking of shafts in 1947, the mine here was open-cast: a deep scar has been incised into the hillside, parallel to the burn. In another landscape – Glen Coe, perhaps – it could pass for a natural gully, but with the softly-bedded sphagnum-lined 'true' burn alongside for comparison, its human origins are evident. By the time the mine closed in the late 1960s, nearly 300,000 tons of barytes had been extracted from these hills.

Hill of Stake, the County Top of Renfrewshire, is unprepossessing in itself, but a fine viewpoint. I can see northwards to the distinctive profile of Ben Lomond, with other hills beyond; to the west, Arran is clear; to the south lie the Galloway hills. Glasgow is intermittently visible between thick white showers bowing out beneath cumulus clouds.

I leave the summit to follow the ridge towards Lochwinnoch.

Almost immediately, the weather overtakes me: snow, in large, wet flakes, explaining the peculiar thickness of the showers over Glasgow.

55I studied briefly at the University of Glasgow, and have remained in loose contact with one of my lecturers, Anne, who still works in the department. Hoping to surprise her with an impromptu visit, I wake early and walk at a brisk pace along the cycle route into Glasgow. The cycle path signs are frequent but discouraging. When Glasgow first appears as a destination, it is thirteen miles away. Then twelve. Then it takes a step backwards, to thirteen miles away, where it persists for what is surely more than a mile, before leaping closer: ten miles, then nine, eight, nine again, eight again... I give up paying any attention to the signage and assume that I will eventually reach Glasgow.

The wind cuts through me in sheets of ice. I am not wearing my waterproof coat to try to prevent it being torn further, but I keep thinking to myself "I should put my fleece on," only to realise that I'm already wearing it. In Bellahouston, I capitulate, don my jacket, and dive into a corner shop with a coffee machine. Huddled in a bus shelter, I try to warm my hands on the paper cup. Either my manners or my smell are obviously offensive to a couple waiting for the bus, who shuffle to the far end of the shelter.

As I climb the short flight of steps leading to the university's East Quadrangle, I am aware of a sense of comfortable familiarity. I feel more of a connection, more of a *belonging*, to Glasgow than to any other academic institution at which I have studied.

Anne is in her office – but only just, having returned the previous day from a work trip to Montreal. We chatter for half an hour or so, during which time she fills me in on changes in the department since I graduated, and we discuss the delicate issue of sponsorship – Anne is one of the few people who understands my decision not to seek sponsorship for this walk.

After visiting the university, I relax with a book in the Botanic Gardens, basking in the warmth of the Kibble Palace, until it is time to check in to my guesthouse in Charing Cross.

"Do you mind if I sit here?" At breakfast the next morning, a portly, bustling lady with a Germanic accent gestures at the seat diagonally opposite me.

I nod in acquiescence. "No, please go ahead."

She promptly sits down directly in front of me. "It is always best to sit opposite someone at breakfast, I think."

I had been reading, and try to continue, but it soon becomes apparent that the reason that it is best to sit opposite someone at breakfast is to talk to – or at – them. The lady introduces herself as a Harley Street Homœopathist, visiting Glasgow "for my appraisal." The 'ai' of appraisal is elongated by a slantwards grimace, leaving me in no doubt as to the Harley Street Homœopathist's opinion of this professional evaluation. She commences a comprehensive and partially-comprehensible lecture on the state of homœopathy in Glasgow, during which I do my best to keep track of the narrative and nod in appropriate places. It's an indication of how settled I have become in my solitude that I find a cheerful conversation over the breakfast table so alienating.

"But you must see the Botanical Gardens!" The conversation changes tack abruptly – or perhaps I missed the linking sentence.

"I have done," I respond, "I spent most of yesterday afternoon reading in the Kibble Palace."

Clearly this is not sufficient. "But you must see the orchids!" The last word is accompanied by a wooshing hand gesture resembling a fountain. "The orchids! [*woosh*] They are wonderful! [*woosh*] Never have I seen such orchids! [*woosh*] So many varieties! [*woosh*] And from the Botanical Gardens one can walk along the Kelvin Walkway. It is wonderful! [*Two wooshes – it really must be wonderful*] It reminds me of my home. The river running through the deep gorge is so much like the Black Forest. Wonderful! [*woosh*] And so clean! I am going to walk there again today."

I reply that I am also thinking of walking alongside the Kelvin today, although in reality I am mentally running through other options for getting out of the city towards Milngavie – walking up the verge of the A809, perhaps?

"Well, I can tell you how to get there. It is very simple! One takes the bus to the Great Western Bridge and then there is a little flight of stairs to take you down to the river."

At the mention of the bus, I feel a surge of relief: I am fairly certain that this means walking into the centre of Glasgow, to catch a bus from the main bus station. If I walk the five or ten minutes from

Charing Cross directly to the bridge, I will have a significant head start. I thank the Harley Street Homœopathist for her guidance, mumble something about needing to pack my rucksack, and then make my escape.

My ploy seems to have worked, as I see few people other than a handful of joggers and dog-walkers on the path alongside the River Kelvin. It is a pleasant enough path, and there is much evidence of work by Glasgow City Council to tidy up the river and surrounding land – but in places the river is an unhealthy opaque turquoise, like muddied mouthwash, and there are too many car tyres lurking beneath the surface of the water for me to sense any resemblance to the Black Forest. Further out towards Milngavie, I catch sight of a dipper bobbing up and down on the wheel of an upturned shopping trolley.

In the Campsie fells, the water is of a very different quality. I drink deeply from a spring – people pay a high price for this when water it comes in plastic bottles. Admittedly I have to lie on my front in a bed of bog asphodel and cotton-grass before I can reach down far enough into a peat-hole to fill my flask.

The air is thick and cloying with the buttery scent of gorse, now in full bloom. Hawthorn and elder are in leaf, and the first velvety leaf-lets are beginning to unfold from the buds on beech trees. And, as I pass the crags of Lewis Hill, where an intrusion of igneous rock presents a barrier-like sill on the south-eastern side of Stirling, a solitary double-call: the first cuckoo of the year.

Ben Cleuch (County Top of Clackmannanshire), Innerdouny Hill (County Top of Kinross-shire), West Lomond (County Top of Fife) and Cairnpapple Hill (County Top of West Lothian)

Stirling to Penicuik. 119 miles, 3,570 metres ascent.
Friday 28th April – Friday 5th May

I have marooned myself at Stirling Motorway Service Station. The road sign depicting the junction resembles a Swiss Army Knife: a long oval with splayed tools and trunk roads. During my rest day, I make several forays into the city centre to re-supply and to explore, each time taking my life in my hands as I sprint across motorway slip roads.

Next morning, I oversleep, waking only at 8.00am, so it is past 9.00am before I set off. My parents are staying in Alva for the Bank Holiday weekend, and I have arranged to meet them there for lunch; the late start means that I have to force my pace.

After lunch the clouds threaten rain and we can see heavy showers sweeping over Stirling, but the Ochils receive only a few tentative drops. We ascend a switchback path over Ben Ever to reach Ben Cleuch, the County Top of the tiny county of Clackmannanshire.[24] Despite a general murkiness in the air, we can see as far as the Forth bridges and the Pentland hills. A shaft of sunlight traverses the new Forth crossing, which smoulders with a golden glow, before the sunlight slides off the bridge into Queensferry.

We part company on the summit, my parents heading down over The Law, while I continue over Andrew Gannell, Tarmangie and Whitewhisp hills, to camp by a burn leading into Glen Quey. Just as I am drifting off to sleep, two distinct gunshots crack only a short distance away. I lie still, wondering whether this will prove to be a very poor choice of campsite, but there are no more shots before sleep overtakes me.

I am relieved not to oversleep again, since I have another rendezvous to make: as I am descending towards the road, a taxi pulls in

---

24 By area, Clackmannanshire is less than half the size of Rutland, the smallest of the English historic counties, and only a third the size of Wales' smallest county, Flintshire.

next to Castle Hill Reservoir and Mark clambers out.

"Excellent – a good drought – good for business." Mark is a water engineer. Callous though his words sound, I catch a glint in his eye to suggest that he is not speaking entirely sincerely – though the water level in the reservoir does indeed look worryingly low for the time of year. Work has brought Mark north to inspect a pumping station near Oban and he has kindly diverted over to Kinross to join me for today's County Top.

My map depicts Innerdouny Hill in the midst of a plantation, un-reachable by any of the forest tracks, so we are thankful to discover a narrow trodden-down path leading us easily to the summit. On the descent towards Kinross, much of the forest has recently been felled, so we are again granted an easy passage.

With Mark on his way back to work, a heavy melancholy delays my departure from Kinross, but quickly dissipates in the warm sun-shine as I follow the shore path round Loch Leven. Heightened by its isolation, the distinctive volcanic outline of West Lomond dominates the view to the east. The hill is tiring just to look at; I am a little wor-ried about whether I will have the energy to climb it, but manage to be on the summit by noon.

The geology is beguiling. Glen Vale cuts steeply through the hills, breaking out into arable farmland between outcrops of calciferous sandstone. Exposed earth is either clayey-white or rich orange; where the two are visible together the contrast is striking, despite the haze-dulled air.

Reluctantly tearing myself away from the hills, I return to Loch Leven, to continue along the shore path as far as the Vane Farm RSPB reserve, before following roads to Ballingry, Loch Ore and Loch Gelly. Though separated geographically by less than a dozen miles, there is a noticeable disparity between the affluence of Kinross, and these former mining villages, which feel as though they have turned in upon themselves, looking away from a world which has forgotten them. They accuse me: of privilege; of belonging to, or believing in, class. I am uncomfortably aware that I am striding along their streets in expensive boots, with a job to return to in November, knowing that I can afford to take eight months out of employment.

I consider camping by Loch Gelly, but the loch shore has been fired, reducing the reeds to a blackened stubble and charring trees,

All three Forth bridges, 3rd May 2017.

bushes and fence-posts. The burnt reeds have exposed layers of litter. Heat-mangled remnants, the origins of which I don't wish to examine too closely, snap or squelch beneath my boots. I soon return to the road, then turn onto a track towards a line of wind turbines. The map shows this track as a minor road, but I have to climb a number of padlocked gates and dip under a strand of barbed wire, before I can continue between the cloud-spewing towers of the Fife Ethylene Plant and the slicing blades of the turbines. Dark shadows race repeatedly across the ground, as though the world is blinking, involuntarily, once per second.

The construction of the Forth Replacement Crossing is evidently running behind schedule – my map marks the new bridge with a line of blue dashes labelled 'Due to open end 2016' – and the area between Inverkeithing and North Queensferry is a labyrinth of past, present and future roads, through which columns of traffic cones march like ants. I'm not certain that my interpretation of the blue cycle-route-diversion signs is correct until I ascend a final ramp onto the Forth Road Bridge. A notice requests pedestrians and cyclists to use the east walkway – but the route through the roadworks has led me to the western side of the bridge, and there is no obvious access to the opposite walk-way other than to cross the carriageways, so I decide that I haven't noticed the notice.

The haze which has been buildings for several days limits visibil-ity along the river, although perhaps my expectations of the weather are unduly high, since Laurence and I once drove across the road bridge in a cloud inversion, with clear blue skies above and tendrils of silver burning off the surface of the river below.

Reaching the southern shore, I head to the Three Bridges Takeaway, where Liam, the proprietor, provides me with a free cup of tea. While Treacle, Liam's dog, licks my boots clean, Liam explains that free drinks to backpackers such as myself are his way of returning the many favours he has received during a lifetime's walking. He proffers water, hot food, first aid supplies… indeed, he seems a little disappointed that he can't provide more assistance than a simple cup of tea.

If I can repay Liam for the tea, perhaps it is by saying this: next time you are crossing the Forth, visit the Three Bridges Takeaway. The food and drink are of a far better quality than you will find at a motorway service station, and much more reasonably priced, and there is nowhere better from which to survey our nation's engineering history.

On the southern side of the Forth, the air is redolent with the scent of sewage works. The metallic grating of banners fluttering outside car showrooms sounds absurdly like the braying of geese. I will be staying in a motel in 'Edinburgh's luxury car village' – not my natural habitat, but a two-night stop within this shrine to consumerism allows me to visit my next County Top as a day walk, without my large rucksack.

I stride out in the morning carrying only a small bag of provisions. Aeroplanes coming in to land at Edinburgh Airport line up almost perfectly with the River Almond railway viaduct, and roads are con-gested with rush hour traffic; all routes converge on Edinburgh.

The view to the west is blocked by a hill resembling an enormous pink blancmange – Greendyke Hill is a 'bing', or slag heap; the ac-cumulated waste of shale mining. Although mining came to an end in the 1940s, the contours of this man-made hill are not depicted on my map. The waste is alkaline – not acidic, like spoil heaps from coal mines – and the bing is now a haven for wildlife. James 'Paraffin' Young, the chemist whose Bathgate factory produced naptha and lubricating oils from shale oil, stares glumly out from the backs of buses running along the A89.

A narrow track leads into abused suburban woodland. Nailed to a tree is a far-from-encouraging handwritten notice:

> "Site closed in the hour's off darkness
> For health and safety"

I tread cautiously, careful to avoid the most suspect pieces of litter. Brambled stonework is visible through the trees to my left. I reach a clearing to find tarmac beneath my feet and a boarded-up building ahead. I notice another, much grander, building behind, then another, then a paved path with a broken handrail alongside. It feels as though I have entered a post-apocalyptic future: an abandoned upper-class estate. I later learn that these are the ruins of Bangour Village Hospital, a psychiatric hospital which operated between 1904 and 2004. A church occupies what seems to be the centre of the settlement. It too, has been boarded up, but fresh wreaths of remembrance have been laid on a memorial in the southern entrance.

Leaving the desolate future behind me, I continue along minor roads towards the Cairnpapple. A prominent hill topped by a pillar is visible from several miles away, but this proves to be the viewpoint on Knock Hill, not the County Top of West Lothian. On Cairnpapple Hill itself, the official summit lies about five metres north east of the trig point, although there are several plausible locations for the highest point; I try to visit all of them, just to be sure.

Not having far to walk the next day, I loiter in McDonalds, knitting with a ball of yarn purchased from a charity shop in Broxburn. I don't have knitting needles, but a pair of tent pegs will be just long enough to knit a narrow scarf – provided the pegs are not required for my tent before I finish the scarf. The side of my coffee-cup bears a tear-off loyalty card and an adhesive token depicting a coffee bean: collect six such tokens for a free hot drink.

The quantity of litter on the road to Balerno is scarcely credible. I feel a surge of anger at people who so wilfully damage the environment in which we live. Much of the litter is McDonalds packaging and I soon realise how easy it would be to collect six loyalty stickers. In fact, with nettles being number one, McDonalds loyalty stickers are probably the second most abundant source of 'food' that can be scavenged from the hedgerows. There is, of course, the issue of then needing to find a McDonalds in order to convert the voucher into calories, whereas nettles require only a source of boiling water.

I begin to seriously consider litter-picking as I walk. My two concerns are firstly my own safety, as I don't have a litter-grabber, and secondly the insurmountability of the task. In a semi-urban area such as this, I could fill a rubbish sack within ten minutes, or less than 500 yards.

Having just endured two indoor nights in the luxury car village, I crave the solitude and safe enclosure of my own tiny tent. To contrive two nights' remote camping, instead of the full rest day on my schedule, I walk only the short distance between the Pentland and Moorfoot Hills, and spend much of the day in Penicuik. I have chosen a good day to visit: Pen-y-Coe Press has recently opened a museum of papermaking, and I receive a guided tour from a well-versed volunteer.

Later, I sit on a bench in the town centre, writing postcards and half-listening to a street busker. After about thirty minutes, the guitar playing ceases abruptly. I look up, to see the busker standing in front of me.

"Thought you'd been here a while. You enjoying the music?"

Although he's busking on guitar, Jez tells me that he also plays virtuoso jazz piano for an up-market Edinburgh restaurant. I've no idea whether he's being truthful or not, but he is clearly trying to impress me. We chat for a few minutes. As well as boasting about his musical accomplishments, Jez talks of his interest in 'rationalising the paranormal' and I can't help but feel a tinge of relief when he resumes his busking.

Two tunes later, he's back, sitting beside me on the bench, this time with an offer of staying the night with him in Peebles. By now slightly uneasy, I politely decline, explaining that Peebles isn't on my route, that I have a tent and that it is good weather to be camping.

"What are you on Facebook?" Jez asks.

"Sorry, I don't use Facebook," I reply, truthfully.

"Email then?"

This time, I lie, showing him my notebook full of jottings and claiming that I am a 'paper person'. When Jez picks up his guitar for a second time, I continue writing for as long as I dare, to give the appearance that I'm not running away – then grab my rucksack and bolt down the nearest alley. Jez's intentions may have been friendly, but I was more than a little uncomfortable.

Introspection: Freedom

A search for freedom in the wilderness suggests an idealism of nature, a yearning for those two states of existence described by Jean-Jacques Rousseau[25]: physical freedom from other people, and psychological freedom from the artificial needs of modern society. Superficially, at least, I ascribe to these aims, and consider myself in agreement with Thoreau when he writes that "Hope and the future for me are not in lawns and cultivated fields, not in towns and cities, but in the impervious and quaking swamps."[26]

But lurking beneath the surface, some primal instinct or ingrained

Frozen footprints, Foinaven.

25 Jean-Jacques Rousseau, *Discourse on the Origin and Basis of Inequality among Men* (1754).
26 Henry David Thoreau, 'Walking', *Atlantic Monthly* IX, no. LVI (1862), pp. 657-74.

behaviour will not allow me to let go of the world. Though my County Tops walk should have been my chance to escape, to prove that "the most alive is the wildest," [27] I found myself clinging to the fringes of society, and searching for signs of others in the wilderness: the cairns on Small Mount; the abandoned drinking flask on the slopes above Loch Choire; the snaw-rink beside Wester Fearn burn. Writing of the snaw-rink reminds me of a winter walk on Foinaven, a mountain which lies twenty miles to the north of Ben More Assynt. Running along the ridge were a line of footprints, not sunk into the snow, but raised above it – the result of loose powder snow having been blown away from compacted, harder snow beneath 'ordinary' footprints, leaving the latter standing proud above the surface. This remains one of the most breath-taking sights that I have ever seen in a mountain environment, and serves as a reminder that there is beauty to be found where people tread, as well as in the wilderness.

---

27 *Ibid.*

Wrapped Between Borders

Midlothian – Berwickshire – East Lothian – Roxburghshire
– Northumberland – Dumfriesshire – Selkirkshire –
Peeblesshire – Lanarkshire – Ayrshire –
Kirkcudbrightshire – Wigtownshire

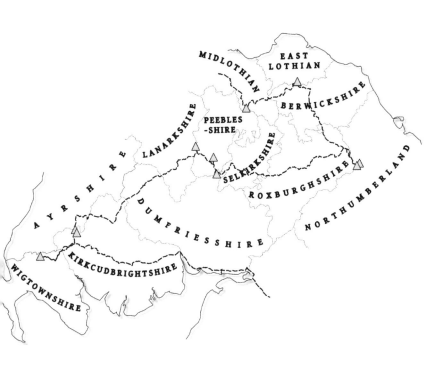

Blackhope Scar (County Top of Midlothian) and Meikle Says Law (County Top of Berwickshire and East Lothian)

Penicuik to Sweethope Hill. 58 miles, 1,860 metres ascent.
Saturday 6th – Monday 8th May

Intricate crustose lichens daub the rocks with colour: buttercup-bright *Xanthoria parietina*; mottled orange *Rhizocarpon oederi*; pale green continents of *Rhizocarpon geographicum*. Despite the gentle gradient and the soft, dry sphagnum beneath my feet, the ascent from Gladhouse Reservoir towards the County Top of Midlothian on Blackhope Scar takes several hours, as my eye draws me away from the path towards ever-more delectable lichens.

Later, in the glen of the Heriot Water, I walk alongside formerly hedged and pollarded roadside beeches, which have been allowed to grow to full height, resulting in some beautifully serpentine contortions. Ivy runs rampant, and there are more lichens to delay me. One large tree – not yet in leaf, so my guess of sycamore is hazardous – is dusted with yellow *Candelariella reflexa* on its northerly side, yet scaled with a grey lichen on the opposite side, revealing just how sensitive each lichen is to its environment.

On Fallago Rig, the interminable rotation of turbine blades plays havoc with the fabric of space-time; slicing and mixing, sweeping away and melding together. Bemused Scottish Blackface sheep are jumbled between tumbledown grouse butts and the stark steel of energy infrastructure. Sections of the ancient Herring Path are excised, spliced between EDF Land Rover tracks, then re-laid on top of rags ripped from the patchwork of heather moorland. The air – and my mind – is overwhelmed by the screams of pain as the present is torn away from past and future. In the mist, it is impossible to tell how many turbines there are. As I climb slowly towards the indefinite summit of Meikle Says Law they surround me like futuristic re-incarnations of Thor and Rán, lashing each other with rain, sleet, wind. Caught in the crossfire, I am soaked long before I reach the trig point and soon begin to question my perception of time. How long have I been on Fallago Rig? Three hours? Three years? I am no longer sure whether the screaming is inside or outside my head.

Lichen, Moorfoot, 6th May 2017.

Descending eventually along the Dye Water, I catch sight of a figure in high-visibility yellow, riding towards me on a small black and white pony. Though Edinburgh's luxury car village lies only a few days behind me, I am already hungry for human contact again, and increase my walking pace. The pony halts, and appears to be turning. I feel a sudden, overwhelming sense of abandonment: *Don't go! Don't leave me here alone!* The pony is persuaded to continue; when I eventually reach the pair, the rider is happy to satiate my hunger with heartfelt complaints about the weather forecast. She enquires after my destination, and responds with "Blumin' 'eck, well, good for you," before resuming her journey, head bent against the wind, up towards the Rig.

The wind backs overnight, becoming a bitter northerly. As I head due south, my rucksack shields me from the wind, yet I still need to wear all my available layers.

Reaching lower-lying arable land, I camp in the shelter of a mixed woodland, amidst sycamore and Scots pine. Croziers of bracken and buckler-fern are beginning to unfurl. The woodland is eerily silent. I hide inside my tent until the flutes and trills of birdsong begin to creep back into the soundscape: the birds have become accustomed to the intruder in their midst. A greater spotted woodpecker flits between favourite drilling spots. I lie back in my sleeping bag, watching the chaffinches and trying to learn some of their many calls. The barking of roe deer serenades the sunset.

Cairn Hill West Top (County Top of Roxburghshire) and The Cheviot (County Top of Northumberland)
Sweethope Hill to Borthwickbrae. 69 miles, 3,020 metres ascent.
Tuesday 9th – Saturday 13th May

A hardware shop in Kelso sells me a litter-grabber and a roll of bin bags; I can now, finally, begin to try to do something to counter my anger at the litter I have encountered since reaching more urban areas. I bring my armoury into service at Proctor's Smithy, a short distance out of Kelso on the road to Kirk Yetholm. But I have seriously mis-judged the amount of litter – my bag is full within a mile, and I have to carry it for a further five. According to a government website, the UK road network totalled 246,500 miles in 2016. This means 493,000 bags of litter to be collected: and this is a conservative estimate, based upon only the right-hand verge of a quiet rural road.

Kirk Yetholm Youth Hostel is unusually quiet – a discord in the tide times has caused the flow of walkers on St Cuthbert's Way to dry up, and it is still a little early in the year for walkers to be tackling the longer Pennine Way – so I have a dormitory to myself. I have the dou-ble luxury of space to spread my belongings, and a lighter load, since I will climb my next two County Tops as a day-walk, returning to Kirk Yetholm for a second night.

I wedge the dormitory window ajar, to let the sounds of the village outside lap gently into the silent interior. The bells of Yetholm Kirk chime the quarter hours. The pattern sounds to be a variation on the traditional Westminster quarters, giving me a sensation of having ar-rived halfway through the performance.

There are two mountain refuge huts in the Cheviots. Although they are ostensibly emergency shelters, I suspect they are most often used by walkers seeking temporary respite from the elements while they eat their sandwiches. They are also all-too-often used as rubbish bins, tending to receive two kinds of litter: walkers nearing the end of the Pennine Way discard anything they no longer need, while southbound traffic leaves items deemed essential when packing but which have now been reclassified as 'excess weight'. Hikers with heavy rucksacks seem adept at deceiving themselves that such littering is well-meant, that some future visitor to the hut might be grateful for their sodden half-empty box of matches – but in the majority of cases, they are simply littering.

Only six months ago I spent a night in the Auchope hut when I climbed The Cheviot by a route that I suspect few others would deem sensible: starting from Carlisle. As I ascended towards Auchope, it became apparent that any attempt to camp would result in the rapid

Forget-me-nots, near Kelso, 9th May 2017.

loss of my tent, probably in a northerly direction at a speed exceeding sixty miles per hour. On that occasion, I found the hut stocked with a folding shovel, a ruptured self-inflating air mattress, a large bag of mouldering teabags mixed with what I assume was once powdered milk and no fewer than three copies of pages 194 to 209 of the Cicerone guide to the Pennine Way. Today, there are a semi-shredded pair of fluorescent yellow over-trousers, a wad of train tickets and a trio of contorted spoons.

The skylarks fall silent as I climb past the scoured gully of Hen Hole; perhaps the very top of the ridge is too exposed for their parachute displays. The County Top of Roxburghshire on Cairn Hill is little more than a junction, where a spur leaves the Pennine Way to visit the summit of The Cheviot, my second County Top of the day. Most of the route is paved with flagstones, recycled from long-defunct mills; the more recently flagged sections are conspicuous for their lack of lichen. The trig pillar on The Cheviot has been repaired since my last visit – once balanced unsteadily on a column of peat, it has been shored up with concrete.

In contrast to the chill wind on the ridge, the next day is almost unbearably hot. Even before I raise the blind on the dormitory window next morning, I can feel that it is going to be sweltering. I need only my t-shirt – and tellingly, no gloves, usually a necessity since my fingers succumbed to frostbite some five years previously – when I step out of the hostel and into the skies of strafing swallows. During their six-week migrations from South Africa, these birds cover in a single day a greater distance than I have walked in the last fortnight.

Approaching Morebattle, I notice the first ash tree coming into leaf.

> *Ash before oak and you're in for a soak;*
> *Oak before ash and you're in for a splash.*

I cast about me for any sign of an oak in leaf. There are lime, rowan, sycamore with its almost autumnal array of colours in the new year's growth, horse chestnut, hawthorn, birch – but no oak. The bunched fingers of unfurling sycamore leaves can look deceptively like the lobes of oak, and a few of these trees lead me to false hope. Eventually, Otterburn provides my much-sought-after oak. I have seen my first leaf-bearing ash and my first leaf-bearing oak on the same day:

better an inconclusive forecast than a pessimistic one.

As St Cuthbert's Way draws me further from the Cheviots, patches of woodland alternate with arable fields, and the suffocating smell of oilseed replaces the perfume of gorse. The heat festers towards a midday head. I find a shady spot to crouch while I eat my lunch. A blue tit hops and bows, possibly in anticipation of crumbs, but is apparently not satisfied with the fare on offer, chirruping "*I*-want-a *cheese*-burger."

Pennine Way, Cheviot Hills, 10th May 2017.

Later, following a bridleway, I fall into a routine with a trio of teenagers on bikes. The three boys zoom ahead to the next gate, dismount, open the gate, remount and continue, by which time I have arrived to shut and fasten the gate. A few hundred yards later, the procedure is repeated. For a few brief miles, our woven trajectories put me in mind again of lichens, and the delicate, filamentous webs created through the symbiosis of algae and fungi.

Laurence's aunt and uncle meet me in the centre of Jedburgh, bringing maps, supplies of clean socks and their ten-month-old rescue dog, Clover, who is proving hard work. Much to our surprise, we find a dog-friendly café. Clover rises to the occasion and is wonderfully – unusually – well-behaved.

The next day, I have another visitor: Laurence makes a last-minute visit to deliver a permit, which I will need to climb Mickle Fell later in the month, and a proxy vote application form for the unexpected general election.

There are limited accommodation options in this part of the Borders, so we have booked a rather expensive B&B for the night. I arrive first, to the consternation of the proprietor, who is expecting us an hour and a week later.

Breakfast here is an elaborate affair. Five different choices of cereal are arrayed in hand-labelled Kilner jars, awaiting individual portions of milk in miniature milk bottles. The table is crowded with jugs of fruit juice, jams and preserves, baskets of bread rolls. Clearly this is what £80 per night pays for. I don't feel comfortable, though: our grubby little Ford Fiesta has gate-crashed a party of BMWs and Audis, and I discover that my walking boots have been removed to outside the front door.

White Coomb (County Top of Dumfriesshire), Broad Law (County Top of Selkirkshire and Peeblesshire) and Culter Fell (County Top of Lanarkshire)

Borthwickbrae to Coran of Portmark. 102 miles, 5,200 metres ascent.
Sunday 14th – Thursday 18th May

My first thousand miles are complete. Having led me across southern Scotland from west to east, my route is now swinging gently back round upon itself. I must cross Scotland again, almost as far as the west coast. Though I have made a brief foray into England, I have more Scottish County Tops to climb.

I had planned to follow a route called the Captain's Road over a pass to Tibbie Shiels Inn, but have difficulty finding the start of the track and end up ascending rough ground on the wrong side of a burn, able to see a wide track on the opposite bank. From the top of the pass, the Captain's Road enters a poorly-drained plantation, and I struggle to keep my feet dry. When emerging into a felled area, the challenge changes, as piles of branches have been strewn across the track. I hop from branch to branch, trying to keep my balance, hoping that the spindly pine-limbs will bear my weight.

Having climbed Broad Law – my objective for tomorrow – Laurence is waiting for me at Tibbie Shiels bikers' café. I swap back to my heavy rucksack and stiff-soled boots. After a morning walking in lightweight shoes, my rigid boots make me feel as though I have plastic buckets on my feet. Laurence also donates his map of Broad Law, which is more detailed than mine.

"It's easy to find the summit," he tells me. "You follow this fence, and keep going up until you reach a trig point with a spaceship next to it."

I follow the A708 towards the Grey Mare's Tail waterfall, reputedly named after the mare in Robert Burns' *Tam o'Shanter*. From the point at which the road enters the modern county of Dumfries and Galloway, I litter-pick, and have a bagful ready to hand over to the National Trust ranger stationed in the car park by the waterfall. The ranger expresses interest in my route, and I tell him that I'm going to climb White Coomb, followed by Broad Law, then Culter Fell, before continuing westwards.

"Are you a bagger, then?" he asks. "I thought you must be, if you know all of the names of the hills."

This is the first time I have seen the Grey Mare's Tail in good weather, so I sit for a while, listening to the voice of the water, before cutting up the hillside to White Coomb, the County Top of Dumfriesshire. Stretching out around me is a landscape of names as poetic and characterful as anything by Burns: Riskinhope, Riskinhope Hope, Drowning Dubs, Carrifran Gans, Muckle Knees, The Strypes.

In the next glen to the north, the Megget Stone marks the boundary between the historic counties of Selkirkshire and Peeblesshire; Broad Law is considered the County Top of both. I climb into the seething cloud and driving rain, following the fence as instructed. Momentary breaks reveal the interminable line of the wooden fence-posts stretching away into greyness, before visibility falls back to just a few feet. The summit feels a long time in coming. Just when I am beginning to wonder whether I might accidentally have wandered onto some other long, flat-topped ridge, I glimpse the unmistakeable outline of a trig point, and, a few seconds later, the 'spaceship' – technically, a VHF omni-directional radio-range beacon – just as Laurence promised.

I pitch my tent early, at 2.30pm, by now so rain-sodden that I cannot contemplate another ascent. I try to segregate my belongings, designating a wet end and a dry end in the tent, then huddle in the middle. My fingers are so swollen by cold and rain that it is difficult to peel my gloves off.

Some clothes will dry better if I keep them on, others if I remove them, so I am fully clad (including coat) from the waist up, and naked below. The back of my jacket and jumper are wetter than the front, having been compressed by my rucksack, but the front of my body dries more quickly, so I turn my top-half clothing after a while. With hoods hanging bib-like down my front, I have to be particularly careful when using the stove. Overnight, everything goes inside the sleeping bag: nothing will dry, but at least the moisture will become evenly distributed.

The patter of the rain stops only when I put my earplugs in and bury myself in my sleeping bag.

I strike camp next morning as swiftly as I can, then scramble up alongside the burn to Gathersnow Hill. As I had hoped, a fence runs alongside the county boundary; I can use the fence as a handrail by which to navigate, and concentrate on forcing my way into the wind and rain, rather than worrying about keeping track of my precise location within the cloud. From the relative shelter in the col at Holm Nick, it takes an hour to complete the two-mile round trip to the trig point marking the summit of Culter Fell, the County Top of Lanarkshire.

I have just passed Hillshaw Head when an unnaturally sleek grey shape looms out of the mist: the bottom third of a wind turbine is hanging like a stalactite from the cloud. I tumble out of the heather onto a wind farm road. Within a minute, an official vehicle rumbles through the cloud to ask what I'm doing. I apologise for inadvertently wandering into the wind farm, explaining that it's not shown on my map and offering the map for inspection as evidence. In return, the driver points out where we currently are on his 1:25,000-scale map – he's wrong, but I don't like to mention it – and offers me water. It has been raining for more than 48 hours – why would I want more water, when every stitch of my clothing is sodden?

Reaching Camps Reservoir becomes something of an exercise in psycho-geography, a term coined in the 1950s by the Marxist theorist Guy Debord, who suggested enigmatic and inventive strategies for exploring urban environments. In my case, I am attempting to navigate the built environment of the wind farm using a map which depicts only the underlying topography.

Once on the reservoir shore, and sheltered from the weather by the surrounding hills, I can hear cuckoo-calls echoing across the water.

A diversion to Abington Motorway Service Station offers a motel, the opportunity to dry out – and the magnetism of the anatopistic. Our paths converge across the rain-swept car park, two alien beings with full waterproofs and outsized rucksacks. Kevin, I learn, is also heading for Land's End, although by a more sensible route than me, having departed from John O'Groats around the time I walked through Glasgow. I had expected more chance encounters such as these, but, with the possible exception of a quiet smile from a pair of walkers crossing the Forth Road Bridge in the opposite direction to me, this is the first time I have knowingly crossed paths with another end-to-end walker.

The rain eventually dries up towards the middle of the next morning, as I approach Leadhills and Wanlockhead, both claiming the title of Scotland's Highest Village. My legs tell me that Wanlockhead is the higher of the two, although I am unable to calibrate them against the rest of Scotland. Leadhills is home to the oldest subscription library in the British Isles, founded in 1741, although sadly (it being Wednesday) closed on weekdays. The soft moorland landscape, as much as the evidence of the villages' lead mining heritage, reminds me of the mining areas in the North Pennines.

From Wanlockhead, I join the Southern Upland Way, which I will follow for the next few days. A wayside box of leaflets advertises the Weymarks project: specially minted coins hidden in thirteen 'kists' along the trail. I have already walked obliviously past the kist at Cogshead, but resolve to look for the others. Later, a Sanquhar resident talks more about the Weymarks and gives me directions to both the Cogshead and Cloud Hill kists. I find the combined directions a little confusing, but over-precise information would take the enjoyment out of the hunt.

Some hours later, I camp on Cloud Hill. After much scouring, the kist proves to be a painted ceramic bowl laid into the ground. A lid of swollen chipboard and shattered terracotta is making a futile attempt to keep the weather out, and the coins inside are rusting badly. Though a coin would definitely constitute excess weight to carry, I have a definite weakness for treasure-hunting, and stow one in my first aid kit.

Also on Cloud Hill, I meet a group of walkers who report that they have left Mars bars in the Polskeoch bothy. I enter the Polskeoch plantation the next day, just as a rather corpulent hiker with a rucksack to match is leaving it – and there are no Mars bars in the bothy. The path here is indistinct, but eccentrically marked by strips of pink towel tied to the branches.

Kirriereoch Hill (County Top of Ayrshire), The Merrick (County Top of Kirkcudbrightshire) and Craigairie Fell (County Top of Wigtownshire)

Coran of Portmark to Gretna Green. 126 miles, 3,530 metres ascent

Friday 19th – Thursday 25th May

I rise at 6.00am and make an early start, wanting to be down from the hills before the thundery showers that have been forecast for late afternoon. Laurence and I once spent a terrifyingly tense night bivvying on a glacial moraine high in the Alps, while thunder rolled and crashed in the mountains around us: I have no desire to repeat the experience.

Walking through Dumfries and Galloway, I hear more cuckoos each day than I have in the first thirty years of my life. The distinctive call of the male carries clearly through the still air, and the broad amphitheatre of the hills around me creates a slight echo, adding a touch of tremolo to the end. Should I, like Anna Akhmatova, ask the cuckoo how many years I will live?[28] Or how many months I will walk for?

Deer run over the hillside with a light, fluid grace. I stumble my way diagonally up a brae, bent under the weight of my rucksack, moving at only a fraction of their pace. Paying attention to my footing, I close my weather eye. When I reach the ridge that will lead me to Kirriereoch Hill, the cloud has thickened, and the bright, hot day has become sullen and chilly.

A county boundary runs roughly east-west across Kirriereoch Hill, so the County Top of Ayrshire is distinct from the summit of the hill itself. The Merrick is only a short distance further along the ridge, and I reach my second County Top of the day as the first ponderous drops of rain are beginning to fall. The Merrick derives its name from the Gaelic *meurach*, meaning branched or fingered; the metaphor has latterly been distended beyond its intended scope to bestow the name 'Range of the Awful Hand' upon the ridge as a whole.

I descend to Culsharg bothy, where I hope to spend the night, to find that previous visitors have treated it with a disgraceful lack of

---

28 Anna Akhmatova, *I Asked the Cuckoo,* (1919).

respect. Bags of rubbish have been stuffed into the fireplace. The sleeping platform is rotten and unstable, and supporting struts have clearly been removed from it for firewood. The door hangs askew, suspended by a single hinge. Such is the sad truth of bothies that are accessible by road.

The Merrick, County Top of Kirkcudbrightshire and Kirriereoch Hill, County Top of Ayrshire, 19th May 2017.

I walk on, searching for somewhere to camp – somewhere exposed enough to avoid midges, but not so exposed as to make me a target for lightning. Unable to find anywhere meeting these over-exacting criteria, and concluding that lightning is worse than midges, I camp in the lee of a low drumlin.

I wake to a pinging noise on the flysheet of my tent. This means either raindrops or midges: it's the latter. My parents have recently presented me with a mosquito-repellent wristband, which seems to be attracting a fair amount of interest from bees but thus far has had no discernible effect on midges – what does? Midges have been the bane of visitors to Scotland since long before hill-walking became a common pastime. An early guidebook provided the following advice:

> …the tourist should make use of [a] thin veil to protect himself from the myriads of mosquitoes, or midges… to strangers the pain inflicted by these creatures is at first quite excruciating.[29]

And remains quite excruciating, I might add.

I walk five miles along Glen Trool to drop off my tent and sleeping bag at a campsite which I will return to this evening. This early in the morning, the only other person in reception is checking out, not in. The campsite warden wishes them well for the rest of their holiday.

"Thank you; and without any more rain and midges, I hope."

Waiting until the door of reception has swung shut, the warden turns to me. "What does he expect? This is Scotland."

A return trip of 21 miles along the Southern Upland Way takes me to Craigairie Fell, the County Top of Wigtownshire. It is a modest hill, only 320 metres above sea level, but a rewarding climb for the wide, free views, the shy delicacy of bluebells carpeting the woodland and the feeling of quiet satisfaction that I have done something unique: I have now walked between the highest points of every county in Scotland.

The next morning is another game of midge-dodging. The midge forecast is predicting 'no flies on us' in Ayr, Dumfries and Stranraer. I curse inwardly. Of course there aren't any midges in Stranraer: it's a coastal town. Why isn't there a forecast for people trying to camp in the Galloway Forest?

On your marks: I pack everything (except the tent) into my rucksack and put on full waterproofs with the hood up and sleeves securely taped.

Get set: I mentally run through the routine. Unzip the tent, throw my bag out, get out myself, get the tent down as fast as I can, grab the bag, and run.

Go!

With the right motivation, I can be on my way in under two minutes – but even two minutes is long enough for midges to feast. And,

---

29 Peter Anderson and George Anderson, *Guide to the Highlands and Islands of Scotland: Including Orkney and Zetland* (Edinburgh: A & C Black, 1827).

once I am moving, to pause for more than thirty seconds gives them time to find me again. For the next two days, I walk to the mental riff *keep moving, keep moving*, preferring exhaustion to the experience of becoming a festival for biting insects.

White Laggan bothy is already occupied by a group of young men, who are overnighting on their way back home after camping on an island in Loch Maree. The stove is blazing, the kettle is boiling and one of the group is frying bacon, sausages and eggs. The temperature in the bothy must be in the high twenties and the smell is mouth-watering, quite unlike the usual damp-sock bothy aroma. I am tempted to sleep here, rather than spend another night playing host to the midges, but I need to keep moving east.

The breeze drops overnight, and once again my tent is crawling with tiny black dots when I wake. I debate whether to forego my morning hot drink, since the stove-heat will act like a beacon, attracting all midges within a hundred-mile radius. Feeling very English, I decide that a cup of tea is worth the risk of a few thousand more midges.

To keep walking without pause is physically and mentally exhausting. I resort to counting my paces, permitting myself a too-brief rest when I have walked at least 1,500 steps. Eventually, Stroan Loch appears, its surface dimpled by a light breeze. The water is a rich, deep blue near the shore, paling further out. On the far bank, this year's bluebells are asserting themselves through last year's cinnamon-brown bracken, creating an illusion of creamy purple.

The line of a disused railway leads me to Mossdale, then continues on to a viaduct across Loch Ken. The bridge greets me with prominent discouragement:

DANGER
BRIDGE LOCKED
NO TRESPASSING

The alternative being a detour of thirteen miles around the northern end of Loch Ken, I determine to find a way across the viaduct. The planks appear a little rotten in places, but otherwise the bridge is in good repair. On the far side, however, when I have crossed the loch but the viaduct is still high above the ground, I reach a tall metal gate: locked, wrapped liberally with barbed wire and with protruding spikes

Bluebells, Galloway Forest, 20th May 2017.

to discourage people from climbing round the sides. Exploratory ma-noeuvres on the side-spikes reveal that the entire assembly has been greased.

Having ascended 14,000-foot mountains in the Alps, I'm not going to turn back from a mere gate – but I don't go mountaineering with a sixty-litre rucksack. I lower my rucksack as far as I can reach on the landward side of the viaduct, then let it drop towards a tree, which I hope will break its fall. Freed of my load, I swing myself around the gate, my woollen gloves giving me purchase on the greased metal. I climb down from the viaduct to retrieve my rucksack. The litter-grabber has snapped, but my belongings seem otherwise undamaged. I am similarly unscathed, although smeared in grease.

Once I leave the Galloway Forest, I find myself walking through pastoral farmland. There are no midges to greet me the next day, only slugs: long, thin, orangey-brown slugs and fat, black liquorice slugs.

It is one of those days when the tracks do not live up to their cartographic reputations and every field contains inquisitive cattle. Dumfries is still many miles away, but I am spurred on by the promise of a full day of much-needed rest and the waiting company of my friend Anne.

Fortuitous coincidence, rather than careful planning, has brought Anne and her husband Richard on holiday to Dumfries for this particular week. We visit the town's museum, a fascinating cornucopia of anything and everything Dumfries-related. From the museum's copy of John MacTaggart's *Gallovidian Encyclopaedia* I learn some useful terminology to describe my recent travels:

Blashy-wather (n):	wet, stormy weather
Dashelled (adj.):	battered by bad weather
Drifflin (v.):	raining slowly
Mochy (adj.):	warm and moist

Sparse rain cools the early morning as I leave Dumfries, but the clouds soon slink away to the east, revealing the blue vault above. Heat beats down from the unbroken sky, becoming heavier and heavier as the day wears on.

My mother arrives by train in Annan. We walk out together onto the saltmarsh of the Solway coast. Oystercatchers wheel and squeal about us. Slipping on slick mud-flats, and hopping over tidal channels, we make slow progress towards Gretna Green, where we will spend the night. On the far side of the firth, the Cumbrian hills stand waiting for me.

Introspection: Loneliness

I had hoped, during my seven-month journey, to escape from an emotion that has haunted me since childhood. For, as I grew into an awareness of my own insularity, and my childhood illusions fled, a new emotion flooded into the freshly-abandoned mental wasteland and pooled in the valleys of my mind: loneliness. Perhaps my use of the term is imprecise, since it connotes physical remoteness from, or lack of contact with, other people – whereas my own loneliness is founded in a fear of being alone in the presence of myself. This fear can be at its most acute when I am not alone in a physical, literal sense, but when the company of those who are natural, comfortable occupants of society brings into razor-edged focus my own inadequacies and inability to belong. I had therefore some reason to anticipate that time spent wandering the hills, alone, would be time free from loneliness and an opportunity to explore my own nature without feeling compelled to compare myself with others.

But loneliness is neither simple nor shallow: in the words of Joseph Conrad, "Who knows what true loneliness is – not the conventional word, but the naked terror?"[30]

When my walk took me away from towns I felt a quiet contentment within my own safe routine of walking and camping, and came to appreciate the subtle gradation of emotions from solitude to aloneness to loneliness. Yet time spent alone served also to heighten my fear of returning to places where I would encounter other people. On rest days spent in populous places such as Fort Augustus or Stirling, my overwhelming emotion was agitation, and a need to escape back to wilder territory. This sensation was described by the nineteenth-century French missionary the Abbé Huc, who spent five years travelling through Central Asia – for the most part, alone:

On re-entering cultivated lands, the agitation, perplexity, and turmoil of civilisation oppressed and suffocated us: the air seemed to fail us,

---

30 Joseph Conrad, *Under Western Eyes* (London: Methuen, 1911).

and we felt every moment as if about to die of asphyxia.[31]

Paradoxically, though, I need to have other people around me. They guarantee my safety by tethering me to reality, preventing me from drowning in the pools of loneliness within my mind. And so, as I have already discussed, I find myself unable to completely let go, and unable to completely yield to the wildness and solitude that I long for.

Stroan Loch, 22nd May 2017.

31 Évariste Régis Huc, *Travels in Tartary, Tibet and China: During the Years 1844-5-6,* trans. William Hazlitt, vol. 1, (London: National Illustrated Library, 1857).

The Places We Know Well

County Durham – North Riding of Yorkshire –
Westmorland – Cumberland – Lancashire –
West Riding of Yorkshire – East Riding of Yorkshire

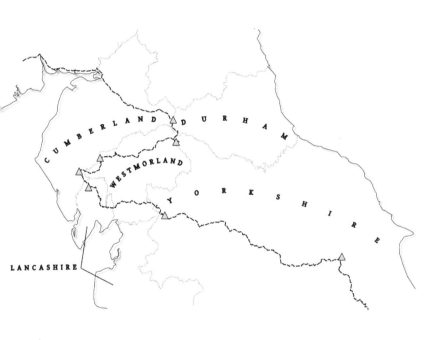

Bunhope Seat (County Top of County Durham) and Mickle Fell (County Top of the North Riding of Yorkshire)

Gretna Green to Dufton. 70 miles, 2,430 metres ascent.
Friday 26th – Monday 29th May

Carlisle. City of gates. City of saltmarsh winds and sandstone wynds. City of the sweet scent of sycamore leaves lying in the gutter. City of my childhood horizons. Though Lancaster was closer to home, it was too accessible, too familiar, to feel like a true city. Carlisle, distant yet distinctly visible, was the epitome of cities, the city against which all others were judged.

Yet now, as I cross the Esk and the Eden, stepping out of Scotland and into England, I am disorientated; I have been away for too long. In the Carlisle of my adulthood, I am "a stranger in town… [and it is] hard to relate what I've found."[32] So, I reason with myself, why try to relate it? I must simply keep walking. I move through my childhood scenery, treading lightly, relishing the soft yield of rubber-soled boots against tarmac, as though treading the oily surface of a soap bubble.

Searing heat makes for a suffocating climb out of the Eden Valley and up towards the Hartside Pass. Clouds boil above me; anvil heads are beginning to form. The sky grows dark as I reach Garrigill. Thunder bursts overhead, then marches around the valley below. Thick raindrops begin to fall. Twice I flinch as forks of lightning rip through the sky over Tyne Head.

There are two County Tops for me to climb in the North Pennines, before I can turn my attention to the Lakeland hills which had beckoned to me across the Solway Firth. As the deluge continues, I pitch my tent in a stream gully close to the ski-tow on Burnhope Seat, the County Top of County Durham: the stream will provide drinking water and the gully will protect me from lightning.

Realising that the best way to dry my saturated clothing is to continue walking, I shelter in my tent until the storm abates, then set off to climb Burnhope Seat, wearing my jacket backwards and flying my

---

32 Striding Edge, 'Wrapped between Borders', *Borrowdale Johnny,* (2007).

waterproof trousers from my rucksack. The absolute summit of the hill lies within Cumberland, and is a couple of hundred metres to the west of the highest point of County Durham, so I am careful to make sure that I visit both 'tops'. The brisk ascent dries me out nicely, but as I descend, so does the cloud, and I return to my tent only a little drier than when I left it.

Next morning, the visibility is less than five metres and it is raining again. By the time I have packed away my tent, I have an audience of curious sheep, standing in pairs on the brow of the gully. Each brace of black faces and dirty grey bodies looks uncannily like a pair of binoculars.

The fog thins as I reach Cow Green Reservoir. As with the Ochil reservoirs, the water level is extremely low; islands have risen from the headwaters and there is a thick rim of exposed sand and peat. I try to pitch my tent on the smooth, warm peat, but it is too soft to allow any tension in the guylines.

The second of my North Pennine County Tops, Mickle Fell – the highest point of both Yorkshire's North Riding and the modern administrative county of Durham – lies on Ministry of Defence land within the Warcop Training Area, so may only be accessed on specific non-firing days. I have permit number 1417 to climb it and instructions to telephone the Guard Room to inform them when I am entering the danger area – but no mobile phone reception.

I cross Maize Beck and ascend along the line of a county boundary to reach the summit ridge, known as the 'boot' of Mickle Fell. A short distance away, a cairn marks the highest point. The clouds have lifted, giving me fine views over the velvetine emptiness of the North Pennines.

Returning to my tent, I spread my clothes and sleeping bag on the heather to dry, then venture into the reservoir shallows to wash. Walking barefoot over the peat is delicious. By the water's edge the peat is slightly yielding under my footfall, and pleasantly warm. The drier areas have a rough crust, which crunches with each step. The air is so still and quiet that I can hear the throb of the lapwings' flight as well as their frantic cries.

The wind is behind me as I follow the Pennine Way across the moor to High Cup Nick, so that I am almost unaware of the constant rain. This is my first encounter with the Pennine Way since its northern endpoint at Kirk Yetholm. Walkers following the National Trail will have walked a little over one hundred miles between those two points, whereas my meandering course has taken me more than three times that distance.

Graham Wilson, who devised his own route between the highest points of the northern English shires, has much to say on the subject of encounters with the Pennine Way. With his characteristic, somewhat hyperbolic, humour, he conveys something approaching contempt for Britain's first, and probably best-known, National Trail.

> You may even... feel a sense of smugness with the superiority of your own path... On the other hand, you are forced to leave go of the safety-blanket of exhaustively detailed guidebooks with explicit directions on the best way to open gates and climb stiles. You will just have to make do with the Ordnance Survey and a compass. At least you will no longer have to worry about tripping over signs warning against the inexperienced leaving the recognised track unless accompanied by someone in possession of a Mountain Leadership Certificate.[33]

Far from sharing Wilson's sentiment, I enjoy re-walking a familiar route, and feel tendrils of memory threading through the mist as I recall my two previous visits to Dufton, on my twofold attempt at the Pennine Way.

For a walker approaching High Cup Nick from the east, the moors guard their secret closely until you find yourself standing on the brink of a great lozenge-shaped chasm, with a windswept waterfall blowing spray up into your face. The poet and artist Anna Adams captures the energy and beauty of this air-and-water dance in her description of how the "streams performed handsprings / on the limestone sill's high edge."[34] Whilst I feel something of Anna Adams' love for the valley,

---

33 Graham Wilson, *Tops of the North. Volume 1: Three Shires Head to Carlisle* (Disley, Cheshire: Millrace, 2008). Wilson has even suggested that, depending upon the exact procedure by which the county boundary reforms of 1974 were carried out, Mickle Fell may also have been the County Top of Cumbria for a few seconds.

34 Anna Adams, 'Walking Downhill, High Cup Nick', *Speak to the Hills: An Anthology of 20th Century British and Irish Mountain Poetry,* Hamish Brown and Martyn Berry (eds.) (Aberdeen: Aberdeen University Press, 1985), p.251.

High Cup Nick, 29th May 2017.

I would perhaps not extend my praise as far as that of Frank Showell Styles, who describes the view down towards the Eden valley as "Alpine, even Himalayan, in its impressiveness."[35] To me, the view is quintessentially Pennine, and all the more beautiful for being so.

Ben, Fiona and their daughter Ailsa have walked out from Dufton to meet me on Narrowgate Beacon, where the path runs high on the edge above High Cup Gill. The gill is barely visible as a narrow silver ribbon winding along the valley bottom – or, to borrow Anna Adams' words again, "far below, the ravelled tinsel strand / of levelled waterfalls." We make a slow descent to Dufton – probably the slowest miles of my entire journey: every few hundred metres, a distinctive plastic popping noise announces that one of Ailsa's wellies has fallen off into the mud. Down in the village, we visit the Post Box Pantry, where an enormous pot of tea provides at least three cups per adult.

---

35 Frank Showell Styles, 'The Way is the Way' *The Journal of the Midland Association of Mountaineers,* IV, no.4 (1966), pp.19-21.

Helvellyn (County Top of Westmorland)

Dufton to Grasmere. 39 miles, 2,000 metres ascent.
Tuesday 30th May – Thursday 1st June

A road sign at the top of the lane reads:

IMPASSABLE TO MOTOR VEHICLES
CLOSED AT THE FORD

Loch Ken has made me wary, but I am not a motor vehicle: I take the risk, and find stepping stones to lead me across the River Lyvennet.

After the ford, though, my footpath becomes overgrown with nettles. I reach a farmyard, where three gates present themselves as equally unlikely candidates for the right of way. As I examine each gate in turn, searching for the reassurance of a yellow footpath arrow, a woman comes to the farm door.

"The footpath's not that way."

Her tone is accusatory, contemptuous. Withdrawing from my inspection of the gates, I walk over to her to ask for directions. She indicates a rusted red gate, its latch concealed deep within a hawthorn hedge, which leads into a field of knee-deep nettles, thistles and docks. Not an obvious path – walkers are clearly not encouraged. Reaching Reagill with scratched and stung limbs, I resolve to stay on tarmac for the rest of the day.

Ahead, sunlight plays over the immutable hills, highlighting first a ridge, then a crag, then the jaws of a valley. Once, I would have been able to trace the skyline with my eyes and put a name to every hill and pass. Now, although I have retained a clear mental map of the Lake District, too many names have withdrawn themselves from my memory. I wonder whether they are buried somewhere deep within me, or have gone forever.

In Shap, a charity shop provides a pair of green cotton trousers to replace my leggings, which suffered from the barbed wire and grease of the Loch Ken viaduct and my more recent tramping through thistles. My friend Becky will be arriving in Shap, to join me for the next few days. To spare her the need to carry camping equipment, we have booked three nights' full board and lodging. Tonight's accommodation, New Ings Lodge, is towards the north end of the village, but I am unsure exactly where. For the second time in a day, I ask for directions. The lady I approach is unimpressed by my inability to navigate a village as small as Shap.

"A bit brain-dead today, are we?"

Perhaps I am. She does, however, point me in the right direction. I arrive at New Ings Lodge with a slight aching sadness that I have encountered this terse hostility only now, when I have returned to an area of the country that I can consider 'home territory'.

The Lakeland poet Robert Southey once observed that "No distance of place or lapse of time can lessen the friendship of those who are thoroughly persuaded of each other's worth."[36] I am privileged to enjoy friendship of this kind with Becky. We last met in person in the final few weeks before I left home for university, yet we re-open our conversations of more than a decade ago as though indifferent to the passage of time. Cheerful chatter with a friend soon dispels my sadness at the truculence of strangers.

Together, we follow the northern shore of Haweswater, then climb alongside half-hidden waterfalls. Tadpoles dart for cover as our shadows fall on the surface of a pool. Becky has an artist's eye for detail, and we delay ourselves in admiration of delicate antlers of reindeer moss and sunlight splintered by running water. The fells around us are painted in infinite shades of green and the view is so distinct that I want to run my hands over the contours.

There have been three significant snowmen in my life.

This phrase has echoed inside my head for years. Yet, now that I come to commit it to paper I find that I can remember only two of the three snowmen – unless the third belongs to Jenny Brunies?[37] As Becky and I descend from Beda Fell towards Patterdale, the sight of Red Screes standing guard over the Kirkstone Pass to the south recalls the snowmen to my mind, on this bright and otherwise snow-free June day.

---

36 Robert Southey, *Thalaba the Destroyer* (London: Longman, 1801).

37 *"With the flat of her hands she beat him firm all around, set him upright, gave him a nose modelled with a few swift strokes…"* Günter Grass, *Dog Years* (New York: Harcourt, 1965).

We met, the second snowman and I, at the top of the pass, in the strange, discontinuous relief of the jostling of upslope against downslope. It was as the bus shuddered over the summit of the public road that I glimpsed him, through the twin veils of breath and twilight. His crazed, arm-splayed chest pressed against the top of the drystone wall; a strip of wet, black grass leading perpendicularly from the grey tarmac marked his passage from the rim of the mountain above.

The first snowman is more a construct of place-attachment. A path leads through my childhood memories, along a valley, between the ash-forest and the reservoir, then ascends to a moor-barren summit with a long-forgotten trig point. And there – in my memory – a girl, delighting in the first snowfall of the year and the joy of being fifteen and free, dancing in the snow, from which she had fashioned a snowman on top of the trig point.

A party of schoolchildren are ascending from Patterdale, porting rucksacks larger than mine – and in some cases seemingly larger than their bearers. "Only 300 more to go," one of the girls exclaims theatrically. I resist the temptation to ask 300 of *what*. Presumably neither miles nor summits

A school friend once expressed concern that she wasn't an experienced enough hill-walker to join me for a weekend walk in the Langdales. She followed in blissful naivety as I led out of the valley and up Jack's Rake, a scrambling route on Pavey Ark. I turned to her as we clambered out of the top of the rake: "Now you're experienced."

Becky's second day of walking with me will take her outside of her comfort zone in a remarkably similar fashion. Despite living her whole life on the shores of Morecambe Bay, this will be Becky's first ascent of Helvellyn. We have chosen the 'Hole in the Wall' route, culminating with the classic ridge of Striding Edge to lead us to the summit.

A red squirrel flushes a blue tit from behind a tree, giving the illusion that the squirrel has transformed into a bird. Clouds flow over the ridge ahead of us like deer leaping a fence: low-bellied, with a kick of the hind legs as the front make contact with the ground. There is a stiff breeze – enough to turn my fingers an unhealthy, sallow yellow, but not enough to make the ridge unsafe.

The clouds clear from the summit shortly before we arrive. We

Summit of Helvellyn, County Top of Westmorland, 1st June 2017. Photograph courtesy of B. Hutchinson.

pause for photographs, celebrating the County Top of Westmorland and Becky's conquest of this well-known Lake District mountain.

This is another place which holds memories of snowmen. Once, walking the long ridge north of Helvellyn in the opening days of January, I met with a moment's confusion on seeing the summit through diplopian eyes, before the extra trig point resolved itself into a snowman standing on the lip of a cornice above Swirral Tarn.

The wind wrings teardrops from our eyes and drives us down to Grizedale Tarn in search of lunchtime shelter. A school of minnows are cowering in the shallow waters at the tarn's outflow. My mind continues to range over snow-capped remembrances, recalling the bitter tang of the tarn when Laurence and I swam here in the depths of winter.

As the day wears on my thoughts turn to the more mundane matter of food. Last night was Sausage Night in Patterdale Youth Hostel. Will it be Sausage Night again in Grasmere? The warden welcomes us into the hostel.

"For supper tonight it is …"

She scurries out of reception into the corridor, skims her eyes over the notice board, scurries back behind the counter, and continues: "… Burger Night."

Later, she explains that menus have been standardised, to prevent hostellers spending a week's holiday walking between successive Sausage Nights. Burger Night marks the end of my full board holiday: it is time for Becky to return to the real world.

Scafell Pike (County Top of Cumberland) and Old Man of Coniston (County Top of Lancashire)

Grasmere to Whitbarrow Scar. 55 miles, 3,740 metres ascent.
Friday 2nd June – Monday 5th June

Rossett Gill pours out of a swirling mist onto greasy breccia slabs. Ahead of me, bare, stern crags melt into the cloud. A well-used path leads from Angle Tarn to Esk Hause, then skirts Great End as it follows the boulder-strewn ridge towards Scafell Pike. I can see barely a few feet into the thick, purpling fog. Although the route is marked by cairns, I can follow it only by paying attention to the sheen of lichen-free rocks, worn smooth by the passage of innumerable boots. I trust my instinct and sense of direction.

Just before the final ascent, where the path dips in deference to Little Narrowcove, I meet a large party of well-equipped Geordies, who are retreating without having reached the summit. Though the fog is thick, the weather is otherwise very benign, and I am surprised that they consider the conditions dangerous.

On the summit of Scafell Pike, I again seem to be the only person confident of navigation. A father and son are about to plunge down the route to Esk Hause when the young boy exclaims "It's not that way, Daddy!" He's right: they are supposed to be heading for Wasdale. I help them to re-orient themselves.

Two girls, suitably attired for the weather, but lacking a map, are being advised by another father-and-son pairing on the best descent route for Eskdale Youth Hostel, having become nervous on their ascent when the visibility dropped to less than the distance between suc-

Map lichen, Scafell Pike, 2nd June 2017.

cessive cairns. The girls photograph the father's OS map, then I walk with them down Little Narrowcove. Chatting as we descend, I discover that they are older than I had thought: close to my own age. Their innocence among mountains had made them seem younger, and I begin to feel awkward in *loco parentis*. I part from them once we have reached the River Esk and the route down the valley is clear.

As the afternoon wears on, the clouds thin and disperse, laying bare the dramatic grandeur of Scafell Pike. A ridge of purple-black crags curves out from the summit towards Slight Side, embracing the meandering Esk in the valley below. After three days among people, I relish the freedom of a night in the company of the fells.

My solitude is short-lived, though.

"Is this the way to the road?"

A lone walker hails me. I am descending Moasdale, heading for the road junction in Cockley Beck – but this isn't necessarily the road that the other walker is seeking.

"Where are you trying to get to?"

"I don't know. I parked the car near the start of a trail."

"In Eskdale, or the Duddon Valley?" I query.

"I don't know. It was a car park near a trail." He's starting to look a little sheepish, "but I suppose they're all like that."

I try to hide my smile. After a few more minutes of questioning it becomes clear that the other walker really doesn't know where his car is. I suggest various routes, aware that a descent into the wrong valley would necessitate a walk over the Hardknott Pass – reputedly the steepest road in England.

Nestling between the Hardknott and Wrynose passes, Cockley Beck is small enough to drown in the word 'hamlet', high enough to give us a flying start for our climb into the Coniston fells. Ray has been fretting over our nebulous arrangement to meet, revealing a lack of familiarity with the area. His friend Chris, who will be our host this evening, ensures that he arrives at the agreed time and place. Chris has also usefully cajoled Ray into lacing his boots properly and swapping his heavy oilskin jacket for a lightweight waterproof coat.

We make a steep, pathless ascent up Grey Friar, then sit on the ridge, admiring the play of shadows over the green of the fells. Skirt-

Scafell Pike, County Top of Cumberland, 2nd June 2017.

Moasdale campsite, 2nd June 2017.

ing Swirl How, we follow the curving ridge to the Old Man of Coniston. Ray comments that it is "like rush hour", inadvertently echoing
Alfred Wainwright's description of the main route of ascent as "the
way the crowds go: the day trippers, the courting couples, troops of
earnest Boy Scouts, babies and grandmothers, the lot."[38] There are
fewer than ten people on the summit when we reach it – relatively
quiet for such a popular hill. This is the highest point of Lancashire,
my home county, although it now lies within the modern construct of
Cumbria. The name is falsely anthropomorphous: 'old' is most likely
to be a corruption of the Norse *alt*, meaning high, and 'man' simply
means hill. An alternative derivation is that the appellation 'old man'
refers to worked-out mines, of which Coniston has plenty. The first
mines in the area were dug in the late sixteenth century, and staffed
by miners from the Austrian Tyrol. By their heyday some three centuries later, the mines extended 900 feet below ground, and up to 500
tons of copper ore were extracted every month.

A whinchat joins us for a picnic lunch among the disused mine

---

38 Alfred Wainwright, *The Southern Fells* (Kendal: *Westmorland Gazette*, 1960).

workings. It stands motionless, a worm trailing from its bill, regarding us warily. Eventually satisfied that we pose no threat, it resumes its parental duties, ferrying food to a nest beneath a nearby rock.

Later, Chris and Carrie welcome us into their home with cups of tea and slices of Carrie's delicious lemon cake. Carrie very delicately drops hints that I might like to take a bath, and offers to wash clothes for me – perhaps she can smell me.

I feel distinctly out of place as I slip between stiff lavender-scented sheets, but sleep soon overcomes my unease. What seems like only a few minutes later, a woodpecker thuds into my bedroom window, stunning both of us. The woodpecker's tree-drilling skull must have protected it from the impact, as it flies off, seemingly not even a little dazed, while I blearily realise that it is time to be getting up again.

8.00am sees the four of us assembled in the kitchen, eating cereal and toast in a wonderfully haphazard fashion. Today is supposed to be a rest day, but questions from Chris and Carrie about my itinerary for the day make it clear that there has been some confusion over the number of nights I am to spend at their house. The day is brimming with sunshine, so to be forced to continue is no hardship. And, if I am honest with myself, I had been regarding the prospect of rest day in company with a feeling of trepidation. I am beginning to feel like a parcel, passed from person to person, or perhaps an intriguing moth, being repeatedly trapped, observed, then tossed back out into my natural habitat for the next lepidopterist to catch. It's not that I don't appreciate the kindness that my friends are showing in supporting me on my journey; rather I find it difficult to re-adjust to company after so long on my own.

The landscape of South Lakeland is comfortingly familiar, but one particular low hummock triggers an avalanche of memories of camping here with my Guide unit. One snowy January, I led my long-suffering patrol for nearly two complete laps of this hill before a kindly local put us on the right track: the recollection serves as a useful reminder that I must be charitable towards those who are still learning to read a map. My navigation has evidently improved since my time in the Guides, as I find my way to the north end of Whitbarrow Scar without walking in circles.

The scar is an outcrop of exposed limestone pavement, ringed by low crags. I intend to camp on the scar, but first I have a diversion to make: to the nearby home of a friend with whom I lost contact when still at school. I am searching for a doorbell when she comes out of the porch.

"Are you lost?"

"No," I reply, "actually, I was looking for you."

Confusion flits briefly across her face before she breaks into a smile. "It's Victoria, isn't it?"

Diana and Martin kindly invite me into their home and ply me with more cake. School yearbooks are dug out from a cupboard. Although I often say that I feel just the same as when I was eleven, seeing photographic evidence of my eleven-year-old self brings home to me how much I have truly changed.

I mention my intention of camping on Whitbarrow and am slightly embarrassed to learn that Martin is a trustee of the charity which looks after the Township Allotment at the north end of the scar – but he assures me that I can cite his name if questioned.

Whernside (County Top of the West Riding of Yorkshire)

Whitbarrow Scar to Home. 69 miles, 2,540 metres ascent.
Monday 5th – Friday 9th June

A familiar pattering on the roof of my tent heralds the return of wet weather. By listening attentively, I manage to get my tent down during a brief lull, which will later prove to be the only dry period of the next two days. I descend from Whitbarrow and make my way towards Kendal. Minor roads offer the easiest route in poor weather, perhaps because I make greatest headway. In the town, I acquire a second-hand plastic mac to wear over my (supposedly) waterproof jacket. The atmosphere quickly becomes rather soupy inside multiple layers of waterproof clothing, but I am warm and sticky with sweat rather than rain-chilled and clammy.

I trudge on towards the motorway service station at Killington Lake. Although the services lie not far off my planned route, the need to cross the M6 and reach their non-motorway access road means a torturous detour. Keeping my double-hooded head down, I pay little attention to my surroundings, simply plodding forwards in a numb, almost trance-like state. I drip into the motel reception, willing to pay any price to be readmitted to the civilisation that I have so recently been longing to escape.

By morning, water is everywhere. Streams tumble down hillsides and sheet over the road. Springs bubble and spout from drain grids and manhole covers. Inspection of my map shows that the rights of way across the River Lune are just that – rights of way only, without bridges. Footpath signs pointing river-ward are suffixed '(Deep ford)'; judging from the water levels I can see, 'deep' could be well over my head. Today is the sort of day when the answer to the question 'Where is it best to ford the river?' is an emphatic 'Don't'. But to cross the Lune at a bridge means a stretch of A-road walking and consigns me to roads rather than hill paths for the rest of the day.

I follow a narrow lane up Dentdale. The surface flow of the swollen, greedy Dee is impossibly swift, creating an illusion of laminar shearing, as though a sheet of water is being swept across the river surface, faster than the current beneath. Where the river eddies, stationary water appears to flow backwards against the terrible speed of the current. The drowning roar is inescapable; so loud that I struggle to hear my own thoughts. In places, the Dee has brimmed out onto the road, deeper than boot-deep. I splash my way through, almost stamping, so that the water slops away from my feet and I have splashed on to the next step before the return wave can overtop my boots.

I pause to watch a fledgling great tit make tentative hops of soggy flight along a hedgerow. The rain accentuates the smell of wild garlic, which is now going to seed beneath the trees. The colour around me is dominated by the vivid, citrus green of the lime and sycamore forming the greater part of the woodlands.

Reaching Dent by early afternoon, I have lunch in the Meadowside Tea Rooms, then explore the Heritage Centre. The latter is a tiny museum, crammed with domestic and agricultural artefacts of varying ages, many collected by the Centre's founders, Jim and Margaret Taylor of High Laning Farm. It is a wonderfully chaotic jumble: so many things to peer at, some invoking recognition and reminiscence, others filling previously unacknowledged gaps in my local history learning. If it wasn't for the smattering of labels and explanatory text hanging in picture frames, it would be as though someone had opened a viewing gallery onto my father-in-law's house.

Heading back out into the deluge, I follow Dent's nature trail up Flintergill, passing the exposed limestone flags in the gill bed, where local women would once 'dance' on the cloth, causing it to waulk, or felt, in the running water. A little further upstream a 'wishing tree' has a passageway through its root structure, presumably formed by erosion around buttress roots. To walk three times clockwise around the central pillar is said to bring good luck – but probably not to those carrying oversized rucksacks.

Next morning finds me back in the Meadowside Tea Room, sampling carrot cake in the company of Ann and Andrew. We had planned that Andrew would walk with me over Whernside, but he is suffering from a bug caught while open-water swimming, and it is obvious that the energy required to sit in a café is more than he can muster. I tarry for longer than I should, given that I have a 2.00pm rendezvous with another friend on the far side of Whernside.

In the warmth of Ann and Andrew's company, I finally come to understand my seemingly chaotic reaction to companionship over recent days. Hills have always provided the context to my life. When I find myself wondering thickly through the fug of early morning: Where am I? Who am I? I look to the hills for an answer. A faint pink tinge blotting up into the velvet slopes tells me: dawn to the east, hills to the west: I'm in Yorkshire, an adult, on my way to work. But, in the days since I crossed the border from Scotland, I have been walking through the landscape of my childhood. Against this backdrop, the company of childhood friends – Becky, Diana, Ann and Andrew – has seemed natural, whereas time spent with Ray, Chris and Carrie, who belong to my adult world, has felt dissonant and awkward.

I set off from Dent at 11.20am, leaving less than three hours to cover the ten miles across Whernside and return to adulthood: I'm going to be late. On the ridge, I hide my bag behind a peat hag, then jog to the summit and back – not a very respectful way to reach a County Top. I haven't run any distance at all in the last three months, so the sudden decision to do so in heavy winter boots comes as a shock to the muscles in the backs of my thighs.

Only twenty minutes behind schedule, I reach Ribblehead Station, where Laura and a two-person tent are waiting. We camp high on a hillside, out of view of any farm buildings, but, as we are finishing our porridge the next morning, our ears catch the thrum of an approaching quad bike. I mentally prepare myself for a dressing-down from the farmer whose land we have camped on, but the quad mows straight on up the hill within a couple of metres of the tent, the driver probably not wishing to prolong his rain-swept sortie by stopping to confront us.

The shopkeeper in Bucken is curious about where we're going "in this weather." Rather than admitting the full details of my walk, I name the reservoir that is our objective for the evening. Hearing Laura giggle behind me, I wish I had kept my eyes on the shopkeeper's face to observe his reaction.

"Should go on the bus," is his verdict.

He also seems to be of the view that the weather will improve tomorrow, mostly on the grounds that "no two days are the same here."

Our next hill is my second Whernside in as many days. This is Great Whernside. Lower, in fact, than yesterday's Whernside, the adjective distinguishes it from neighbouring Little Whernside. We don't summit the hill, but take a rising traverse on a bridleway, which, despite its proximity to home, I have never previously managed to follow successfully; past attempts to cross the ridge at this point have been frustrated wanderings, my feet tripping through Yorkshire fog grass, my head swimming in Yorkshire fog. Laura doesn't seem pleased to hear this admission.

It is wet enough for me to seriously consider sleeping in the public toilets at Scar House Dam: they're clean, and spacious enough to pitch a tent inside. Again, Laura is unimpressed – sleeping in public toilets is not what she had in mind for a walk through the Yorkshire Dales. Instead, we find a flat, comparatively sheltered spot beside Woo Gill, and trample around in the bracken to create space for our tent.

A party of children in blue overalls and hard hats is trooping up the dale, led by a man with a rope slung over his shoulder; presumably this is the start of a day of caving or ghyll-scrambling.

"Have you heard the election result?" the instructor calls cheerfully over to us. "We're marching to Scotland to get out of the way."

"What he doesn't realise," Laura comments, when we are out of earshot, "is that you've just come from Scotland."

I had quite forgotten the general election – the vote called when I passed through Killin – and in our privileged isolation we actually have no idea who has won. For a brief period we are autonomous, beholden to no-one – but any elevated thoughts of national politics are soon superseded by more immediate local concerns.

The first herd we meet are a little too friendly, but don't cause us any serious trouble. The second cattle-field, though, is far too confining for the number of young bullocks penned within it. My accustomed technique is to talk to the cows, and move towards rather than away from them, which usually throws them off balance. But no sooner have I sent this herd packing than they have run a complete circuit of the field and are back for another investigation. Each time the bullocks return I raise the volume of my voice and wave my arms more vigorously, making myself progressively louder and larger. My aim is to keep the bullocks far enough away to give Laura time to reach the exit gate.

Half way across the field, Laura freezes.

There is a limit to how loud and large I can make myself, and our safe time in this field is running out. "You need to MOVE!" I yell at Laura as well as the cattle. We sprint the last few yards to the gate

105

and slam it shut against the pressing mass of bovine noses.

After this experience, I can't persuade Laura into any more fields of cows, even though the next herd we encounter are Friesians – dairy cows are generally used to being handled, so rarely cause trouble unless provoked. A farmer catches us as we sneak up a farm lane to reach a nearby road, but lets us off the hook when he learns that I live in the next village.

Bishop Wilton Wold (County Top of the East Riding of Yorkshire)

Home to Elloughton Dale. 73 miles, 1,070 metres ascent.
Saturday 10th – Wednesday 14th June

Two days at home is too little and too long. Too little time for me to appreciate the infinitesimal joys of my home life, and too long for me to remain in one place, when I crave the freedom of walking.

Reading over some of my husband's walking logs, I am struck by the stark contrasts within our shared experiences. Writing of the walk he and I know most intimately – the mile from the front door of our cottage to the crest of a nearby ridge – he focuses on the visual clues to the history of our village: the peculiarly low, languid arch of the bridge over the beck; the exposed rock outcrop suggestive of quarrying; the elevated situation of the parish church overlooking the oft-flooded willow carr where the Methodist Chapel once stood; the low ridges in the far fields indicating where (before the coming of the black death) the other half of the parish resided – perhaps the reason why ecclesiastical activity in the village is now limited to one Sunday in the month.

This perspective on the world may come naturally to Laurence, who studied history at university. For me, however, each visual feature is so ensnared with historical ties that I struggle to follow the overall narrative: I can't see the woods of the past for the trees of the present. I know this same mile just as intimately as my husband, yet there is startlingly little common ground in our common ground.

I know the rhythms of the puddles formed where the run-off from the low-arched bridge can't quite make it into the beck. I know the soft ground where sodden catkins mix with sawdust whenever the willows go the same way as their Methodist antecedents – *thou return unto the ground; for out of it wast thou taken*. I know how the crunch of gravel beneath my feet changes at the point where the lane splits, then bends slightly right to cross another bridge. In truth, I know this so well that I can run along here on a moonless winter night, and the soles of my feet tell me whenever I've strayed too far to the side, or when it's time to turn.

Home lies on the boundary between dale and vale, where the Yorkshire Dales give way to the Vale of York. The high, raw green of the moors is far behind me, and I walk out of our village through arable fields, where swathes of poppies nod amongst wheat and barley.

Shortly after crossing the A1(M) I fall into conversation with another walker. In response to the routine questions about my destination, I reel off a Viking-inflected list that roughly aligns with my route for today: Whixley, Cattal, Tockwith, Rufforth, York.

"You don't need to go to Whixley to get to Cattal!"

My conversational companion sounds incredulous, as though this is a preposterous idea. "Look, we're here," she says, pointing at the floor, which doesn't strike me as a very auspicious start to a set of directions, "Whixley's over here," a swimming motion with the left hand, "and Cattal's over here," the right hand completes the swimming stroke. "So, you'd be going a long way round to go Whixley then Cattal."

Knowing that Whixley is south east of our current location, and Cattal is due south of Whixley, I decide to pay no attention to the woman's directions. My main aim is to bring the conversation to a swift conclusion and get back on my way. This is not easy, since a long description of how to get to Cattal without straying too near to Whixley ensues, accompanied by more swimming, and is repeated a full three times before I can escape. I know that it is best not to argue, but to accept and ignore the directions, especially in light of the fact that they are being unnecessarily justified with a refrain of "because I used to live there."

From Whixley, I decide not to visit Cattal after all, partly out of a perverse enjoyment of disregarding the lengthy directions, and partly because the day has now warmed up and Green Hammerton Post

Office sells ice cream.

Before leaving home after my two-day rest, I swapped my winter boots for a pair of lightweight trainers, but am beginning to wonder whether this was a wise decision. By the time I reach Green Hammerton my feet are sore, but blister-free. By Rufforth, however, I have large, painful blisters on both heels. By Acomb I am limping badly, and I do not reach the Youth Hostel in York until 5.30pm.

I have barely enough time to bag a bunk and shower before I need to hobble back into the city centre, where Laurence greets me with a selection of potential emergency footwear. Gingerly easing my feet into each of several pairs, I conclude that I need to return to the pair of boots that I thought I had just discarded. Wearing winter boots, in June, in a city centre, I add a further level of absurdity to the situation by trooping into an Italian restaurant for an evening meal in the company of colleagues Alan, Adele, Thurstan, Jan and Sharon.

Bishop Wilton Wold is a low hummock on the horizon, where the Vale of York inclines grudgingly upwards to become the Yorkshire Wolds. Also known as Garrowby Hill, the County Top lies adjacent to the A166. A trig point lurks in the corner of a fenced compound surrounding an underground reservoir, sulking because a clump of trees are occupying the highest ground on a nearby tumulus. In a lay-by opposite stands a modest memorial to the lives lost when a Halifax bomber crashed here in February 1944, killing all seven crew and the driver of a passing lorry.

The view back towards York has been immortalised in vibrant, strident geometry by David Hockney's 1998 painting *Garrowby Hill*. Today, though, high-pressure haze and the throb of my blisters take the edge off the pageantry on display in the farmland below me. I descend from the Wolds feeling that I have merely brushed against them. The roads have recently been surfaced with loose chippings, which are agony to walk on with blistered feet. A short limp away from Pocklington, Jan and her family are helping me to ease back into my walk by providing accommodation for the night.

Colleagues Thurstan and Caroline provide further moral support the next day. By the time I have eaten a plateful of Jan's delicious toast and then walked back into Pocklington, they are waiting for me outside the town's library. Caroline's birthday is approaching, so I have brought slices of cake and candles. The cake is more than slightly misshapen, having been carried in my rucksack for the past couple of days, and the wind blows out the candles faster than Caroline can make a wish, but I think she at least catches a glimpse of flame.

It is a joy to walk with people who take notice of the world around

Memorial to World War Two Halifax bomber crash, Bishop Wilton Wold, 13 June 2017.

them. We listen to bird song, watch a wake of buzzards soaring on a thermal and a swift collecting mud from a roadside puddle, admire the shades of lichen on a sycamore.

We part after lunch in a café in Market Weighton. The heat of the afternoon is pitiless and impersonal, emphasising aloneness rather than solitude. The air is a claustrophobic cordial of sweet, sticky elderflower and I begin to appreciate the feeling of suffocation described by Colin Fletcher as a "sudden, aching vacuum,"[39] that lies between the familiar and the unknown. I have a reservation for a campsite on the southern bank of the Humber, but my feet refuse to reach the Humber Bridge. Instead, I camp in broad-leaved woodland close to the river's northern bank.

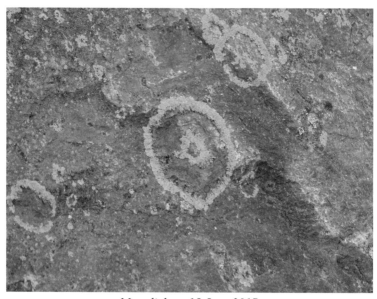

More lichen, 15 June 2017.

39 Colin Fletcher, *The Thousand Mile Summer* (New York: Vintage, 1987).

Introspection: Poetry

There is much poetry within these pages. When I first showed a type-script of this book to Thurstan, his response was a question: "Do you write poetry?" I cannot claim anything so accomplished, yet perhaps I might say that I write fragments of poetry. I find that it is only when I commit words to paper, and then try to rearrange them until they express exactly what I mean them to, that I come to realise what it is that I am trying to say. This is one of the reasons that I love writing, for it helps to bring clarity and understanding to my thoughts. It can be comforting to create something beautiful from even the darkest of thoughts or the most painful of memories – in Thurstan's words, this is writing as "exquisite torture."

And, of all writing, I love poetry in particular for the very same reason that I love high and wild landscapes: freedom. When you are walking amongst the hills, exploration is as important as destination, an idea alluded to by T. S. Eliot in his conclusion to the Four Quartets: "We shall not cease from exploration / And the end of all our exploring / Will be to arrive where we started / And know the place for the first time."[40] *Similarly, when you are writing poetry (at least in some forms) there may be no sense of needing to build a narrative or argu-ment, as there so often is with prose. The poem need not even form a coherent or unified whole, if there are fragments within it which cap-ture or convey thoughts and ideas perfectly – indeed, perhaps a slight air of mystery or enigma makes the whole even more tantalising. Eliot, again, explores the perfect conveyance of ideas through poetry, defin-ing the "sentence that is right" as one in which "every word is at home / Taking its place to support the others... The complete consort dancing together." For me, 'dancing' is the crucial word here: the freedom to dance is part of what sets poetry apart from prose.*

As examples of perfect capture, I cite Dave Gingell's description of a valley as the "dark arms of silent sleep,"[41] *or M. L. Michal's*

---

40 T. S. Eliot, *Little Gidding* (London: Faber & Faber, 1942).
41 Dave Gingell, 'The Valley', in *Speak to the Hills: An Anthology of 20th Cen-tury British and Irish Mountain Poetry,* Hamish Brown and Martyn Berry (eds.) (Aberdeen: Aberdeen University Press, 1985), p.3.

(evocation of "brown-green, blue-brown, blue-grey, grey ghost mountains."[42] I often find that when I come across lines with such simple perfection as these, I will carry them around in my head tasting the flavour of the words on my tongue and listening to their rhythms as I walk. Indeed, I often find myself so entranced by what I read that I wonder with some seriousness whether it would be possible to reconstruct a list of my reading material during my County Tops walk based upon the writing styles I employ and ideas I explore throughout my diary: I leave this as a challenge to the reader.

It might be argued that in quoting extensively from other writers I am somehow fraudulent, or insufficiently diligent with my own writing. It is certainly not my intention to give this impression; rather, I feel that when another writer has captured an image or emotion in such exemplary language it would be churlish to attempt to say the same thing, only less well. Or to put it another way: if you don't have anything (new) to say, don't say anything at all. With a due sense of irony, I quote Arthur Sidgwick, a classical scholar and keen walker, who was killed in action near Ypres a century before my long walk:

> How vain my effort, how absurd,
> Considered as a symbol!
> How lame and dull the written word
> To you the swift and nimble!
> How alien to the walker's mind,
> Earth-deep, heaven-high, unfillable,
> These petty snarls and jests ill-laid
> And all the profitless parade
> Of pompous polysyllable![43]

Moreover, I believe that it is through writers citing other writers that we come to discover new authors, as, for example, has recently been the case with the books of Robert MacFarlane helping to inspire new interest in Nan Shepherd. So, there is much poetry within these pages: poems by other writers that I carry around in my head, and those few fragments of mine that I dare to contribute.

---

42 M. L. Michal, 'From Skye, Early Autumn', in *Speak to the Hills: An Anthology of 20th Century British and Irish Mountain Poetry,* Hamish Brown and Martyn Berry (eds.) (Aberdeen: Aberdeen University Press, 1985), p.493.

43 Arthur Sidgwick, *Walking Essays* (London: Edward Arnold, 1912). I love Sidgwick's writing for its simple, direct humour: "It is thus clear (if it is not, I decline to argue)…"

Always Summer, Always Alone[4]

Lincolnshire, Parts of Lindsey – Nottinghamshire – Cheshire – Derbyshire

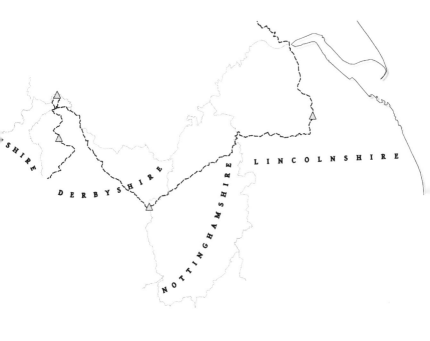

---

44 "If it could only be like this always – always summer, always alone, the fruit always ripe and Aloysius in a good temper…" Evelyn Waugh, *Brideshead Revisited* (1945).

Normanby Top (County Top of Lincolnshire) and Newtonwood Lane (County Top of the North Riding of Nottinghamshire)

Elloughton Dale to Tibshelf. 96 miles, 1,470 metres ascent.
Thursday 15th – Monday 19th June

I have more than thirty miles to walk today, so set my alarm for 5.00am, hoping to be walking within an hour of waking. The heat begins its assault as soon as I have left the shade of the woodland. Blue damselflies dance ahead of me, like sparks flashing in my eyes, causing me to question my balance. Sunlight glimmers brightly on Larkin's gull-marked mud as I cross the Humber Bridge a half-day behind schedule. The bridge's pedestrian walkway is suspended at a lower level than the road, giving a strangely asymmetrical sense of being alone: I walk a tightrope between the blank isolation of a road undercarriage and a vast estuarine emptiness.

I stop for lunch in Bigby, where I refill my water bottle from a churchyard tap. In Caistor, I buy more food, then sit on the ground outside the supermarket to eat. An elderly man shuffles towards me, leaning heavily on two wooden walking sticks decorated to their full height with hair-ties, elastic bands and coloured ribbons.

"Going far?"

"Normanby," I answer.

He looks as though he would like to stop for a chat, but dare not pause in case his twin sticks lose their rhythm. "That's the highest point in Lincolnshire up there," he observes, nodding in agreement with himself.

I smile. "That's exactly why I'm going there."

"There's a trig point, but you need to go along the edges of a couple of fields to get there," he adds before he has shuffled so far as to make further conversation impractical.

He's right about the fields. On the northern flank of the hill, I find a fallow field, sparse with thistles, so I can reach the trig point and the County Top without too much vegetative difficulty. The next field to the south has been planted with wheat, but a wide margin has recently been trimmed. My feet crunch on the hollow, musical stems of hogweed. Too tired to continue further, I pitch my tent in a field

Normanby Top, County Top of Lincolnshire (Part of Lindsey),
15th June 2017.

corner next to a radar tower.

Lincolnshire, like Yorkshire, has historically been divided into
three parts – Lindsey, Kesteven and Holland – an arrangement which
existed from the late nineteenth century until the widespread boundary reform of 1974. Normanby Top is the highest point within the
county as a whole, but the County Top of Lindsey only; I will have
two more Tops to ascend when I return to Lincolnshire later in the
year, although this will not be until after I have traversed Wales from
north to south. Delving further back into history, Lincolnshire was
actually partitioned into wapentakes (an administrative unit roughly
synonymous with the 'hundred'), known as Elloe, Kirton and Skir-
beck; thankfully, the highest points within wapentakes are not also
considered County Tops, or I would have little hope of ever reaching
Land's End.

I sleep badly, waking often with a queasy feeling in the pit of my
stomach. At first I diagnose heat stroke, but then it occurs to me that
my water source of yesterday afternoon may not have been a particularly sensible choice: in future, I will chlorinate any water that I take

from a churchyard.

To add to my worries, I am beginning to develop an ingrowing toenail, probably because my feet have been trapped in heavy winter mountaineering boots for so long. I clean the affected toe with TCP and trim the nail as short as I dare, but am aware that there is little I can do to remove the cause of the problem.

Either the inhabitants of Lincolnshire are more concerned for the well-being of travellers than people in the counties I have hitherto passed through, or my series of 5.00am starts is showing in my face, because everyone I pass asks whether I am lost – even when I am standing outside a supermarket in Market Rasen. My reply of "Not yet" raises a brief smile.

Perhaps this local concern has developed in response to Lincolnshire's predilection for recycling place names. I walk from Market Rasen to Middle Rasen to West Rasen. A signpost offering options of Toft-next-Newton, Newton-by-Toft or New Toft is more than my sun-burnt mind can cope with; I stare stupidly at it for several seconds before I settle upon which road to follow. Much of one day is in fact spent walking from Normanby(-le-Wold) to Normanby(-by-Spital).

The town centre of Gainsborough is bi-partite: the older, more traditional streets surrounding the marketplace contrast with the newly-redeveloped Marshall's Yard. The former hosts what I regard as the useful shops; the latter is trendier, with pavement cafés and fountains where semi-clad children are running around, screaming, while exhausted parents loll in the heat on lavender-backed benches.

The temperature and the vegetation are both rocketing skyward. By 8.30am, as I leave Gainsborough, the river-front is busy with people in little or no clothing, while on the opposite bank I flounder my way through fields of grasses, nettles and thistles. There is no visible indication of a path, but the feel of a smooth rut in the ground beneath my feet keeps me moving in the right direction.

A footpath closure forces me onto a tarmac road. I am not sorry for the easier terrain, but being a little way off my planned route I accidentally bypass South Leverton, where I had intended to replenish my drinking water.

As I press on towards Grove, a clear-cut path tempts me into a cornfield. The next field, however, is deep oilseed, with only a strip of broken stems to suggest a right of way. With every step I must lift my feet to knee height to clamber over the plants. By the third field I feel as though I want to sit down and cry; instead, I cheat and trespass along the hedgerow to return to the road.

I stagger into Grove, desperate for water. There is no shop. The churchyard has no tap. Gated driveways advertising guard dogs and CCTV prevent me from even approaching a front door to ask for a drink. I am taunted by the chime of an ice-cream van in the distance – or perhaps my mind. Nearly an hour later, in allotments on the southern edge of Retford, I quench my thirst, refill my water bottle and douse my t-shirt with cool water, probably breaking several by-laws in the process.

Later that afternoon I lose myself in the woods of Clumber Park to camp. My head is throbbing – this time it is definitely heat stroke – so I try to soothe the ache by pressing the cold metal of a gas cylin-der against my forehead. Even with the door unzipped the heat inside my tent is unbearable. Ruminating longingly on the cooler weather of only a week ago, I find a stark white image presenting itself in my mind's eye: the third snowman, the missing element of my thoughts when surveying the Kirkstone Pass on my descent to Patterdale. The third snowman inhabits a memory of camping in Knoydart, a remote peninsula on the west coast of Scotland, when heavy snowfall pre-vented Laurence and me from climbing the mountains that had lured us there. As I found in the Lake District, I am haunted by snow-ghosts in hot weather.

I toss fitfully through the sweltering night, until it is time to start walking again. My throat feels as though it has been sandpapered and echoes of my footsteps ricochet off the inside of my skull. The dam-selflies flashing in front of my eyes are almost painful to look at; by mid-morning their straight bodies are beginning to look curved, like electric-blue airborne parentheses. Even the dark satanic mills of Pleasley Vale are sunburnt.

In the afternoon, I follow cycle trails along disused railway lines. Common spotted orchids are blooming amongst bird's foot trefoil, stitchwort and bindweed: a reminder that not all hedgerows are over-run with nettles and goose-grass. The pink-and-white carousel flowers of bindweed evoke such potent memories of childhood sweets that I am certain they must be strawberry-flavoured.

Newtonwood Lane is an uninspiring County Top – a high point

The road which gives its name to Newtonwood Lane, County Top of Nottinghamshire, 19th June 2017.

next to a communications mast only a hundred metres from the road from which it takes its name. A mile to the north, a spoil heap from Silverhill colliery also contends for the title of the highest point within Nottinghamshire. Recent surveys being inconclusive, I have chosen the natural hill rather than a man-made feature. I have been warned of fly-tipping on Newtonwood Lane, as well as an aggressive holly at the entrance to the field. There is no evidence of fly-tipping today, but the holly is every bit as vengeful as described – painful on sunburnt limbs.

Black Hill (County Top of Cheshire) and Kinder Scout (County Top of Derbyshire)

Tibshelf to Hope. 72 miles, 3,010 metres ascent.
Tuesday 20th – Saturday 24th June

After the lower-lying County Tops of Lincolnshire and Nottinghamshire I am glad to be returning to the higher hills along the spine of England. The path climbs a little higher with each rise. I can feel the moors of the Peak District awaiting me. Though the land here is still under cultivation there are bracken and foxgloves in the hedgerows, and I can sense that it would soon revert to moorland, were farmers to pause in their work. Then: gorse heralds my return to the true moorland, though the yellow blaze has dimmed to a smoulder. The vibrancy of dandelions, too, has been replaced by pale and intricate clocks, standing intact in the still, sultry air. Brambles are now in flower, as are clover, dog-rose and honeysuckle. Bees feed greedily on wild geraniums.

The hot fug has curdled the air, reducing visibility and making everything appear much further away than it really is. I can only just make out the outlines of the edges ahead of me until I am almost upon

The road to Sheffield, Moscar Moor, 21st June 2017.

them. The clouds grow jaundiced and fuzzy, until at last the sun burns through and blue sky becomes palely visible through thin haze.

The track leading away from the Derwent Reservoir narrows to become a footpath, then a sheep trod. From the map, it appears to be the sort of path that doesn't fit logically into any sensible walking route, and I suspect that it doesn't see much foot traffic. It comes as something of a surprise, therefore, to round a bluff and see a string of seven or eight walkers, who are clearly having some difficulty following the twists and turns of the faint path through the bracken and heather. Since I am about to cut off the path up the hillside I decide to first catch up with the group, in case my abrupt change of direction would otherwise cause consternation in the context of their already fragile route-finding.

"Afternoon," I greet the two men at the back of the line. "Where are you heading to?"

"Mick at the front's got the map," one informs me. This does not bode well: Mick is a long way ahead of the rest of the group. "He's looking for a path onto the ridge, then we can follow the ridge back down to the car park."

I know which 'path' they are looking for: in fact it is just a right of way, with little evidence of a path on the ground, but can easily be identified by the stream gully which it follows. We have already passed it, a good mile back down the valley.

My explanation of this is met with a shrug of resignation. "Mick's got the map."

The walkers in the centre of the group have much the same reaction. When I eventually catch up with Mick and suggest that the route he wants might actually lie behind us, he reacts grumpily. "Well, I'm not going back down now I've come this far up. We'll just have to follow this path up onto the ridge."

"But I don't think this path actually does go onto the ridge. Look," I indicate the map, "it just stops in the middle of the bog. If you want to get onto the ridge, you either need to backtrack, or scramble up somewhere it doesn't look too steep."

Mick replies with "Well, I'll let you get on ahead, then," from which I infer that the interview is over. I leave him to sort out the rest of his party, which has regrouped further downstream beneath a cloud of mutiny.

Black Hill is the historic County Top of Cheshire, although in modern divisions of the country it now forms part of the border between the borough of Kirklees in West Yorkshire and the High Peak district of Derbyshire. The hill is also known as Soldier's Lump, a name bestowed upon it in the nineteenth century by surveyors from the Royal Engineers, who reputedly experienced some difficulty in finding solid ground on which to erect the trig point.

I ascend using the more navigationally challenging route over Westend Moss, then take the easy way down on the Pennine Way. The hills are swathed in cloud all day, making it difficult to be certain of my exact position, but 'up' is 'up', even in mist.

The Pennine Way is my guide for much of the next day, too. The recent hot weather is fading into the recesses of memory. The air is damp, but peat hags provide just enough shelter to prevent the rain from driving. There is nothing to see and little to mark my progress against, other than the alternation of path surface between stone flags and gritstone-strewn peat.

From Snake Pass, the Pennine Way ventures onto the Kinder plateau, passing Mill Hill and Kinder Downfall. The trig point at

Yet more lichen, Kinder Scout, 23rd June 2017.

Kinder Low does not mark the highest point of the plateau, so I strike off the path into the bog to find the County Top of Derbyshire. I follow a bearing as closely as the rough terrain permits, wondering how I will identify a 636-metre peat hag amongst 635.9-metre peat hags. Eventually, I come across a small cairn in what seems to be the right place, and deduce that this must be the Top.

Summit of Kinder Scout, County Top of Derbyshire, 23rd June 2017.

After leaving the summit, I take another bearing to guide me to Crowden Tower, where weather-sculpted gritstone pillars line the edge of the plateau. I skirt the edge of the moor until I can descend to Edale, then a final ascent over Hollins Cross leads me to Hope, and Laurence, and a day of rest.

My boots are worn out and no longer even remotely waterproof. Hesitant to risk blisters again, I have asked Laurence to bring me a new pair of boots, identical to the ones I am currently wearing, but without the built-in swamp. The need to break in new boots provides justification for a walk, even on my rest day: we climb back up to Hollins Cross, then follow the ridge to Castleton to sample the local ice cream.

Introspection: Escape

At the halfway point of my journey, peeling myself slowly away from home, friends and familiar landscapes, I sought to escape the real world, just as I did at the start of my walk some three months earlier. I sought to escape, much as I ran away from the Harley Street Homœopathist and her enthusiasm for orchids; from Jez the busker; from the lady who helpfully tried to direct me to Cattal without travelling via Whixley...

Perhaps the pattern is clear to the external observer, but I had certainly not acknowledged it myself until Thurstan drew my attention to the frequency with which I escape uncomfortable situations by running away.

Once he had broached this subject, I realised that he had stumbled upon something fundamental to my character. From my early teens, I recall having an escape kit packed and ready beneath my bed. Though looking back with the eyes of a seasoned wanderer I see the stark inadequacies of my equipment – and skills – I remember also time spent planning and considering exactly what I might need to survive alone. Learning from experience, I saved diligently until I could afford to buy a warmer sleeping bag, which came in an unfortunately garish orange, and then fretted over how best to conceal this bulky, brightly-coloured object from the eyes of my family.

One of my clearest memories of my teenage years is of the almost paradoxical sense of elation when, following a heated argument with my mother, I grabbed my escape kit and set off walking east into the Forest of Bowland. (My anger cooled by moorland freedom, I telephoned home from the Youth Hostel in Slaidburn to request a reconciliation, and my mother walked out to meet me on my return crossing of the fells.)

Perhaps my whole walk was nothing more than running away? If so, from what? In seeking freedom, I was certainly fleeing the real world – or, as Sidgwick so insightfully terms it, the 'blind world'[45] –

---

45 Arthur Sidgwick, *Walking Essays* (London: Edward Arnold, 1912).

123

but was I also running away from the constraints of society, from responsibility, even from myself? And, if this was indeed an unconscious desire, was I also unconsciously aware of the fact that I would, eventually, have to make the equivalent of a telephone call from Slaidburn, and return home?

Beyond Hope

Staffordshire – Flintshire – Anglesey – Caernarfonshire –
Montgomeryshire – Denbighshire

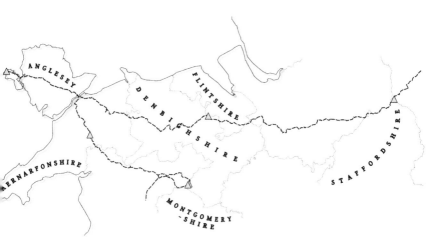

Cheeks Hill (County Top of Staffordshire)
Hope to Hope. 79 miles, 2,050 metres ascent.
Sunday 25th – Wednesday 28th June

The limestone beneath my feet is slick and slimy. Cyclists travelling both up and down dale are pushing their bikes, unable to get any traction. The head of Cavedale is gated: a metal five-bar with a type of 'latch' that I haven't previously encountered – a single light touch and the gate falls face first, prone in the mud. Shutting the gate behind me is less easy.

I pass through Buxton, then use the Dane Valley Way to climb Cheeks Hill, which just sneaks into Staffordshire and claims the accolade of County Top, though it is surrounded by higher Derbyshire moorland. Close by, Staffordshire, Cheshire and Derbyshire meet at Three Shire Heads, a tumbling confluence in the headwaters of the River Dane. A packhorse bridge of gritstone rubble marks this as an important route for traders travelling between Flash, Hollinsclough and Macclesfield. John Lomas, a Hollinsclough silk trader, founded the Methodist Chapel in Flash in 1801: Lomas is my mother's maiden name, so its appearance on headstones is a sign that I am entering the area from which my maternal ancestors hail, even if I feel no particular connection to it myself.

Perhaps there is something in the waters of the Dane, for I am not the only hunter of County Tops to be able to trace my ancestry back to this part of England. Graham Wilson records in his book *Tops of the North* that his mother's family once farmed at what would later become the Rose and Crown Inn at Allgreave. It is also from Wilson that I learn that 'Flash' is a seventeenth-century term for counterfeit money; the abutment of three counties providing a convenient opportunity to hop across administrative boundaries, at a time when police were authorised to act only within the limits of their own counties.

I meet no Flash men today; instead, the damp air by the river provides ideal conditions for midges. But these English midges are beggarly beasts in comparison to their Scottish cousins. When I camp, they tootle over the outside of my tent, making no attempt to find a way in, even when I unzip the inner tent and reach into the porch: in Scotland, an arm venturing into the porch would instantly be tarred with a thick, black midge-coat. When I light my stove, expecting this to attract further clouds of insects, I instead hear a gentle patter of dead midges falling into the roof of the tent as they succumb to the heat.

The bluebottles, though, are orchestral. As I cross a field of cows, a throbbing, buzzing disc levitates above each cow pat with a unison hum which rises in pitch and volume, then fades as I walk on past and the flies resume their faecal feasting.

The current of the Dane washes lines from Beowulf through my mind. Despite the likely etymology of the river's name being from the Welsh *dafn*, meaning trickle, I instead think of "spear-armed Danes in days long sped" – although sometimes my inner tongue strikes off at a tangent and follows this with "in fair Verona where we lay our scene." I find it easier to recall Seamus Heaney's interpretation of Beowulf than any more faithful or literal translation, perhaps because of the memorable surroundings in which I first encountered it. I read Heaney's telling of the tale whilst bivvying high on an Alpine mountainside, in readiness for a push to the summit the next morning. Beowulf seemed apt literature for such a magical location, and I read whilst watching the orange glow of sunset slip from the snow-covered peaks. Rising before first light, I was mesmerised by the twinkling of torches on the opposite side of the valley; beads of light strung in pairs, threes, or fours, inching their way up the dark, blank faces of pre-dawn mountains.

All paths lead to the Cloud. The Dane Valley Way is joined by the Gritstone Way and later the Staffordshire Way, all three Ways converging on the summit of the Cloud. The Cheshire Canal Walk seems intent on joining us, but makes a last-minute change of direction, realising that a diversion up a 343-metre hill is a little tenuous for a canal walk. The Cloud is a prominent, distinctive outcrop and an excellent viewpoint. I'm not climbing it because it's a County Top – it's not – but because it's there. Like the trails, I find myself drawn towards the hill. From the summit, I recognise the distinctive outline of Mow Cop, a familiar landmark from the poetic novels of Alan Garner. Garner is another family name, and a cousin with a keen interest in genealogy believes that our family may be related to the author – an inference which I would dearly love to be true.

I skirt the fringes of Congleton and make for Sandbach. Both place names are familiar from the canon of family history: one Lomas ancestor owned a silk mill in the area, and another was headmaster at a school in Wheelock, a village on the fringes of Sandbach. In the town centre, a charity shop provides a complete outfit – dress, jumper and tennis shoes – for £6.27. I'm now suitably re-attired for an evening meal with three generations of relatives at Sandbach Old Hall.

This part of east Cheshire has a surfeit of stiles – some hedge-crossings have been awarded two. Most, though, are lacking one or more vital components, and each adds a couple of minutes to my journey as I carefully negotiate safe passage for myself and my heavy rucksack.

I am already frustrated by my slow progress, and my mood does not improve when a herd of young bullocks refuse entry to their field, forcing me onto the verge of an A-road. Here, I sense an air of stolid indifference about the tirade of traffic, the hostile houses behind rusting automatic gates, the grass verges littered with coffee-cups; a sense of desecrated rurality that I find repulsive. Hand-scrawled signs, peeling white paint on soggy plywood propped by the roadside, appeal to drivers to pull off the road and purchase whatever offscourings are in surplus:

Topsoil

Sand-Stone

Rabbits ECT *[sic]*

Everything about this landscape is making a statement: nobody cares. Near Church Minshall, I escape the wasteland onto the towpath of the Shropshire Union Canal – the first canal of my walk, despite my recent encounter with the Cheshire Canal Walk. The canal is a haven, a rose-tinted window onto a tranquil life. Narrowboats queue politely at locks and putter gently between bridges, casting green ripples on the opaque, sandy water. Most boats have saccharine names: *Dreamboat, Tom Bombadil, Lotus, Another Venture...* and almost all are piloted by a gentleman with seafaring beard, red or blue waterproof jacket and flat cap. The roadside litter has been supplanted by tubs of flowers. Only the bloated body of a small deer – muntjac? – floating in the water suggests anything other than manicured gentility.

Away from the canal, I follow the Bishop Bennet Way, which is well-waymarked – until I reach Milton Green. Here, two men are chatting next to a signpost pointing north. I stride confidently off in this direction, but my intuition brings me to an abrupt halt after only a few paces. Turning round, I notice another waymarker some distance to the south.

"That sign's pointing the wrong way," I gesture at the offending sign, feeling that my about-turn requires an explanation.

"It got knocked over and put back the wrong way," one of the men replies. "It's an initiative test. Is it the Bishop Bennet Way you're after? It's very overgrown down there."

"Good," I respond sardonically. "Well, better nettles than cows."

"Oh, plenty of cows too," he smirks. "Have fun."

After this commendation I choose another route to reach Aldford.

Having successfully avoided the cattle, I hold the Duke of Westminster responsible for my next diversion: his Eaton Hall estate sits plumb across my line of travel. From Aldford, I must plod three sides of a rain-soaked rectangle in order to by-pass Eaton Hall: north to Ecclestone, west towards Belgrave, then south again, before I can resume my westward progress.

Though the environs of Eaton Hall are as gentile as the canal towpath, the path begins to deteriorate as I approach the A483. A dog-rose with back-pointing thorns snares me as I try to clamber over one of the double-stiles and it takes me several minutes to disentangle myself. Fighting through bushes to reach the road, I then have four lanes of speeding traffic to negotiate. On the far side, the vegetation is even worse: I suspect that no-one has walked this way since the council employee marking the route with yellow arrows. I trip through brambles and crash through rosebay willowherb to the railway – where a notice affixed to a metal barrier informs me of a 'temporary' suspension of the right of way, from 2015 until 2019. The notice concludes with the helpful statement:

THERE IS NO ALTERNATIVE ROUTE

Neither do I have an alternative: the Welsh border lies only a short distance away and I can already see the bosky slopes of Hope

Mountain veiled in cloud ahead of me. Walking from Hope to Hope has taken me from Derbyshire to Flintshire, from the southern tip of the Pennines to the fringes of North Wales. This second Hope of my walk offers additional hope: a B&B on the slopes of the mountain has a vacancy. No doubt I would survive another night camping in the rain, but since I have the option of indoor accommodation, I decide to take it.

Moel Famau (Count Top of Flintshire)

Hope to Betws-y-Coed. 49 miles, 1,870 metres ascent.
Thursday 29th June – Sunday 2nd July

The morning sky is rain-smudged and bleary. I trudge slowly towards the inescapable greyness shrouding the Clwydian hills. I write post-cards in the warm shelter of the café at Loggerheads Country Park, which nestles against the lower slopes of Moel Famau, enjoying the opportunity to legitimately write "I am at Loggerheads," but wishing that I had a companion to name. An interpretative panel illustrates the official version of the view, but Moel Famau has wandered out of sight, like a caged zoo animal hiding from prying public eyes.

Leaving the visitor centre at 3.00pm, I follow a well-signposted, if indirect, route to the summit of the County Top. The cloud thickens as I gain height, so that I do not see the Jubilee Tower that crowns the summit until I am only about five metres from it. Commissioned to commemorate the golden jubilee of George III in 1809, a lack of funding meant that it was never completed. Suffering storm damage in 1862, the unfinished tower was partially demolished to reduce it to a safe level.

By the next morning, the rain has eased a little, and visibility now extends to about thirty metres. I am tucking into my breakfast porridge when my tongue encounters a smooth, slightly slimy, lozenge. I gag involuntarily, horrified at the thought that I have a slug in my mouth, before I detect the sweet, musky flavour of a wine gum, and I recall having mixed some sweets in with my dried fruit last time I stocked up on supplies.

Over recent days I have been eschewing overgrown footpaths in

Moel Famau: the official view, 29 June 2017 and, below,
Moel Famau: the actual view, 29 June 2017.

favour of minor lanes, but in Cyfflliog I notice a waymarker for the Brenig Way. Since I am aiming for Llyn Brenig, this seems a sensible option. The path winds seductively between limestone outcrops edged with clumps of purple foxgloves, above the singing of the Afon Clywenog. Overhanging alder branches shower me with water as I push through them, but the trail is perfectly passable. Perfectly passable, that is, until I reach an isolated farmstead and quite suddenly lose all trace of the path. Without the guidance of waymarkers, I resort to climbing a series of padlocked gates and following forest tracks that I know are not rights of way to join a public byway higher up the hillside.

Reaching the byway, I glance down to find my clothes and ruck-

First night in a bird hide, Llyn Brenig, 30th June 2017.

sack crawling with greenfly. There are too many insects to contemplate removing them individually, but I trust the persistent rain to wash them away. I also realise how cold I am, in sodden clothing on an exposed hillside, but decide that the best way to warm up is to keep moving. I will need the dry jumper in my bag when the air cools this evening.

The byway crosses a minor road where, in defiance of topological logic, the waymarkers reappear, informing me that I'm back on the Brenig Way. On the shores of the llyn I find a small bird hide: a little damp, but dry enough – much drier than anything about my person – with a solid bench running beneath the window. Though it is only 3.30pm I decide to spend the night here rather than in my soaking wet tent. By tying my air mattress on top of the bench I can create just enough width to sleep off the floor, out of reach of any rodent room-mates.

To my surprise, I survive the night without falling off the bench, and am woken at first light by a sheep butting against the exterior wall. Sixteen hours after entering the hide, I step outside, back into the enduring rain. Clouds float mournfully over the reservoir, dragging their tails towards the water's surface.

Unfamiliar birds with wings the colour of parkin are making a peculiar racket from their thistle-top perches: chirp-chirp crunch-crunch-crunch, chirp-chirp crunch-crunch-crunch. Perhaps they are simply ordinary sparrows, but I have never before noticed this odd combination of the melodious and the percussive in their song.

A right of way marches with Roman geometry across my map. I know from experience that such an idealised path never exists – the reality is tussocky moorland, sliced by an electric fence. I use sheep tracks whenever these move in vaguely the right direction, but otherwise trip through the tussocks until a small llyn opens out before me. Next to the llyn stand a ruined cottage and a man-made platform occupied by a dark, hulking shape: an osprey. As I draw closer the osprey takes to the skies, circling languidly overhead. I stand and watch as the circles drift serenely northwards until the bird disappears from view. Walking on, I glance back every few minutes in the hope that the distinctive silhouette has reappeared – but no; I was lucky to arrive at the right time.

From Capel Garmon the road plunges endlessly to Betws-y-Coed.

I haven't been above an altitude of 400 metres all day; with this much descent I must surely now be below sea level. My feet are screaming at me. My ingrowing toenail is affecting my gait, putting more pressure on the outer edges of the balls of my feet, where corns are beginning to develop. The steep downhill gradient intensifies the pressure and the pain. I arrive in Betws-y-Coed through the railway station and collapse into the buffet car café. I slip my boots off under the table as discreetly as I can, hoping that the aroma of my feet will go unnoticed amongst the greasy tang of fried food and the warm, stuffy smell of British Rail upholstery.

I have arrived in Betws-y-Coed on the second day of the Snowdon Challenge event, and a steady stream of trekkers are tramping through the tourist crowds. Snowdon, the County Top of Caernarfonshire and the Challengers' objective, is only a few miles from the village, but before climbing it I must walk out to Holyhead Mountain on the far west coast of Anglesey, then back to Snowdonia. Although I enjoy the feeling of moving 'under the radar', playing outside the rules, my arrival in a supposedly civilised place such as this brings a sudden crushing loneliness. The emptiness before sleep arrives is the dangerous time, when thoughts come unbidden and memories surface. Why is it only the bad times that haunt me? I remember only reasons to loathe myself, not the days I have loved and been loved.

The next day is a rest day, and my mood is buoyed by the arrival of friends Maggie and John on an early afternoon train. We head to a garden centre a short distance away from the main shopping parade, in the hope of finding a quiet place for coffee. Even here, we are lucky to secure seats.

"Whatever that was," John indicates a bucket-sized red mug left by the previous occupants of our table, "I want one." It transpires that the bucket contained a large cappuccino: Maggie orders three, along with coffee, lemon and chocolate cakes, which are gleefully devoured before they have a chance to wilt in the heat.

Later, John investigates the miniature railway, taking photographs "for my grandson," while Maggie and I chat. All too soon it is time for them to re-embark and continue their train journey towards Porthmadog.

Just enough time remains for me to scour Betws-y-Coed's many outdoor shops until I find a pair of walking shoes made by the same manufacturer as my current boots, and with a very similar fit. They're half price, having been returned by their first purchaser. No information has been provided about the reason for their rejection, but I don't see any obvious defects and I am desperate to change footwear: it is now July, yet I am still wearing crampon-compatible winter boots. I definitely don't want blisters again, though, so will carry my boots with me when I leave Betws-y-Coed, to give myself the option of changing my mind.

In a further effort to improve the comfort of my feet, I operate on my ingrowing toenail and succeed in pulling a splinter of nail out from the flesh of my toe. The throbbing subsides almost immediately and I begin to feel more optimistic about my onward journey.

Holyhead Mountain (County Top of Anglesey)

Betws-y-Coed to Bangor. 81 miles, 2,680 metres ascent.
Monday 3rd – Thursday 6th July

Bands of teenagers are ranging through the woods, evidently on training exercises for the Duke of Edinburgh's Award Scheme. While they learn to navigate, I am granted a rest: at every junction a group of young people pore over a map, their backs towards the way they have come, showing me which path leads to the National Mountain Centre at Plas y Brenin, near Capel Curig.

I enjoy a leisurely game of leapfrog with an elderly cyclist on the byway between Capel Curig and Ogwen Cottage. He opens our conversation with "My knee hurts," and I am momentarily concerned, thinking that I'm going to be called upon to put some of my first aid skills into practice. But this is simply the start of his explanation for the bicycle – a keen walker in his younger days, he cycles now that his knees prevent him from climbing mountains. That is, he cycles downhill, but dismounts to push the bike at the first hint of an uphill gradient, hence the fact that we keep overtaking each other over the next few miles. Each time we pass, he greets me with a jovial accusation of "You're catching me up," and bids me farewell with "well, take care."

From the base of Tryfan, I turn off the byway to ascend into the Carneddau mountains, scrambling up Y Braich to Pen yr Helgi Ddu and on to Carnedd Llewellyn. This isn't a historic County Top, but a modern one, the highest point in Conwy, so I have climbed up here partly because it adds no appreciable extra distance to my route, and partly to re-trace memories of walking in Snowdonia with Laurence and other friends. We have both climbed Carnedd Llewellyn many times, usually in foul weather in early January. Today it is cloudy and a little damp, but not otherwise unpleasant. I meet two further Duke of Edinburgh groups on the ridge – one just approaching the summit of Carnedd Llewellyn, the other trying to re-trace their steps to the shelter on Foel Grach. The latter group have abandoned their attempts to reach Carnedd Llewellyn in low visibility and have opted instead to take their 'escape route' down to Cwm Eigiau. We find the shelter together, and I make sure that they are oriented for the descent before parting from them.

I descend northwards over the rocky summits of Yr Aryg, Bera Bach and Drosgl. My toe has been much less painful since yesterday's surgery, but now I bash my foot against a sharp piece of slate and am in agony for a few minutes until the pain subsides. I can also feel a deep bone-ache at the base of my spine, which I suspect is caused by the extra two-kilogram weight of the boots in my bag.

Descending past a group of shepherds busy on the col between Drosgl and Gyrn Wigau, I find myself within a theatrical set constructed entirely from slate: purpureus flakes lie in heaps on the hillside; greying lichen-encrusted plates have been stacked to form walls; a narrow lane is laid with tiny purple fragments. Sea and sky, too, reflect the same dark timbres. For some days I have been meditating on whether the landscape alone apprises me that I am walking through Wales. In lowland agricultural areas, I was unsure (bilingual signage aside), but this world of slate is definitively, unambiguously Welsh.

Walking through Bangor, I am refreshed by the euphonious fluidity of the Welsh language. My incomprehension of the conversations being carried on around me lends an illusory, unreal quality to my passage, so that even though I am walking through a civilised, urban area, I don't feel the isolation of Betws-y-Coed. In utterly flawed logic: I am not really here, therefore I cannot feel alienated.

My mind jumps to make (usually erroneous) links between Welsh and other languages. The word for eagle, *eryr*, is close to eyrie, for example, and *draig*, dragon, occurs in the Irish name *Pádraig*. Sometimes a leading Y feels like an acute accent on a French E: *ysgol* = *école*, *ystad* = *état*. The few loan words that I come across give the impression that the English are responsible for anything and everything bad: *Dim Parcio; Dim Tipio; Dim Trespasu*.

I cross the Menai Straits on Telford's suspension bridge, pausing to admire a pair of egrets stalking haughtily through the exposed low-tide mud. Though my map depicts Anglesey as an island veined with footpaths, I have seen enough of the rights of way in the locality to be distrustful of their existence, so stay on lanes until I can join the Lôn Las Cefni cycle route at Llangefni.

Arriving at the Llyn Cefni reservoirs, I pause to read an information board – and am instantly spotted. A lady in shorts and hiking boots, but without a rucksack – sure signs of a local resident – strides confidently over: I am reading the sign, and must therefore be lost.

"Where are you heading to?" The accent confirms my identification.

I hesitate. My intention is to continue a short distance into nearby woodland, then find somewhere to hide my tent, but I don't want to admit this, being unsure of local attitudes towards wild camping. Nor do I want to even attempt to pronounce the name of the village at the far end of the path. My equivocation confirms that I am in need of help. The lady asks to see my map, which makes matters even worse, since our current location is about five millimetres from the edge of the page, next to a prominent handwritten annotation detailing the opening hours of Llangefni's Asda. My rescuer opts for a lengthy description of how to follow the path towards the unpronounceable place, but then loop back to end up at Asda. I decide that the best option is to let the explanation run its course and then express my gratitude.

Satisfied that she has been of assistance to a stranger in distress, the lady now becomes more generally conversational.

"I've just walked round the small lake," she tells me. "I was going to go all the way round, but the weather doesn't look great, so I came back along the railway line. You've got to watch out for raptors, though, but I think it's too cold for them today."

Raptors?

Maybe I have mis-heard, but raptors are either birds of prey, which do not usually cause trouble to walkers, or velociraptors. I certainly don't want to meet any of the latter, so am relieved if the weather is too cold for them today.

By smiling and repeating my thanks for the irrelevant directions I eventually manage to withdraw, nip round the corner, and pitch my tent in the woodland. Just in time, as it is starting to rain again.

I am developing a strange reluctance to write my diary. I don't know whether it has become a chore, or whether I am struggling for things to say at a time when much of my walking is mechanical leg-work, propelling myself perpetually onwards. For most of the next day, I plod along roads from Llyn Cefni to Holyhead, knowing that I will need to re-cross the island again only a day later, probably by the same route.

The bold granite wedge of Holyhead Mountain appears quite suddenly, rising up from the low-lying island as I approach the Holy Isle causeway. Though it attains a height of only 220 metres, I can see immediately why it has been awarded the title of 'mountain'.

Summit of Holyhead Mountain, County Top of Anglesey, 5th July 2017.

A fine lacework of routes has been draped over the hill, extending down to the South Stack lighthouse and Breakwater County Park. By the time I reach the summit, the day has grown hot. I sit for a while, watching a ladybird crawling over bird's-foot trefoil at my feet, while tiny ladybird-sized ferries sail in and out from Holyhead. The hazy outline of land is just discernible across the Irish Sea. Judging its direction in comparison to the ferry routes, I conclude that it must be the Isle of Man rather than Ireland.

They say 'it takes one to know one', but in this case I think it is obvious. The man striding down the lane towards me, bent slightly forwards beneath an oversized rucksack, head covered by a piratical red scarf, and using a furled flag as a walking staff, is clearly playing the same game as me. His objective, I learn, is South Stack lighthouse; he has walked all the way from Bristol, carrying the flag of Anglesey with him. It's a charity venture, he informs me – only later do I realise that I have forgotten to ask which charity he is supporting.

In Y Fali, I post my winter boots home, committing myself to the lighter walking shoes from now on. As I step out of the Post Office, I make an impromptu decision to re-cross Anglesey by a different route. This will make the return to Bangor longer than my westward journey, and will lead me off the edge of my maps, but the idea of reprising the tarmac miles of the previous day is almost unbearable. However, a footpath alongside a railway line deposits me in a clump of wiry gorse, so I resign myself to roads again. The roadside hedges are aromatic with lilac, honeysuckle and lavender, tinged with salt from the sea breeze – but their skirts are thick with accumulated litter, in quantities that I haven't seen since the outskirts of Edinburgh.

Later in the day, I decide to risk another footpath, hoping to walk through the Cors Ddyga marshes rather than along the A5. At the bottom of a lane, metal posts look suspiciously as though they might once have borne footpath signs, and gates have been secured uninvitingly with blue twine. I am fairly sure that I can work out where the right of way is supposed to run, but a young woman is digging in an adjacent garden, and politeness dictates that I ask for clarification.

Amy has only been living here for a fortnight and is unaware of the existence of the right of way. She tries very hard to be helpful, scrutinising my map, and then walking me back up the lane – effectively pointing me back the way I've come. I find an alternative path, marked by yellow arrows affixed to posts deep within the undergrowth. I wade through a bed of nettles, negotiate three rusted gates, edge round a field, scramble over a wall… and eventually reach the well-kempt paths of Cors Ddyga.

When I first catch sight of Snowdon the summit is clear, but soon a thick blanket of cloud begins to creep up from the base of the mountains, as though they've pulled the duvet up and are going back to sleep. Behind me, Holyhead Mountain bears the same cloud blanket on its western, seaward side – a moist sea breeze must be rising over the hills, the moisture within it condensing as the air cools.

It is nearly 4.00pm by the time I reach Gaerwen. Needing to make faster progress, I stomp down the edge of the A5 to Llanfair P.G. and the Menai Bridge. My map shows an area of woodland on the southern fringes of Bangor. What it doesn't show is that this woodland belongs to Bangor University Botanical Gardens – hardly an ideal choice of campsite, but after more than ten hours of walking, I am too tired to continue further.

⚠

Snowdon (Yr Wyddfa) (County Top of Caernarfonshire), Moel Sych (County Top of Montgomeryshire) and Cadair Berwyn (County Top of Denbighshire)
Bangor to Bala. 70 miles, 3,730 metres ascent.
Friday 7th – Tuesday 11th July

The tent is on more of a slope than I had realised when I pitched it, and everything keeps sliding towards one corner. My legs ache with being curled up for too long, but I don't want to stretch them out in case I put my feet through the tent fabric.

Once again, I walk predominantly on tarmac. The one footpath that I do risk is only 500 metres in length and usefully cuts the corner off at a road junction. Within those 500 metres the path descends into a bog, crosses a rotten bridge whose planks disintegrate as I step on them, then crashes through a stand of eight-foot-high bracken. The only aspect of the path that seems well maintained is the slate wall bounding it on both sides, crushing any dreams of escape. I have learnt my lesson, and resolve to stay on the road.

From Llanberis, I ascend Snowdon by the path alongside the railway – a route I haven't walked since I was about ten years old. On that occasion, on a family holiday run by the Field Studies Council, two groups climbed Snowdon by different routes; the minibus drivers swapped keys on the summit, before each group descended by the other's route of ascent. Starting from Llanberis, our group parked the minibus at such an angle that the diesel slumped to one side of the fuel tank, and the other group were unable to start the engine. Needless to say, they were not best pleased with us.

Like an inverted iceberg, the top half of Snowdon lurks within the cloud. Rain sets in. Visibility falls to between five and ten metres. I can always hear other walkers approaching before I see them, and at one point can smell the train descending the mountain only a few feet away, although it remains invisible to me.

On the summit, a trainload of tourists are being unloaded into the midst of a crowd of drenched hikers. After they have recovered from the initial bewilderment of seeing so many people who have actually walked up the mountain – in this weather! – the train passengers divide into two groups: one braving the few steps to the summit cairn, the other making straight for the coffee machine.

Back outside in the driving rain, a scene from Scafell Pike is being re-played. A small boy pipes up, "Dad, it's not that way!" as his father strides off towards the Watkin Path. I ask which way they're heading: the Miners' Track – the boy is right.

As though to taunt me, the weather makes an abrupt change as soon as Snowdon is behind me. The next day is warm, with skies the colour of an Adonis butterfly. A plume of cloud is burning off the summit of Snowdon as I ascend the opposite side of Nant Gwynant. Ahead of me rises another pyramidal peak, formed by the same glacial processes as those which shaped Snowdon: Cnicht takes its name from the knight's helmet which it supposedly resembles. For me, it is not a resemblance of things known, but an enticement to new exploration. In areas where I have climbed extensively – Glen Coe, Loch Lomond, the Lake District – I bypassed hills without hesitation.

Here, though, I am captivated by new crags, and it is heart-wrenching to walk on past. I remind myself of the importance of conserving my energy, and do not permit myself any diversionary peak-bagging.

My path descends through mine workings above Ffestiniog. Aware that I'm behaving recklessly and that a false step could result in serious injury – or worse – I make a precipitous scree-run down the face of one of the huge slate slag heaps, racing my own exhilaration and the cascade of loose flakes that I set in motion.

Snowdon, County Top of Caernarfonshire, 8 July 2017.

There were midges at my campsite last night, and I am plagued by horseflies as I walk. I brush the insects away each time I sense them, but always too late; my arms and legs are soon blotched and swollen. Once I have pitched my tent I cool the smarting stings in the running water of a stream, but another horsefly bites while I bathe.

Reaching Bala by late morning the next day, I check the weather forecast. Rain is forecast again, so I decide to reverse the loop I have planned for the next two days, giving a long walk over two County Tops today, then a shorter return to Bala in the rain tomorrow. I climb on a B-road to the top of a pass, close to the point where the modern-day counties of Conwy, Denbighshire and Gwynedd come together. Only halfway to the top of the pass I have almost run out of water, having not realised quite how hot the afternoon would become. A stream flows beneath the road at Pont Cym Pydew. The water is opaque and orange, but I tell myself that this is probably just a mineral deposit – iron? I climb a short distance upstream of the road, away from the area where passing motorists might throw litter or stop to urinate. A dead sheep lies in the stream, back arched, teeth bared, like a vision of Dante's inferno. Hoping that the sheep didn't die as a result of drinking the orange slime, I climb further uphill before filling my bottles.

Now with a heavier bag than I'd like, I continue on to the top of the pass, where a board-walk leads along the ridge. Some cautionary advice, dispensed in the form of a humorous ditty by older friends, shuffles out of the recesses of my memory and begins to dance about, dictating a rhythm for my footsteps:

> *The day was hot*
> *So he drank his fill*
> *From the flowing waters*
> *Of Sour Milk Gill.*
> *But little he knew*
> *That out of view*
> *And splitting the rushing stream in two*
> *Were the rotting remains of a Herdwick ewe.*[46]

In an effort to conserve my 'drinking' water, I squeeze moisture from clumps of sphagnum moss onto my headscarf, and use this to cool my head. The board-walk leads to a good path, then to the County Tops Moel Sych and Cadair Berwyn. The latter hill has two summits: one (the higher) with a cairn-like structure next to a craggy outcrop, the other a slightly lower top bearing a trig point.

I follow the ridge a little way further to camp. A stiff breeze is blowing, so the sodden tent dries in less than ten minutes, although if the forecast is correct it will be wet again before morning. I lose a

---

46 I know neither the author nor title of this poem. Another refrain, which I find comes to mind more often, starts with the words "*It rained and rained and rained and rained...*" and expands upon this theme for several verses.

tent peg in the deep heather; surprisingly, the first one I have lost since setting out on my walk.

The forecast is proved correct. I wake to thick fog, which amplifies everything around me, as though to compensate for the obfuscation of detail. The dim outlines of imperial pines resolve into a scrubby patch of thistles as I approach. With little to look at, I find myself speculating on Welsh etymology again. Could the word for litter, *sbwriel*, be related to the similar-sounding 'spurious'? Why does the English *garth* refer to a gate or gateway, but the Welsh *gardd* denotes a garden, and the Cumbrian *garth* means an enclosure?

From Llandrillo, eight miles of road-walking brings me back to Bala. I try to walk facing the oncoming traffic, on the right-hand verge or the outsides of bends, but some sections of road contrive to be left- and right-hand bends at one and the same time. I wonder whether I might make myself more visible by walking along the central white line and throwing myself into the appropriate hedge whenever a vehicle approaches.

Friends might describe the Bala hostel warden as straightforward and honest; a less charitable choice of adjectives might include brusque or forthright. The hostel is run as a tight ship. Instructions on acceptable behaviour paper every available surface, from shelf-edges to the walls of toilet cubicles:

> Please keep the Games and Books TIDY!
> Please Do Not Touch the Painting
> Irresponsible People must be supervised to
> Keep Books and Games Tidy Please
> WATER IS METERED Every Drop Counts Keep Costs Down

Idly browsing the internet, I discover a Facebook group for people who have 'survived' a stay at this particular hostel. Since the warden is currently holding my clothes hostage in the laundry, I tread lightly, going out of my way to maintain a good relationship with her.

Introspection: Connections

At a fundamental, geographical level, my walk was about making connections – finding footpaths to link the counties and their highest points. On a more personal level, it was also a means of making connections with people. In some cases this meant re-casting the links of existing friendships, as with Maggie and John, who contrived their own cross-country journey to intersect with mine. In other cases the connections were with people previously unknown to me – or even with people that I am unlikely ever to meet.

A sense of common purpose meant that my brief communions with Kevin at Abington Service Station, and with the lone walker with the Anglesey flag, felt more real – and crucially, more meaningful – than the evening spent in the company of relatives in Sandbach. Although I did not realise it until later in my walk, another adventurer, Alex Staniforth, was active in the area at the time. In 2017, Alex connected the highest points of the modern British counties by bike and on foot, as part of his 'Climb the UK' challenge. Alex had reached the summit of Moel Famau only a few days before me, but in rather different weather conditions, which he described in an email to me as "probably one of the clearest and most pleasant days I had besides Ben More Assynt."

Many months after I had returned to civilisation, and shortly after I had received an offer of publication from Hayloft Publishing, I discovered one further connection in another of Hayloft's books. In Hugh Symonds' 'Running High', an account of his 2,000-mile run connecting the 3,000-foot mountains of Britain and Ireland, I came across a line describing "the icy crossing to Conival," and was hit by the sudden realisation that Hugh, like me, had approached Ben More Assynt from the east. I suspect that any roll-call of people who have climbed Ben More Assynt from Glen Cassley rather than using the conventional route of ascent from Inchnadamph would struggle to reach double figures. Snowdon, only a few days behind me at this point in the narrative, was Hugh's final summit of the British mainland, and from his description I get the impression that the weather on that occasion was very similar to the day of my ascent. After Snowdon, though, I was still less than halfway through my list of County Tops, whereas Hugh's journey continued to Ireland. The County Tops of both Northern Ireland and the Irish Republic await me still.

Connections: morning dew on a spider's web, 17th July 2017.

"It has been known to rain in Wales"

Merionethshire – Cardiganshire – Pembrokeshire –
Glamorgan – Carmarthenshire – Brecknockshire –
Monmouthshire – Herefordshire – Radnorshire

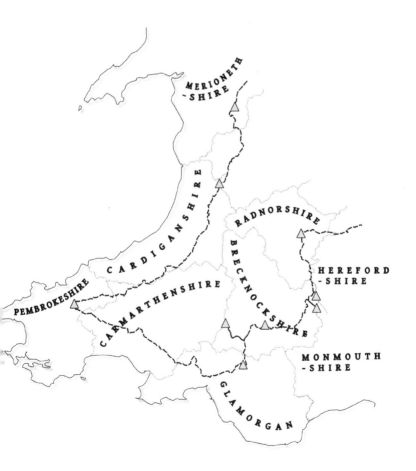

Aran Fawddwy (County Top of Merionethshire) and Pumlumon Fawr (County Top of Cardiganshire)

Bala to Llanybydder. 83 miles, 3,360 metres ascent.
Wednesday 12th – Saturday 15th July

A formative experience from my teenage years was a day wasted walking eastwards through Grizedale Forest, when the compass-bearer had confused their cardinal points, and the rest of our group were too inexperienced to identify other signs that we were not, as we believed, heading west. That particular misadventure instilled in me a wish to see Ordnance Survey grid references displayed on foot-path signs and waymarkers. Though the advent of GPS-enabled smartphones has perhaps rendered my idea obsolescent, here, on Aran Fawddwy, it is finally granted: each stile bears its own grid reference. The ridge is a steady, elongated, climb, and I wonder whether the many false summits might be the reason for this grid-reference-labelling.

I reach the County Top of Merionethshire shortly after midday. To my west, the ridge line of Cadair Idris might have been transplanted from Sutherland. Beyond is a heavy blue horizon so perfectly level that it can only be the sea. To my east, veins of quartz glitter on bulbous hills, folded like smoothly kneaded bread dough. The blue of the sea and the red of the hills bring to mind a poem by Edward Thomas:

> She is dead, Eluned,
> Who was part of Spring,
> And of blue summer and red Autumn,
> And made the Winter beloved;
> She is dead, and these things come not again.[47]

Though elsewhere 'blue summer' might suggest despondency or low spirits, here on the Aran ridge, the poet's choice seems entirely natural in evoking the muted, melded colours around me. Jim Perrin manages to similarly encapsulate the Welsh landscape in a few sparse words when he writes of the "gilded calamity"[48] conveying perfectly the reflection of sunlight from rain-washed crags, or the glinting of the

---

47 Edward Thomas, *Beautiful Wales* (London: A. & C. Black, 1905).
48 Jim Perrin, *On and Off the Rocks* (London: Victor Gollancz, 1986).

Summit of Aran Fawddwy, County Top of Merionethshire, 12th July 2017.

quartz and pyrrhotite here on this ridge. Perrin, though, is writing from the intimate perspective of a rock-climber, and it feels more intuitive to me as a walker to observe the landscape through Thomas' wider field of view.

A solitary figure ahead of me bears a superficial resemblance to a friend. I manage to swallow an involuntary cry of "Holly! Wait!" before it escapes my mouth. Perhaps this is a sign of loneliness, or of my inability to comprehend how many people there really are in the world. Even back in the ordinary world, I often find that my mind tries to classify new acquaintances as being 'the same as' people I already know, a tendency which I suspect is being compounded by my current eremitic existence.

Descending towards Cwm Cywarch, I pass several groups toiling up the track; each comments that I am the first person they have met on their walk. They, too, seem unable to comprehend how many people there are in the world, or at least on the Aran ridge, and steadfastly refuse to believe that there might be other walkers on Aran Fawddwy today.

Down in the valley, a care-free fox is trotting down the road towards me – the first that I have seen during my walk, although I often hear foxes at night. The fox's nose twitches almost imperceptibly as it scents me. It freezes, then vanishes into roadside woodland.

Gorse is still flowering among the heather near Moelfre; I thought I had seen the last of it, but Eluned is not quite dead yet. I pause to dry my tent, but drops of rain begin to fall almost as soon as I have pitched it, forcing me to move on. I can see back towards Cadair Idris and the Aran ridge – strange to think that only a day has elapsed since I climbed Aran Fawddwy, which now looks much further than a day's walk away. Ahead, I catch a brief glimpse of Pumlumon Fawr before clouds descend onto the summit.

The sight of a sheep jumping over a cattle-grid near Glaslyn triggers the tune of 'Hey Diddle Diddle', which cycles through my mind for the rest of the day. Reaching the llyn, I hesitate over my choice of route, deliberating over how far I should press on before dark. I fortify myself by eating most of my remaining rations – probably not a wise decision, as it leaves only a handful of dried figs for the rest of the day – and ascend over trackless, rough terrain.

I pass the sources of the Severn and the Wye before I reach the summit of Pumlumon, the County Top of Cardiganshire. I descend a short distance past the summit to camp next to twin tarns. The water feels tepid and I am tempted to swim, but I am barely warm enough myself, so cannot risk becoming colder.

Something of a pattern is beginning to develop: though it is not raining when I wake, the familiar soundtrack of raindrops on the roof of my tent returns as I am eating my porridge. The tent is very rarely dry when I strike it.

Since Bala, I have been walking generally south through the centre of Wales, heading for the hills that lie along the south coast: the Preseli Mountains and Brecon Beacons. A friend will be joining me to traverse the Brecons, but until then I travel alone. I descend from the wild moors of Pumlumon to the road that will lead me to Devil's Bridge, where I plunge once more into civilisation. Tired after yesterday's long walk, I rest in a café next to Rheiddol steam railway. I have just finished an egg bap and a mug of tea, and am looking over my maps for the next section of the walk, when one of the railway volunteers comes over to my table.

"Are you walking?"

I nod.

"Where from?"

"I camped on Pumlumon last night."

"And where were you before that? Machynlleth?"

I cast around for a place name that I can pronounce. "Dinas Mawddwy." Not quite accurate, but I don't trust myself to try saying Mallwyd.

"Dinas Mawddwy," the man marvels, "that's *further* than Machynlleth." He shuffles away, murmuring 'Dinas Mawddwy' under his breath – and returns, a minute later, to present me with a second cup of tea and a bar of chocolate. My attempts to pay are waved away: "You'll need the energy."

My destination for the day is Cors Caron, according to the National Biodiversity Network the best-preserved raised bog in the United Kingdom. Unlike the vast expanses of exposed peat I encountered in Caithness and the Pennines, Cors Caron is green and gramineous, with stands of alder and willow amongst swathes of sedge and purple moor-grass.

Type-written slips of paper bearing Welsh names have been pasted onto the bird identification chart on the wall of a hide beside the causeway. Reed warbler = *Telor y eyrs*; Grey heron = *Creyr glas*. I am momentarily surprised by the second, until I remember that the Welsh *glas* means blue, not green, as it does in Gaelic; a blue heron seems a more natural description than a green one.

No-one joins me in the hide, so I decide to spend an indoor night here, where I have the space to sit upright or pace about as I choose, in celebration of the fact that I have now walked more than 2,000 miles. After four months on the road, my hair has grown down below my shoulders, and has been driving me to distraction. Abruptly, I realise that I can stand it no longer: I grab clumps of hair with my left hand and hack at them using the tiny scissors from my first aid kit. I have no mirror, but from my dim reflection in the windows of the hide it is clear that I have made a particularly bad job of it.

I sleep badly – perhaps because a fear of falling off the bench has pervaded my dreams. Coupled with the fact that I stayed up late in case a deputation of Cors Caron nature enthusiasts arrived for a bat-watching session, I wake feeling distinctly un-rested. My mood is not helped when I try to brew tea with raspberry-flavoured iced tea, purchased because the Pontrhydfendigaid village shop didn't stock water in appropriately-sized bottles, and my powdered milk curdles into a lumpy yellow scum.

Second night in a bird hide, 14th July 2017.

The walk from Cors Caron to Lampeter is a string of village-to-village hops. In honour of the first day of the school summer holidays, it's raining. I enjoy the freedom of walking into the wind, leaving my hood down and letting my hair get soaked now that it doesn't drip down the back of my neck. Kites are constant companions overhead, and interpretative panels have come into bloom, proffering information about heritage, history, industry and religion. I feel I would benefit from an interpreter of road signs, to assist me in correlating the Welsh and English place-name counterparts.

> Lampeter
> Llanbedr
> Pont Steffan

Is this one place, or two, or three?

Foel Cwmcerwyn (County Top of Pembrokeshire)

Llanybydder to Carmarthen. 61 miles, 2,170 metres ascent.
Sunday 16th – Wednesday 19th July

I walk along roads so narrow and infrequently used that the two wheel-tracks are divided by a velvet stripe of green moss. The road is flanked by laid sycamores that have been allowed to grow out: the horizontal trunks are each as thick as a human torso, and the vertical shoots tower above the few wayside houses. The road passes through patches of woodland – some of it old, to judge from the coppiced birch and surrounding high wood-banks. At one point, the woods have been colonised by ancient cars. A line of them queue along a forest track, bumper to bumper, and less-sociable vehicles are secreted between the trees. Some are covered by protective plastic sheeting, others have been left to brave the elements alone, and one has its own thick mossy blanket. All are extremely rusty; an MOT would be out of the question.

I spend a relaxed afternoon in the National Wool Museum at Dre-Fach Felindre. It being Sunday, none of the machines are running, but it is nonetheless an interesting exhibition. I stand rapt at the spinning machine, wondering how such an intricate mechanism could ever have been dreamt up.

By the time I leave the museum, it has stopped raining, and blue sky soon washes in overhead – long may this last! I camp in a triangular area of heathery scrub bounded by two roads and a coniferous plantation. Desiccated brambles snag my tent, and I notice that the left shoulder-strap of my rucksack is beginning to fray. I coat both tears with glue to try to prevent them from propagating.

Morning dew picks out skeins of spider-silk draped over the heathland. Grasshoppers are singing from recently-trimmed hedges. Brambles have regrown most quickly, their long arms reaching into the road like a caricature of a crowd awaiting royalty. There is a hint of salt on the breeze, and I almost expect to see the sea, but the Preseli hills shield the horizon from view.

Sometimes, when walking alone, I catch aspects of myself that I recognise as belonging to other people. I'll place my foot a particular way, or see a shape in my shadow, and think *that's Rachel, that's Suzanna*. How much of my identity is no more than a reflection of those I have come into contact with? Am I somehow less substantial than other people? Or is existence merely an illusion, and this is the closest I come to breaking the surface?

A vein of brightly-clad figures trickles over the ridge ahead and insinuates itself into my introspection. It looks like a school trip – perhaps a class outing for the end of term. The trickle broadens. This is more young people than a single class: a whole school, and a large one at that. A few of the younger children smile and greet me with *Bore da*, but many of the older ones are playing music from mobile phones and mp3 players. The flow eventually dwindles, until there is only a dribble of stragglers being chivvied along by their teachers. Barely has the sound of chattering children receded when the whole procession repeats itself. I begin to wonder whether every child in Wales is walking the Preseli hills for the end of term.

Eventually, Wales runs out of children, and by the time I reach Foel Cwmcerwyn I have the hills to myself once more. I pitch my tent so that it opens towards the west, and stay up late to read a recently-acquired copy of James Joyce's *A Portrait of the Artist as a*

Sunset from the Preseli hills, 17th July 2017.

Young Man, munch ginger-nuts and drink the sunset. An amber cause-way shimmers on the surface of the sea, but fades as the sun sinks behind Ireland. To the south west a patch of high cloud blushes a deep crimson.

I sleep badly again. Too many ginger nuts? Or too much Joyce hammering round inside my head?

A dead kite lies in the road, wings hunched, eyes bright. Kites are scavengers, so I suspect that this one has dived for road kill only to succumb to the same fate. Part of me wants to pluck a souvenir tail feather, but such behaviour would seem disrespectful towards so dignified a bird. I walk on along the road.

High banks and hedgerows restrict my view of the landscape around me, removing any distinctive sense of 'Welshness' from my walk. Devoid of context, the roads feel very much like the lane leading from my village, and the woodland is reminiscent of Dufton, now a distant memory. These lanes, though, lead me to Carmarthen, not home.

In Carmarthen, I queue at the post office, to send an extremely belated birthday present to my sister's partner. Ahead of me in the queue a woman is changing travel currency. Though the transaction is being carried out in Welsh, I notice that numbers are spoken in English. I wonder whether 'five hundred' becomes particularly cumbrous in Welsh, or whether the young man serving is not a native Welsh-speaker and doesn't want to risk making a mistake.

After the Post Office I find a hairdresser and make an appointment for an emergency haircut, to repair the damage I inflicted upon myself in the Cors Caron bird hide. The salon can't fit me into their schedule until late afternoon, so I send a text message to Matthew to advise him that I may be late to meet him from his train.

"What's the emergency?" comes his reply. "Hair down to the ground?"

Quite the opposite problem – but the hairdresser does an excellent job of tidying up my short spikes of thatch, so that I now feel I can walk about the town centre without my headscarf and not attract comment.

Matthew's train is cancelled owing to a points failure, so he arrives over an hour later than planned. I walk circuits of the station car park, unable to bear the incessant announcements in which the only decipherable phrase is *Arriva Trenau Cymru*. There often doesn't seem to be time to fit in the equivalent English-language announcement before the next flurry of Welsh begins.

Craig y Llyn (County Top of Glamorgan), Fan Foel (County Top of Carmarthenshire) and Pen y Fan (County Top of Brecknockshire)

Carmarthen to Danywenallt. 100 miles, 4,970 metres ascent.
Thursday 20th – Monday 24th July

Looking over my planned route, Matthew is surprised at how much of it follows roads, when the surrounding countryside is apparently well-supplied with paths and tracks. Against my better judgement, I allow myself to be persuaded onto a byway. A tarmac lane leads to a house, but from here the continuation of the right of way is not obvious. Noticing us pause to check the map, the owner of the house comes outside to point us in the right direction and to warn us that the path becomes increasingly overgrown as it reaches land owned by the neighbouring farm.

"You're welcome to try to get through," he tells us, "though I don't know that anyone's managed it since I've been living here."

We try, fail, retreat, and resign ourselves to roads once more.

In the late afternoon we leave the tarmac again, to take a bridleway from Pontarddulais: a beautiful, well-trodden path through bracken and heather. Half an hour beyond the town, the path is blocked by an access road for a new wind farm. The construction work has severed several rights of way and leaves us no option but to return to the road – meaning a lengthy diversion.

Crossing two final fields to reach Matthew's accommodation, I stumble from a stile and land awkwardly. Pain shoots up the front of my right ankle when I put weight on it, but I continue walking, working on the principle that most pain goes away if ignored for long enough. Dusk is beginning to fall by the time we reach the B&B. I limp a short distance further to camp on open moorland.

There is a lump on the outside edge of my right foot and pain when I flex my ankle, but I'm not ready to give up yet: I still have more than a thousand miles to walk. Trying to remember to tread carefully on rough ground, I return to meet Matthew outside his B&B next morning.

"Have you seen the weather forecast?" I enquire, somewhat tentatively. Seventeen millimetres of rain are expected in Neath Port Talbot over the next six hours. "You might want to put your waterproofs on."

Matthew is, as ever, stoical. "Well, it *has* been known to rain in Wales."

It rains. And rains. And rains.

By the time we reach Neath, we are both soaked to the skin; this is more water than our supposedly waterproof coats can withstand. The road through the town seems interminable, a sensation that is probably heightened because I'm so cold. We huddle in a bus shelter, getting steadily chillier as we eat lunch.

"Excuse me, but do you know where Morrisons is?" A car driver pulls up alongside.

We apologise, really having no idea. A few yards further down the road, however, Matthew stops.

"I think I know where Morrisons is now."

Dark green lettering is coming into view on a building ahead: first M, then O and R… We plodge into Morrisons café and try to warm up with multiple pots of tea. A small pond soon forms beneath our table. I stand at the hand-dryer in the ladies toilets for several minutes, until a Morrisons employee comes into the room and I decide that I may have outstayed my welcome. "When we go back outside," Matthew says, "I wouldn't mind wandering up the high street in case there are any shops that might sell me a new waterproof coat."

When we do step back into the deluge, however, we don't find any likely shops. We climb onto a ridge by way of a cycle path, which leads into a coniferous plantation. I pitch my tent on the site of a Roman marching camp on Carn Caca, while Matthew heads back downhill towards a B&B in Resolven.

We make a late start the next day, Matthew having been chased by a herd of bullocks on his way to re-join me at the Roman camp. It is still raining, and we are soon soaked, but today's forecast is for showers rather than a ceaseless downpour, so we hope that we may be able to dry periodically.

It takes a little longer than I'd hoped to find the summit of Craig y Llyn, the County Top of Glamorgan, mostly because of a bridleway which does not bring us out in quite the place we had expected. The sun puts in an appearance just as we finally locate the trig point on the edge of a forest clearing. I look at Matthew.

"You're steaming."

I expect I am too.

We emerge from the plantation at the top of the switchback road ascending Mynydd Beili-glas. There is a snack van in the viewpoint car park; I decide that this is an opportune moment for lunch, so trade up my squashed malt loaf for a cheese-and-pickle sandwich and mug of tea.

"Bit wet for walking," the vendor observes.

"Better than yesterday."

"I didn't even come out yesterday," he admits. "Stayed indoors all day."

Matthew's face suggests that he approves of this sentiment, although he is too polite to comment.

Refreshed, we plunge off-piste down the incline in the direction of Pontneddfechan. The forest possesses more tracks than are shown on my map, but we follow hoof-prints to ensure that we stay on the bridleway. I am beginning to become conscious of a disadvantage of Matthew's 1:25,000-scale Explorer maps: since they show precisely where a path ought to go, we are angry and confused when it doesn't behave as depicted. My Landranger maps, at 1:50,000, are much more vague, so I am disappointed only by those paths which fail to exist.

From Cefn Rhos we turn down a minor lane which appears on the map to allow us to cross the A465 and access Pontneddfechan. It doesn't. The lane becomes narrower and more overgrown until we arrive at the top of a steep embankment – almost a cliff – overlooking the dual carriageway. Thick tangles of brambles and scrubby birch trees run along the base of the cliff. There is no sign of a continuation of the lane on the far side of the A465. On my own, I would probably have forced my way through; with a feeling of responsibility towards my friend, however, I deem it prudent to retreat.

By the time that we eventually reach Pontneddfechan, Matthew is beginning to develop blisters on both feet and decides that what he terms a "supernumerary day off" is required. We part, with a plan to reconvene the following afternoon. At 7.00pm, just as I am reaching the area where I would like to camp, the heavens open with a heavy, thundery shower. My clothing is saturated within a minute: I am as wet as I was on Friday, but without Morrisons' tea and hand-dryers to warm myself with. I somehow manage to pitch the outer tent, then huddle inside it to partially hang the inner tent and transfer belongings to it from my rucksack. Then all I have to do is shuffle out of my sodden clothes and into the inner, without getting my sleeping bag too wet. Water is seeping up through the tent groundsheet.

I think maybe I drowned during the night, yet my ghost continues the pursuit of the County Tops.

Since it usually begins to rain while I am eating breakfast, I try to outwit the weather by getting up half an hour earlier than usual. This works to an extent: it starts to rain as I'm taking the tent down. Everything is sodden. I dry my socks by balancing them on top of the stove as I boil water for tea, but they become wet again the moment that I step into my boots. My sleeping bag is wet on the outside and the inside.

In the rain, below the cloud, the air has a clarity peculiar to thundery showers. Once I climb into the cloud, though, it's thick fog. I follow the Beacons Way over limestone outcrops to the Ogof Ffynnon Ddu nature reserve. The map depicts what appear to be small tarns: these prove to be yawning sinkholes, many larger than those I am familiar with from the Yorkshire Dales. Ogof Ffynnon Ddu itself is the second-longest cave in Wales, and popular with cavers; the path brings me out at the South Wales Caving Centre. The weather becomes a little better as I descend on the western side of the ridge: the rain is easing and the clouds seem to be lifting.

I ascend Fan Hir, the beginning of the ridge which will lead me to Fan Foel, flying my tent like a spinnaker sail. This probably makes me look very unprofessional, but the sodden tent dries to a point where it can be described as merely damp, making the prospect of another night camping seem almost bearable.

Reaching the summit of Fan Foel a little before midday, I continue a short distance along the ridge to a small cairn surrounded by a ring of rocks. This unprepossessing location is the County Top of Carmarthenshire, a county known in Welsh as Sir Gaerfyrddin or, more simply, Sir Gâr.

Retracing my steps along the ridge, I make a speedy descent, causing a trio of walkers to comment that I'm "going at a good lick" and ask whether I'm training for anything. I hope not: if this is training, then I don't want to experience the real thing.

Matthew is waiting in the café at the National Cave Centre. His feet are demanding a second supernumerary day, so we rummage through first aid supplies, peruse bus timetables and work out where to meet the next day. He descends into the subterranean world while I climb back into the hills, using the Sarn Helen Roman road to re-cross the morning's ridge.

The ridge arcing to the north of Fan Fawr seems to have been reserved for the experienced and intrepid. Pairs and small groups are striding out over the moorland, usually with trekking poles and other items of expensive equipment. Everyone I meet contributes to a collective commiseration over the weather on the day that Matthew and I sheltered in Morrisons – evidently still a painful memory.

I cross the A470 where it runs past the Storey Arms and step into a far less elitist world of walking. From the National Trust car park at Pont ar Daf the path to Pen y Fan is crowded with people in all manner of attire, from swimsuits to Scout uniforms. A sign suggests that the summit is two hours away. I steam up in a third of that time – after two thousand miles on the trail, I'm probably fitter than I have ever been. I smile to myself at overhearing a snippet of conversation:

"We've burned one hundred and eighteen calories already… but… oh… we've only come half a mile."

Two popular routes of ascent converge on the summit of Corn Du. Unfortunately, a fair proportion of the assembled crowd seem to be under the impression that they've reached the summit of Pen y Fan,

Summit of Pen y Fan, County Top of Brecknockshire, 24th July 2017.

although the highest point is actually the other one of Pen y Fan's distinctive twin tops, which bears a helpful National Trust sign labelling it as such.

"I think I'll tweet from up here," a woman says.

Aside from my inward recoil at the idea that tweeting belongs in the hills, I also think that this woman risks losing something essential to the spirit of hill-walking. If you wait until you next see your friends to tell them about your ascent of Pen y Fan, it can become almost folkloric, a tale to tell and re-tell, expanding with each recounting: The Time I Climbed Pen Y Fan. If, however, you condense your achievement into a 140-character tweet, you've succeeded in summarising and trivialising it at a stroke. You have slain Eluned, and these things do come not again.

Chwarel y Fan (County Top of Monmouthshire) and Black Mountain (County Top of Herefordshire)

Danywenallt to Glasbury. 35 miles, 1,620 metres ascent.
Tuesday 25th – Thursday 27th July

Having re-joined me at Danywenallt Youth Hostel, Matthew walks with me again today. A gently-ascending bridleway leads us into the Black Mountains without too much effort. I think – I hope – Matthew's feet appreciate the soft turf and level surface. Once on the ridge we sit to eat our YHA packed lunches, watching a kite being mobbed by crows while a buzzard makes the most of the opportunity to glide freely about.

We climb over Waun Fach, at 811 metres the highest point of the day, then walk in a distended U-shape around the Grwyne Fawr watershed to reach Chwarel y Fan, the County Top of Monmouthshire (or Sir Fynwy). The name Chwarel y Fan means 'quarry of the beacon'; Matthew's map shows a disused quarry close to the summit, although we have difficulty distinguishing hewn rock-faces from natural outcrops.

There is no source of water on the ridge so I descend with Matthew to Llanthony, a village in the Vale of Ewyas, thinking that I will either camp there, or, if there is no space in the campsite, collect drinking water before returning to the ridge.

When we find Matthew's accommodation, it is deserted. A young boy traipsing about the village informs us that "she's expecting Jan, Chris and Nathalie tonight," referring to the proprietor as 'she' with a slight awkwardness that suggests he is too embarrassed to utter the word 'mum'. Jan and Chris arrive by bicycle soon afterwards. When 'she' eventually returns to the village, we reach the conclusion that 'Nathalie' is probably a mis-heard 'Matthew'.

Matthew has a four-bedded cabin all to himself – for a whole five minutes, before I book myself into one of the other bunks. The local pub has decided not to serve food tonight, so we improvise with bowls of porridge, then sit watching swifts wheel against a backdrop of pink-tinged cloud.

Our traverse of the Black Mountains has finished off Matthew's feet. Despite our remote location, he succeeds in conjuring a taxi for the next day's journey; while I climb the highest hill in Herefordshire, he rides over the highest road in Wales. The name of the Gospel Pass (*Bwlch yr Efengyl*) is said to refer to the crossing of the Black Mountain by twelfth-century crusaders. At a similar time in history, a Norman nobleman by the name of Walter de Lacy founded Llanthony Priory on the site of a ruined chapel in the valley. Today, much of the priory lies in ruins; a rib-cage of great stone arches rise from the mist that Allen Ginsberg famously described as "a wavelet of Immensity, lapping gigantic through Llanthony Valley."[49]

On the ridge, I re-join the Offa's Dyke National Trail, which I last encountered on Moel Famau nearly a month ago. On the Welsh side of the border our route of yesterday is just visible, but where England ought to lie there is only a bank of cloud. Black Mountain itself is an elongated hog's-back, making it difficult to be sure exactly where the County Top lies. Hay Bluff has a much more distinctive summit. Red dragons have been stencilled onto the four faces of the trig point. When the rain is not driving too hard, I can see along the edge of the escarpment to Lord Hereford's Knob.

Though this is my first visit to the celebrated bookshops of Hay-on-Wye, I show great self-restraint in purchasing only one lightweight paperback novel. Matthew acquires more books than he can comfortably carry the four miles to our accommodation in Glasbury, so has to arrange for his reading material to be posted home.

Matthew is due to depart on a late-morning bus the next day. In keeping with previous days, it is raining thickly and heavily when we walk to the bus stop. This is a rest day on my schedule, so I spend most of the remainder of my free time lurking in a garden centre.

---

49 Allen Ginsberg, 'Wales Visitation', *New Yorker,* 11 May 1968.

Great Rhos (County Top of Radnorshire)

Glasbury to Aymestry. 39 miles, 1,600 metres ascent.
Friday 28th – Saturday 29th July

My perception of today's rain is coloured by the fact that staying in indoor accommodation means a later start, and therefore more time exposed to the afternoon downpour. Before checking out of the guest-house I make a ritual sacrifice of the small tube of sun-cream that I have been carrying since Yorkshire.

Retracing my footsteps to Hay, I pick up the Offa's Dyke path again. Two other long-distance walkers are sheltering beneath a tree.

"We're just waiting under this tree until the rain stops." The man makes a show of consulting his watch. "I think we're stuck here until Saturday morning."

Leaving Offa's Dyke at Newchurch, I continue in a northerly direction to the fringes of the Radnor forest. Signs try to tempt me from my route to see the Water Break-its-neck waterfall and "some of the largest trees in the Radnor forest." But I simply want to get to the end of today's walk and out of the rain as quickly as I possibly can: ignoring both diversions, I follow a bridleway along a cloud-filled valley, then climb onto the whale-back of Great Rhos, the County Top of Radnorshire.

When the track feels as though it has reached the broad, flat top, I strike out across the heather and bilberry, aiming for my best guess at the highest ground. I snap a quick shot on my camera, then continue north following a compass bearing. Two minutes later a patch of cloud resolves itself into the regular outline of a trig point – I obviously hadn't been on the summit after all.

I had intended to camp near a spring marked on my map as the Shepherd's Well, but can find no water, despite the rain; not even the gullies alongside the forest tracks hold enough water to fill my bottles. I press on until I reach an inky pool in the root-ball of a fallen tree. The water is the colour of porter, but odourless; in the absence of alternatives, I deem it potable.

I have finally completed the Welsh County Tops – but will it ever stop raining?

I lie in my sleeping bag, listening to rain sweep across the tent like a stiff broom. Suddenly, I start: light is filtering through the canopy.

I look at my watch: I have slept – and overslept. It is already 7.30am, and I have an arrangement to meet Laurence in Presteigne at midday, so I will need to hurry. I wriggle out of my sleeping bag and start trying to pack my belongings as swiftly as I can. My rucksack and waterproofs are still in a sodden bundle in the tent porch, where I left them last night. I unzip the inner tent and reach out for my rucksack. Why are there shreds of tissue everywhere? Something – a mouse? – has eaten a sizeable hole through the inner tent and into my bag of rubbish. Clearing up the tattered strands of tissue and biscuit wrappers from my campsite delays me even further.

Eventually, I am ready to set off, and am grateful to find that my route through the forest exists and is easy to follow.

The season of summer is announced by ripe blackberries and even a few wild raspberries in the hedgerows. But the verges tell a different story: unable to bear the weight of their accumulated raindrops, the tall grasses have collapsed. Their sodden seed-heads have the appearance of a carpet of foam.

I make it to Presteigne just in time. Laurence has brought dry clothes and a spare waterproof jacket. In the shelter of the public toilets, I strip off my sodden layers and gratefully re-dress. We have lunch together, then Laurence takes my large rucksack in his car, leaving me to walk with just a light day-sack for the rest of the day. Having swapped waterproofs, I am now wearing the jacket bought when I was about thirteen, "to grow into." Over a decade and a half later it still dwarfs me. The bright blue coat with red-maroon trim makes me feel like Paddington Bear as I stomp along.

Introspection: Turning Points

*Turning back east from Foel Cwmcerwyn in the Preseli hills filled me
with an emotion that I cannot put a name to, a feeling that contained
at once a sense of wholeness or finality and yet also incompleteness
– perhaps this is the very nature of a turning point. I had experienced
similar emotional discords on Holyhead Mountain, and before that
Craigairie Fell, when, having been walking west for several days, I
touched the top of a hill, performed a volte-face and set off in the direction from which I had come. In contrast, the easternmost turning
points of my walk – Mount Battock, The Cheviot, or (still to come
within this narrative) Ditchling Beacon – possessed no such sense of
momentous oddity (or do I mean odd momentousness?).*

*I wonder to what extent I can ascribe this difference to the allure
of the western horizon in comparison to its eastern counterpart. My
western turning points have often been closer to the sea (though
Ditchling Beacon lies on the south coast, my instinct is that only proximity to the east or west coast is relevant) and the associated imagery
of the Atlantic expanse (albeit shielded by Ireland). But the need for
parenthetical qualifiers within the previous sentence, coupled with
the fact that I am rather nervous of the sea, suggests to me that this
is not the primary reason for the increased significance of west over
east.*

*The association of the western horizon with the setting sun may
be of more relevance, particularly in the case of Foel Cwmcerwyn,
where fair weather and wide, open views combined to create an arresting and deliciously prolonged sunset. I certainly find myself agreeing with Thoreau when he observes that "Every sunset which I
witness inspires me with the desire to go to a West as distant and as
fair as that into which the sun goes down."*[49]

*But Thoreau's argument is that to journey west, not to look west,
is the desirable object: "Eastward I go only by force; but westward I
go free... It is hard for me to believe that I shall find fair landscapes*

---

50 Henry David Thoreau, 'Walking', *Atlantic Monthly,* IX, no LVI (1862),
pp.657-74.

or sufficient wildness and freedom behind the eastern horizon. "[50] *In addition to the discordant feeling at turning my back on the horizon of freedom, I should, therefore, have felt a concomitant emotion at the easternmost turning points of my walk, when I turned once more to face in the direction of wildness. I cannot honestly say whether this was true; on Ditchling Beacon my overwhelming feeling was of tired relief that I could finally start walking, without further zigzagging, in the direction of Land's End.*

I am sure that another contributory factor is the fact that I grew up on the western side of the Pennines, yet now live on the east – a transition from Lancashire to Yorkshire that some inhabitants of both counties regard as criminal. Though my accent is not distinctively Lancastrian, and I have now lived on the eastern side of the country for more than a third of my life, I am still asked, frequently, in a tone that is only partly jocular, whether I have a passport. So, my repeated crossing of the country's spine from west to east to west, was an alternation between childhood and adulthood.

Oddly enough, many of the places that Laurence and I walk now – Pendle Hill, Ingleborough, Blubberhouses moor – are the very same places that I walked with my family as a child, and it took not a little mental adjustment to accommodate the same geography seen almost as a mirror image when we first settled in Yorkshire. As I realised when my friends Ann and Andrew visited me in Dent, the spatial relationship between myself and the hills gives me some feeling of context in life. I work (when not away walking the length and breadth of the country) in the relatively flat farmland of lower Wharfedale, and I recall the sense of fulfilment, and of grounding, when I discovered that if I climbed one of the taller staircases in our building, and peered through the arrow-slit windows in the stairwell, I could make out the hulking shadow of Great Whernside far away to the west.

---

51 *Ibid.*

Illegal Freedoms

Shropshire – Worcestershire – Gloucestershire –
Warwickshire – Northamptonshire – Leicestershire –
Rutland – Lincolnshire, Parts of Kesteven – Lincolnshire,
Parts of Holland – Northamptonshire, Soke of
Peterborough

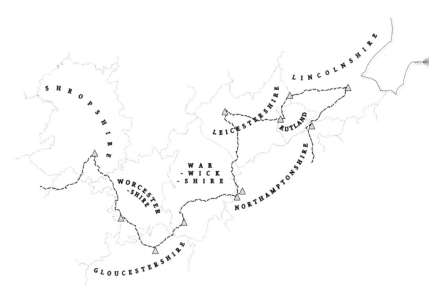

Brown Clee Hill (County Top of Shropshire), Worcestershire Beacon (County Top of Worcestershire), Cleeve Hill (County Top of Gloucestershire) and Ebrington Hill (County Top of Warwickshire)

Aymestry to Alveston. 129 miles, 4,170 metres ascent.
Sunday 30th July – Saturday 5th August

There are two pieces of visual evidence to testify that I have returned to England. Above me, soaring kites are being gradually supplanted by moth-eaten buzzards. Closer to earth, standing unconcernedly amidst the self-conscious grandeur of half-timbered mock-Tudor houses, each village hosts a single Church of England establishment, rather than a plethora of chapels for divergent denominations.

A third change is that rights of way depicted on my map seem also to exist on the ground. The Mortimer Trail is well-waymarked, to assist with navigation through the overgrown vegetation. I disturb an adder from its coiled repose within the long grass, but encounter few other walkers, although at one point I hear voices emanating from the bracken slightly uphill:

"I say, who put this jungle in my way?"

I know that I have walked some of this route before. Some tracks feel familiar, but this could be the common appearance of woodland paths and I cannot honestly say whether I recognise them or not.

Capped with erosion-resistant igneous dolerite, or dhu-stone, the Clee hills stand proud of the surrounding land. Titterstone Clee Hill becomes visible once I have walked through Ludlow, then Brown Clee Hill rises into view as I climb onto a ridge. Shropshire's County Top appears much nearer than it is in reality, and I need to consult my map to remind myself that I still have a long way to go. Perhaps I have not yet made the mental adjustment from lifting my eyes to the higher Welsh hills.

Thick curtains of rain are being dragged out of Wales. For the most part I am lucky and the showers blow through along the valley, touching me with only a few light drops. Then, when I have only a mile to go, I glance over my shoulder to see a screen of rain drawn across the sky: I cannot possibly hope to avoid this squall. The end of the day's walk becomes a race against the sweeping rain. Although I have been

laden with two and a half litres of drinking water since Ludlow, I realise just how fast I can move when the alternative is another soaking.
Nearly at the summit of the County Top of Shropshire, I drop my bag
in the lee of a wind-twisted hawthorn, then cast about, almost franti-
cally, for somewhere to pitch my tent. My campsite is far from perfect
– sheltered from neither sight nor wind – but my tent is up before all
my belongings get drenched once again.

Tent pitched, I visit the multiple potential summits. The three-
spoked theodolite mounting plate and flush bracket from a dismantled
trig point have been embedded in the steps leading to a viewpoint,
but a nearby grassy knoll looks higher.

A moth drowns in my mug overnight. I ladle it out with my spoon
and spend some minutes trying to work out whether the sodden wing-
patterns are those of a mottled grey (*Colostygia multistrigaria*), before
abandoning my amateur lepidopterology in favour of brewing tea. In
Presteigne I swapped my fingerless gloves, which had shrunk to a
size where it was becoming increasingly difficult to prise them off
my fingers, for an older, thinner pair. I think this new pair are of a
synthetic fibre rather than pure wool, so I daren't use them to pick up
my hot kettle. Instead, I wrap my fingers in a sock, which immediately melts itself onto the handle of the kettle, leaving a generous hole
in the back of the heel.

As with yesterday, I can watch showers sweeping in from Wales.
I have time to judge: how long before the rain reaches me? Is there a
chance that it might miss me altogether? When I arrive in Neen Sol-
lars no showers loom imminent, so I pitch my tent on the village green
to dry. I sit on a wooden bench, reflecting on the need to take this expedition one day at a time. I have reduced my needs to the most basic
level: by the end of each day, I need a dry tent, drinking water and a
safe place to camp. If all three can be achieved, the walk will be sustainable. I realise also that I am counting down the days until August
4th, when only two months of my walk will remain.

That night, I camp on Woodbury Hill, thereby continuing a tradi-
tion that dates back to the Bronze Age. The most famous camper is
probably Owain Glyndwr, whose combined Welsh-French forces occupied the hill here in 1405, during an eight-day stand-off with the
English army of Henry IV – until lack of food supplies and, it is said,
continuous rain, forced both armies to retreat. Towards the close of

the same century the hill was occupied by the Duke of Buckingham when a flooded River Severn prevented him from striking against the forces of Richard III.

In keeping with the historical precedent it rains all night. With the evening's meandering search for a suitable campsite, then the need to regain the path in the morning, I must have completed two full laps of Woodbury Hill by the time I finally leave the woodland. It would be easy to become disorientated here, and I am grateful for my innate sense of direction.

I join the Worcester Way, a long-distance footpath which will take me as far as the Malvern Hills, and the best-marked route I have yet encountered; even sections along public roads have waymarkers.

I seem to be noticing fewer changes in the vegetation than I did earlier in the year. I wonder whether the pace of change, like the lengthening of the days, is slowest in mid-summer; or whether differences are simply harder to discern now that everything is in leaf. Something that I do notice, though, is the ground, or more specifically the mud. In the morning, thick rust-orange earth sucks at my feet, but by the afternoon I am sliding over a slick blue-grey surface. The challenge of maintaining my balance is compounded by the fact that I have by now worn smooth the tread on the shoes I bought in Betws-y-Coed.

I also realise that, as on Anglesey, my relationship with my diary is changing. Earlier in my walk, I found myself dwelling on tiny details, perhaps compelled to do so by the sheer scale of the landscape; the candid expanse of moor and mountain cannot be captured within mere words. Now, in more crowded surroundings, it is easier to describe my itinerary, to attempt to provide that overview and sense of breadth which, further north, was intrinsic to the land itself.

The Worcester Way descends from sylvan ridges into orchards: apples (not yet ripe), pears (nearly) and a type of tree that I surmise might be plum. I draw nearer to the "curious bubblings-up"[52] as William Cobbett described the Malvern hills in 1826. On a modern map, the Malverns appear more like a rash, covered with a confusion of red dots, dashes and diamond shapes as paths converge on the

---

52 William Cobbett, *Ride, from Malmsbury, in Wiltshire, through Gloucestershire, Herefordshire, and Worcestershire* (1826).

highest point in Worcestershire. From the summit of Worcester Beacon, I can trace my route since Hay-on-Wye over the hills to my west, and look ahead to Cleeve Hill and Ebrington Hill, County Tops that I have yet to climb.

Worcestershire Beacon, County Top of Worcestershire, 1st August 2017.

It is drizzling hesitantly as I leave the Malvern hills, and the rain grows heavier and steadier. I trail the River Severn from Upton to Tewkesbury; this is my first encounter with the river since its source on Pumlumon Fawr. Escaping Tewkesbury is harder than entering it: a new housing development, a jungle, a footpath unacknowledged by the landowner. Eventually, a little nettle-stung, I resume my journey in the direction of the County Tops seen from Worcester Beacon.

Cleeve Hill claims three height records. In addition to being the County Top of Gloucester it is the highest point in both the Cotswold hills and the Thames drainage basin. The summit is marked by a trig point and marred by a car park and three tall radio masts. Camping is not permitted on Cleeve Common, but dusk is falling and it is raining heavily, so I would be surprised to meet anyone else out walking; I descend towards Postlip Warren and worm my way into the midst of a gorse thicket to wait out the hours of darkness.

The gorse provides inadequate shelter from the tumult of wind and rain which lash the common overnight. With my belongings saturated once more, the morning sees me plodging soggily through Winchcombe to Hailes Abbey, where I am joined by Naomi, a friend and former colleague. The last time that Naomi and I met in person, her son Jacob was just learning to use a spoon. Jacob is now only a few weeks away from starting school, and Naomi will shortly return to work after the birth of Jacob's younger sister Flora; we have much catching up to do.

We follow the Cotswold Way to Chipping Camden, allowing ourselves shortcuts whenever the National Trail feels the need to descend from the ridge only to re-ascend almost immediately.

Cobbett seems to have been less enamoured with the Cotswolds than the Malvern hills, describing the former as:

> …an ugly country …there are, for a mile or two together, no trees to be seen, and, as the surface is not smooth and green like the downs, this is a sort of country, having less to please the eye than any other I have ever seen…[53]

But I enjoy chattering with Naomi so much that I forget to pay attention to the scenery, so am unable to judge whether Cobbett is justified in his criticism. Our topics of conversation range wildly: gender and identity, teaching Jacob to wipe his bottom, condensation in one-person tents, parents and parenting.

The next day is the day that I have been anticipating since camping on Brown Clee Hill: only two months, and less than 1,100 miles, to go. There is no real significance to these numbers, but I feel reassured to have passed another mental milestone.

Ebrington Hill is the second of the County Tops that I sighted from Worcester Beacon. The trig point stands on the Gloucestershire side of the border; I must ensure that I also touch the highest point in

---

53 William Cobbett, *From Ryall, in Worcestershire, to Burghclere, in Hampshire* (1826).

Warwickshire, which lies in a nondescript field on the opposite verge of a minor road. Between the two sits a large block of Cotswold stone, one of eight boundary markers installed by the parish of Ebrington to commemorate the Queen's Diamond Jubilee in 2012; at the time, these were the first new parish boundary stones in Gloucestershire in over a century.

Descending through the villages of Upper and Lower Quinton, my walk changes in character when I leave field paths and join the Stratford Greenway, a tarmac-surfaced cycleway which makes a beeline for the city. With the same indifference to my surroundings as the cycle path I disregard Stratford's tourist attractions and head straight to an outdoor shop, to purchase my fourth new set of footwear since March.

"These are a good pair." The sales assistant holds up a pair of blue canvas boots for my approval. "Even if you're walking every day, if you look after them and clean them well they'll stay waterproof for many years."

"No," I promise, "they won't." I know I will destroy these boots, as I have destroyed their predecessors, but I will be satisfied if they fit me reasonably well and don't give me blisters.

I take my new boots to the till, along with a map – Ordnance Survey Explorer 222 (Rugby and Daventry) – which I will need to find the campsite I have booked for Monday night.

"Planning to scale the heights of Rugby?" the man serving on the till questions me wryly.

"Actually, yes." I show him the twin County Tops of Nottinghamshire.

When I emerge from the shop another rain shower is toying playfully with the town centre. Tourists scatter, shopping bags and newspapers held aloft as improvised umbrellas as they dive into shops, only looking up once inside to find out what is being sold. I duck into a doorway to change my boots, then try to disassemble the shoebox so that I can manoeuvre it into a public bin.

It is a long two miles out of Stratford to the Youth Hostel at Alveston. I am allocated to a bunk in room 23. Up two flights of stairs. All the beds are occupied. Back down two flights of stairs. Back up two flights of stairs, this time with a member of staff, to try to work out which bed should be mine. There are six beds in the room, and six keys to the door: I have a key, therefore there must be a bed for me. A young Italian girl returns to the dormitory and helps us to identify the un-tenanted bed. Back down the stairs to acquire a fresh set of sheets. Back up the stairs, and – at last – a shower!

The next day is a rest day, but, although I have little to do today, force of habit has me up soon after 7 a.m. I fidget restlessly in the self-catering kitchen, trying to spin out a bowl of cereal and a crossword from Thursday's newspaper. Without recourse to a dictionary or thesaurus, I soon admit defeat. I prowl the Youth Hostel's drying room, searching between rows of mop-heads and tea-towels, hoping in vain for old newspapers that I can raid for further crosswords.

My grandmother lives in a village to the south of Stratford, so my parents bring her to Alveston for lunch in the Ferry Inn, where we are joined by my sister and her partner. After lunch we walk back to the Youth Hostel, for coffee in an atmosphere where it is acceptable to linger without feeling any guilt for taking up a table.

In the evening I stroll round to Alveston School, where my grandfather, who I never knew, was once headmaster. My father tells me that a tree was planted in the school grounds in his memory. Though there are several trees outside the school, none obviously bears a commemorative plaque; not wishing to draw attention to myself by nosing around a primary school, I return to the Youth Hostel unfulfilled.

Arbury Hill and Big Hill, Staverton Clump (County Tops of Northamptonshire) and Bardon Hill (County Top of Leicestershire)

Alveston to Birstall. 86 miles, 1,530 metres ascent.
Sunday 6th – Wednesday 9th August

I meet my parents again in Charlecote, and they walk with me for the rest of the morning. Hand-painted signs try to entice us from our eastward route with promises of cream teas and strawberries. The air is bright, with high cumulus clouds, though cumulonimbus heads are beginning to form and rain is forecast to return by evening.

We picnic in Chesterton Green. Since my parents' first visit in the snow-capped Cairngorms, I have come to notice a correlation between my mother's anxiety and the number of fillings she manages to compress into sandwiches: today's contain cheese, tuna, coleslaw, salad and chutney, a sign of her concern for my safety as my walk brings me to the populous mid-shires.

Back in a part of the country where wild camping is impractical as well as illegal, I make for a formal campsite in the village of Napton-on-the-Hill. No sooner is my tent up than a flock of small blond girls swoops down upon me, with cries of "Hello-who-are-you-what-are-you-doing?" My miniature tent is a particular point of interest: Is it big enough for me? Would they fit in? (easily tested) What's that (indicating one of my groundsheet repairs) – is it bird poo? Can they demonstrate their skipping please? Where have I come from? Did I earn all of those badges (pointing to my rucksack)? This last question helps me find my bearings within the conversation.

"Do you go to Brownies?"

I have guessed correctly. Blond heads nod enthusiastically. "We go to the same Brownies," bubbles Megan.

Kirsty looks bemused: "Do we?"

"What's this trowel for?" Megan resumes the interrogation.

"Er, it's in case I need to dig a hole."

Megan squeezes her left eye slightly shut and tilts her head to the side as she considers my evasive statement. "Oh, I get it. It's in case you need to bury your escramint. It's a scientific word, that is, es-cramint."

A green woodpecker skims about the campsite, laughing at our idiocy.

In contrast to Ben Macdui and Meikle Says Law, which each rewarded me with two County Tops for a single ascent, today I have two Tops to climb for just one county – both ascents illegal. The Ordnance Survey have decreed that Arbury Hill and Staverton Clump are exactly the same height – 225 metres, or 738 feet – so far as it's possible to tell when Staverton Clump is wooded and it looks as though someone has been digging up the hill fort on Arbury Hill to create a motor-cross track. This poses an interesting question: if Arbury Hill attains its height by virtue of earthworks, should that make Staverton Clump the County Top, since its height is 'natural'? Does the answer depend upon whether the highest point on Arbury Hill is an embankment from an iron-age hill fort, or a dirt ramp on a modern race track?

The trespassing involved to climb Arbury Hill is minimal. The hill

Common Blue butterfly, 6th August 2017.

lies just to the north of an old byway, so it is the work of only a few short minutes to hop over a fence and nip up to the summit. A herd of grazing cows is untroubled by my presence (although their owner might be less incurious): the cows simply stare apathetically through the drizzle as I flit between the two or three potential highest points before disappearing back in the direction whence I came. More green woodpeckers swoop from trunk to trunk, their slightly arched bodies reminding me of smooth-worn wooden hammer handles. I hear, too, the malicious cackling of jays, but don't see them.

Staverton Clump requires a little more off-piste exploration. I climb the second County Top from the north. A field boundary leads uphill and provides gates to allow me to pass between fields without the need to scale fences or hedges. One such gate is a decayed wooden affair, with a sufficiently large breach between the cross-bars that I can actually duck through it, rather than going 'through' the gate in the conventional sense.

Now that I have ticked both of Northamptonshire's County Tops off my list, I have walked more than 2,400 miles and have less than 1,000 miles to go. As Matthew said when he departed from Glasbury, "You'll be happier once you've got the distance down into treble figures."

It rains again overnight, and is forecast to continue raining all day – and Wednesday too, but for once I don't mind, since I will be staying at campsites or motels as I traverse the urban sprawl of central England. Tonight's destination is Leicester Forest East motorway service station. Leicester Forest East holds me in some kind of occult thrall: wherever I am in the country, wherever I am driving to or from, the moment that I pull off the motorway into the slip road of a service station, it transmutes into Leicester Forest East. It seemed fitting, therefore, when planning my walk, to schedule an overnight stay here.

First, though, I must pass through Lutterworth. I have a choice of paths: either a footpath, or a byway which then becomes a bridleway. I opt for the latter, but soon regret my decision. The bridleway drags me through a field of high-spirited bullocks, then washes me up on the shores of a freshly-ploughed sea of mud. A blue arrow gestures across the field, indicating a direction perpendicular to the advancing waves of furrows. My tread becomes more and more clogged as I lagger across the field, until great rims of loam are sticking out from my boots.

I stagger from the bridleway onto a footpath, which crosses a golf course on the southern edge of Lutterworth. Yellow-topped posts lead across the fairway, and, though some bear arrows pointing in the wrong direction (one tries to direct me through an ornamental pond) the route is reasonably simple to follow. Until I try to leave the golf course, that is. The exit path is an impenetrable thicket. I search for an alternative – if I can reach the car park, then I can walk out along the driveway. I can, but this involves poking about an area festooned with warning signs and CCTV cameras, then climbing over a locked gate. I am relieved that no-one challenges me during my escape.

Further north my route shadows the motorway and revives my sense of slipping though other people's lives unobserved, as I plod through fields only a few feet away from the unsuspecting drivers of speeding vehicles.

The path narrows, channelled between high fences. This is the sort of place where people get raped and/or stabbed: there is nowhere to run, no-one to hear a scream above the roar of the traffic. Brooding on this as I walk, I try to reassure myself that there are unlikely to be any rapists or murderers about on a wet Tuesday afternoon. Nevertheless, I feel a wash of relief when the land to my left opens out to a cornfield.

My path crosses a bridge above the M69, then reaches a minor road. I am supposed to turn left along this road, but a large sign proclaims:

BRIDLEWAY CLOSED EXCEPT FOR
ACCESS TO FARMS BY ROAD
NO PEDESTRIANS BEYOND THIS POINT

I don't fully understand how bridleway restrictions can have been imposed upon a public road, but decide that it is probably in my best interests to seek an alternative route. I continue to walk parallel to the motorway, until my revised choice is also barred. There is evidence of ongoing construction work in the area, and a map affixed to metal railings indicates that all rights of way in the vicinity have been curtailed.

Left with little alternative – I need to get further north – I ignore the signs, climb over the fence, and continue where the footpath formerly ran. A short distance further, a new road has appeared. I scramble up an embankment towards the tarmac, bringing Leicester Forest

East into view. The field immediately to my north appears to extend almost to the services, and there is a wide margin around the crop of beans, so I decide to trespass along the field and make a beeline for the services. I slide down the far side of the embankment to find a wide, overgrown ditch separating me from the bean-field. I am almost ready to despair when I notice that a footpath marker-post (still with yellow top and arrow) has been lain across the ditch, creating a narrow, precarious bridge.

I reach the edge of the services, then stalk round the perimeter until I find somewhere I can climb in – behind the Starbucks Drive-Thru. With the assistance of motel Wi-Fi, I learn that New Lubbesthorpe, 'a complete community' comprising over 4,000 houses, is under construction in the blank space on my map. The new road is so new that even Google Maps doesn't know about it.

Edward ('Ted') Moss, one of the first people to show an interest in the County Tops, described how: "the permitted route to the top of Bardon Hill was a footpath from the [Copt Oak] chapel… on the main road (A50) and passing to the east of Bardon Hall. A deep quarry to the west has cut very close to the summit."[54]

This was in 1947. Seventy years later, the quarry has eaten away almost all of the hill.

My approach route leads away from the A511 close to the village of Stanton-under-Bardon, to terminate abruptly at a high metal fence. Beyond lies an ocean of sticky red mud.

CONSTRUCTION SITE KEEP OUT

Diversionary arrows turn me eastwards, then spit me back out onto the road I have just left. A map depicts the areas of Bardon Hill currently being quarried: most of it. Footpaths labelled as A-B, B-C-D, D-F, E-F-G-H have been suspended. The stump of a path that I have just traversed is a new 'alternative' right of way, an attempt by the aggregates industry to extenuate their excavations by providing a new

---

54 Edward Moss, 'The County Tops of England and Wales', *Rucksack Club Journal* XI, no. 4 (1951), pp.319-27.

path – which, to judge by the height of the vegetation, nobody wants to walk.

Moss' 1947 route is now a private drive. I would gladly trespass, but it too lies within the quarrymen's quarter, and heavy trucks are shunting about the foot of the hill. I am forced to walk nearly three-quarters of the way around Bardon Hill before I reach a path that remains open – and even this has been diverted.

The roots of mature oaks have been exposed by erosion on the re-routed path, and I wonder how the trees will cope with this additional stress on top of the effects of the quarrying. In places, the path vanishes beneath deep black pools. To circumvent the floodwaters, I climb over a fence into an area of refilled quarry, an artificially smoothed landscape colonised by silverweed and sorrel. I reach the County Top, complete with radio masts and more warning signs, more than hour after I passed Stanton.

The afternoon quite literally bears fruit: an apple tree, growing wild just a few yards from the A50. The apples are hard, tart, with lemon-yellow pips, but I pick several of the least unripe and walk into my motel with bulging pockets.

Once I escape the suburbs of Leicester, though, my roadside discoveries are rather less pleasant. A4 black-and-white photographs lie in the verge at intervals of about fifty yards. Most of the pages have curled with shame, with the image facing inwards; the few left unfurled are definitely of an intimate nature, depicting things I would really rather not see. The stark white of the paper keeps snagging at the corners of my vision, but I force myself to keep my gaze fixed upon the tarmac.

Cold Overton Park (County Top of Rutland), Viking Way (County Top of Lincolnshire, Parts of Kesteven), Pinchbeck Marsh (County Top of Lincolnshire) and Racecourse Road (County Top of Northamptonshire, Soke of Peterborough)

Birstall to Bedford Purlieus. 95 miles, 1,140 metres ascent.
Thursday 10th – Monday 14th August

It takes me a full ten minutes to work out what is different about today. Then I look upwards and realise that there is not a single cloud in the sky – the first such weather that I can recall since I walked through Sherwood Forest. This doesn't last: the air is humid after the recent days of heavy rain. By late morning the sky is a marina for flat-bottomed cumulus barges, moored in lines parallel to the high-level wind.

Cold Overton Park, the County Top of Rutland, is a broad swathe of grass. Rutland is the smallest of the UK's historic counties; the nearby village of Cold Overton, and a wood of the same name, both lie in Leicestershire. A trig point lurks beside a hawthorn hedge. It is not on a right of way, but there are no animals grazing in the field, so I trespass over to it. There is no sense of elevation here, no indication that I am on the summit of a hill, just a gentle downward slope eastwards towards Rutland Water.

Just outside Buckminster lies my second Lincolnshire County Top, for the Parts of Kesteven. As with Cold Overton Park, this doesn't feel like a summit: it is a nondescript point on a tarmac road, close to a water tower. In fact, its elevation is less than that of Buckminster, but the village is just over the county boundary in Leicestershire.

Walking through fields towards Colsterworth, I reach a dead end. Assuming that I must have followed the wrong side of the hedge, I backtrack until I can poke my head through into the next field. That, too, meets a blind hedge. I resort to technology and retrieve my smartphone from my rucksack; an online map confirms that my location is correct and that I do need to cross the blind hedge. To retrace my steps then walk round by roads to Colsterworth would be a lengthy diversion, so I find a place where there is a small tunnel beneath the hawthorn, slither through on my belly, then drag my rucksack after me. I continue eastward, using the detailed map on my phone to ensure that I stay precisely on the route of the right of way.

The next hedge-crossing is overgrown with nettles; it is impossible to tell whether the collapsed jumble of wooden fence-posts was once a stile. At the next crossing, wooden bars have been nailed across the gap between an oak and a hawthorn. At the next, I can see a finger-post, but a wire fence has been strung in front of it.

I give up: it simply isn't possible to remain on the correct side of both the hedge and the law. I am now so close to Colsterworth that I can climb over a couple of gates and escape onto a road.

Colsterworth is home to Woolsthorpe Manor, birthplace of Sir Isaac Newton. With hours wasted grubbing about in hedgerows, I don't have time to look around the manor house, but have something else in mind: my A50 apples. I bite into one as I walk through the village, waiting for the flood of insight into the nature of gravity and the fabric of space-time. Nothing, except the obvious observation of the effect of gravity upon my rucksack.

I have walked past Irnham, and am only a mile from the woodlands where I intend to camp, when quite suddenly my left ankle gives up. It has been feeling weak since I changed back from shoes to boots in Stratford, but now it becomes too painful to bear any weight. After a minute I can limp on, resolutely ignoring the daggers of pain shooting up my leg. Gradually, I feel able to resume my normal stride, but remain aware of the feeling of weakness and worried in case the collapse recurs.

Beneath the spreading beeches of Callan's Lane Wood, I pitch my tent and lie listening to the rasping of fallow deer and the low interrogative hooting of tawny owls. The background throb of agricultural machinery continues well into the night, and I am almost surprised not to hear the machine running when I wake at 6.30am.

I have crossed the A15 and walked a mile east from the village of Dunsby when a familiar blue van draws up alongside. This is bad timing, for my ankle gives way again just as Laurence pulls the van off the road, and he sees me hobble the final few yards to meet him.

"That limp doesn't look like you should be walking to Spalding, let alone Land's End."

Inwardly, I agree that I may be reaching the end of my walk, but

I refuse to give up while I can still make any progress, however slow. We stow my large rucksack in the van, allowing me to continue with my much smaller day-sack, carrying only food, water and painkillers.

My route involves a short distance of trespassing, to connect public roads which extend into Dunsby Fen from east and west, but leave the Forty Foot Drain unbridged. I am relieved that there are no other people in sight as I creep along the embankment of the Drain to cross by a private farm bridge.

The road on the eastern side of the Drain is a ribbon of tarmac, pulled taught between compass points. Endless fields of cabbages stretch to a horizon punctuated only by the Pinchbeck water tower and the spire of Surfleet Church. Rectangles of reflected light sliding along the skyline allow me to track the movement of vehicles through this map-like landscape; variations in their speed reveal road junctions hidden from sight.

Ahead, a tractor is inching through the field, dragging a small marquee, which appears to be planting rows of cabbage seedlings in its wake. It is only when I have passed the tractor and look back over my shoulder that I see a tight line of hunched figures inside the marquee, clad in various fluorescent shades: the whole resembles a giant piano accordion being dragged across the field. At the end of the field, the accordion keys clamber out, briefly resuming human form while the tractor turns.

As the name suggests, the land beyond Seas End has been reclaimed from the North Sea. The third County Top of Lincolnshire – Parts of Holland – the lowest County Top of them all, at only eight metres above sea level, sits on an embankment running parallel to the River Welland. There is no public access to the embankment, so I wade through the fringes of a grubby potato field and scramble up the dyke in what I judge to be the correct place – the only variation in height discernible to the eye being due to the growth of brambles and hawthorn.

The next day means another early start: we rise at 6.30am to be walking by 7 a.m., so that Laurence can transport my rucksack for the morning and I can make as much progress as possible towards Stam-

The lowest top: Pinchbeck Marsh, County Top of Lincolnshire (eight metres above sea level), 12th August 2017.

ford carrying only a light day-sack. Neither of us feels confident about my ankle, but I have the option of changing to what I term 'public transport rules' – to proceed as a series of day-walks, using public transport to return to a basecamp each evening – if my ankle would otherwise prevent me from continuing. Walking with only a day-sack has the additional benefit of allowing me to escape the endless fields of cabbages more quickly.

The road alongside the North Drove Drain swells imperceptibly between two and four metres above sea level. I am approaching a trig point (at only two metres above sea level, surely one of the lowest in Britain) when a black 4x4 rumbles up alongside me.

"Do you know where you're going?"

"I think so: straight on here, then right, and left at the next farm."

The driver looks a little taken aback. "Most people don't know. We don't get many walkers out here."

"Does that mean the path's a bit overgrown?" I query.

"You could say that," the driver replies. "In fact, there isn't a path at all really."

185

I am concerned that I am about to be told that I should turn back, but my fears are unfounded.

"You can walk on the field margins if you like."

I thank the driver for this concession, which proves essential when the right of way shown on my map disappears into a weed-filled drainage ditch. Instead of staggering up the ditch, I can skirt a field of barley, then sidle between rows of sweetcorn to emerge onto the next public road – and return to the panoramic cabbages.

Stephanie is due to arrive in Stamford on the 15:04 train the next day. When I reach the railway station, her train is marked 'Delayed' with no revised arrival time. I settle down to wait, assuming that it will, eventually, appear.

15:04 comes, and goes.

At 15:15, the status of the train changes from 'Delayed' to 'Cancelled', then quietly disappears from the arrivals board. The 16:04 inherits the label of 'Cancelled'.

A would-be passenger succeeds in contacting National Rail Enquiries, to learn that a goods train has derailed somewhere in the

Common Blue damselflies (blue male and green female),
13th August 2017.

vicinity of Peterborough, and that services out of East Anglia are to be cancelled for the rest of the day. I telephone Stephanie: she has been advised to travel via Stevenage, a journey which would take an additional three hours and would therefore put us in the undesirable position of needing to walk along the A1 at dusk. We hastily revise our itinerary, deciding that Stephanie should instead join me in Oundle, a day later than planned.

I would rather not walk along the A1 at all, in dusk or daylight, but the County Top of the Soke of Peterborough lies on Racecourse Road, only a few yards away from its junction with the A1, so this is the obvious way to access it. I walk in the cycle lane, but the traffic thundering past feels frighteningly close. Racecourse Road is a far-from-impressive County Top: a bend in the road, overshadowed by a chestnut tree.

I continue alongside the A1 to Wittering, to purchase water, then camp in Bedford Purlieus. The woodland hosts a diverse mix of tree species: some – elm, ash and native species of oak – the regrowth of medieval coppice stools; others – larch, Scots pine – post-war planting by the Forestry Commission. I choose an area of beech to pitch my tent: beech trees are usually well-spaced, but their dense crowns permit little ground vegetation (crucially, no nettles, brambles or bracken) and provide effective shelter from rain.

Introspection: Challenge

Though I had long been aware of Edward Moss and his interest in the County Tops, I did not succeed in tracking down a copy of the Rucksack Club Journal[55] *in which he detailed his ascents until after I returned from my own walk. By coincidence, Edward's son Richard contacted me soon afterwards, in response to a piece that I had written for the journal of the Long Distance Walkers' Association, and kindly provided me with a scanned copy of the same article.*

Richard informed me that in addition to visiting the County Tops of England and Wales, his father had climbed all of the 2,000-foot hills of these countries. Since there are something like 250 of these (depending upon the exact criteria used to select hills), this was in many ways a more challenging undertaking than his round of the County Tops, particularly given the fact that Moss had to identify qualifying hills by examining Ordnance Survey maps himself, rather than being able to enjoy the benefit of modern guidebooks such as the lists compiled by John and Anne Nuttall.[56] As I write, it occurs to me that a natural progression from my County Tops walk would be a continuous round of these 2,000-footers, or perhaps even Land's End to John O'Groats via the 2,000-foot hills of England, Wales and Scotland, although I can envisage no realistic possibility of ever having sufficient time to attempt such a journey, and therefore leave this prize for others to claim.

Another challenge that I did not learn about until after I returned home was the (literally) staggering feat of Stanley Bradshaw and Brian Ripley who, in 1968 completed a continuous walk – that is, without sleep – between six of the County Tops of northern England. Starting at Langley Fold in Northumberland early on Good Friday,

---

55 Edward Moss, 'The County Tops of England and Wales', *Rucksack Club Journal* XI, no. 4 (1951), pp.319-27.

56 John Nuttall and Anne Nuttall, *The Mountains of England and Wales,* vol. 1: Wales (Milnthorpe: Cicerone, 1989); John Nuttall and Anne Nuttall, *The Mountains of England and Wales,* vol. 2: England (Milnthorpe: Cicerone, 1989).

the pair traversed The Cheviot, Burnhope Seat, Mickle Fell, Helvellyn, Scafell Pike and Coniston Old Man, before descending to the Walna Scar road above Coniston on the following Tuesday. Having placed The Cheviot earlier in my itinerary, I walked from Burhope Seat to Coniston Old Man over the course of eight days; Bradshaw and Ripley took 73 sleepless hours and 145 miles. The furthest I have ever walked without sleep is a mere (by comparison) 100 miles, but even this is sufficient experience to ensure that – tempted though I may be to recreate Bradshaw and Ripley's journey – I will not advocate a non-stop attempt to connect all of the County Tops.[57]

---

57 See: A. H. Griffin, *Long Days in the Hills* (London: Robert Hale & Company, 1974). Stanley Bradshaw continued to be a famous name in fell-running circles until his death in 2010 at the age of 97; Brian Ripley was tragically killed in an expedition to Karakorum later in 1968.

Forgotten Familiarities

Huntingdonshire – Cambridgeshire, Isle of Ely – Norfolk –
East Suffolk – West Suffolk – Cambridgeshire – Essex –
Bedfordshire

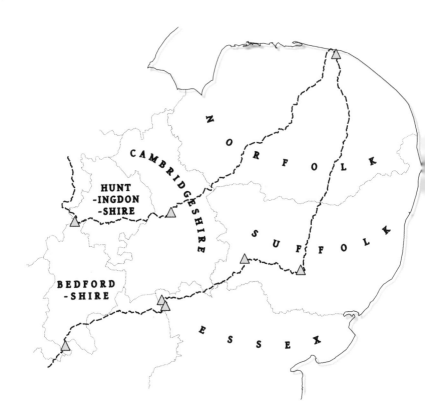

Boring Field (County Top of Huntingdonshire) and Haddenham village (County Top of Cambridgeshire, Isle of Ely)

Bedford Purlieus to Sheringham. 132 miles, 1,260 metres ascent.
Tuesday 15th – Sunday 20th August

My sleep is disturbed by heavy rain in the middle of the night. The beam of my torch catches what appears to be a foot-long slug sliding up the inside of the tent. I recoil in horror before realising that it is a trick of the light, and that what I am actually looking at is a slug of comparatively normal proportions, with a trail of slime in its wake.

In the morning, the canopy is still shivering water droplets onto my tent, so I don't immediately realise that the rain has abated. Even at 7am sunlight is shafting down through the trees, and the sky is a brilliant blue behind the leaves. Daybreak is a beautiful time to walk through woodland. I am saddened to see orange-tinged leaves on chestnuts around the perimeter of the wood – probably a sign that the trees have been attacked by leaf-miners, larvae of the *Cameraria ohridella* moth, rather than the early onset of autumn. Since they were first reported in the UK in 2002, leaf-miners have spread throughout most of England and Wales. Though they have yet to reach the part of Yorkshire where Laurence and I live, each journey to the south of England serves as a reminder that it is only a matter of time until they do.

⚠

Coming back to East Anglia is like returning to a familiar foreign country. The landscape does not speak in my mother tongue, but I have a working knowledge of the language, enough to be able to decipher signs and navigate everyday transactions. I spent five years in the fens as a student – years which, at the time, I regarded as purgatorial – and, although weekends were devoted to exploring the expansive landscape, I never could bring myself to look towards the rows of distant Lombardy poplars with the same love I felt for the hills of my childhood horizons. Yet East Anglia is an area to which I return, time and time again, because friends, like Stephanie, Matthew and Mark, have dispersed less widely than Laurence and I.

Stephanie hops down from a bus just as I reach the town centre of Oundle. We redistribute kit, so that each of us has a similar load to carry, then set off south together. In order to protect my ankle I want to avoid carrying water for long distances, so, rather than camping illegally in a patch of wayside scrub, we divert from my planned route and walk to Molesworth, where the Cross Keys Inn also runs a camping field.

Being slightly off-course means that we need to backtrack east again the next day in order to reach the County Top of Huntingdonshire. Boring Field is less boring than its name implies, but only a little less – hardly something that can be considered a reward for the morning's extra miles. A suspiciously man-made-looking mound stands in the yard adjacent to Windy Barn Farm – if the mound is artificial, should the yard itself be the County Top? A sign in the nearby village of Stow Longa suggests that the church spire attains a greater altitude; a credible claim since the village lies at least seventy metres above sea level and the official height of Boring Field is just eighty-one metres.

On the shores of Grafham Water, we rest for lunch. Pausing in its acrobatic display, a dragonfly alights on our bench, its glossy abdomen reflecting the midday sun like red enamel.

"Thank you for the slug," Stephanie says, opening the bag of provisions I supplied her with in Oundle. I benefit rather unfairly from the exchange of food. Stephanie has baked a delicious four-layer chocolate cake, in celebration of it being approximately mid-way between our respective birthdays. We also mark the (approximate) three-quarter point of my route: I have walked over 2,600 miles, and there remain only about 800 before me.

Ely Cathedral sails like a ship onto the far horizon, helping us to keep our bearings in this unendurably level landscape. That the Isle of Ely even possesses a highest point is implausible, yet the Ordnance Survey have managed to track down the County Top to the village of Haddenham. We pause briefly in acknowledgement of the County Top, but there is little else to interest us in Haddenham, and we are soon on our way again.

Our accommodation for the night is a motel on the Ely ring-road. After draping our room with damp tents and foetid socks, we walk on into the city centre, to meet a group of friends for an evening meal.

More interesting than the name suggests? Boring Field, County Top of Huntingdonshire, 16th August 2017.

Stories of the South Wales Ordeal have reached East Anglia ahead of me, but Matthew is present to help me refute most of the wilder tales.

Next morning, the Hereward Way leads us through Prickwillow, where we decline to visit the drainage museum, and then around two sides of a triangle to Shippea Hill; a permissive path alongside the railway between these two villages would be extremely useful.

A dead-end road brings us to a private farm track, which bridges the Little Ouse, then evolves into a public right of way on the far bank. The nearest public bridge is six miles downriver, beside Lakenheath Station. We walk steadily and purposefully past the 'Trespassers Will Be Prosecuted' sign, past workers outside the potato storage sheds, over the bridge and onto the public right of way beyond. No-one challenges us. I would prefer to seek the landowner's permission, but it is not readily apparent which farm the bridge belongs to.

Though the day is bright, a strengthening wind ushers in thundery showers from the south west. As we walk through Feltwell, a grim gothic archway of cloud rakes through the sky overhead; we can see heavy rain to north and south, but feel only a few droplets. Our meteorological luck runs out between Methwold and Northwold, however. A sudden silence descends over the forest around us, then fat, viscous globules begin to burst through the foliage. It is a soaking rain, yet the air temperature is sufficiently warm that we soon dry once the clouds blow on.

Time saved by not visiting the drainage museum is spent in the village of South Pickenham, where we enjoy the simple splendour of the village church – one of the very few in the country to boast a round tower surmounted by an octagonal belfry. Most round-tower churches were constructed between the eleventh and fourteenth centuries. Of the 180 or so surviving to this day, 124 are within the county of Norfolk; it has been suggested that this localised architectural style developed in consequence of the difficultly of shaping quoins, or corner stones, from East Anglian flint.[58]

Our next break is less rewarding. Stephanie is suffering from blisters on her heels and examination of her socks reveals threadbare fabric at the back. The long, level miles are taking a toll on feet and footwear: I notice a visible degradation in the soles of my boots with each passing day. We delve into our food-bags to fortify ourselves, only to discover that the remaining slices of cake have grown a blue velvet covering.

A group of women stroll by in the lane and pause to ask us all the usual questions.

"Where are you heading to?"

"Sheringham, but not until tomorrow night."

"But that's about thirty miles away!"

We nod agreement, but I am secretly thinking that the remaining distance is probably closer to forty miles. By the time we reach Dereham, Stephanie looks exhausted and seems to be trying to walk without her feet touching the ground. We stagger on to our campsite, a little way east of Swanton Morley. The site is vast, and busy with holidaying families, so our tiny tents attract much attention, passers-by unaware that we are smiling to hear ourselves commented upon.

"They're a bit small. How do you even get in there?"

---

58 'Round Tower Churches Society', n.d., http://www.roundtowers.org.uk.

"Maybe you just lie down and pitch the tent on top of you."

"That's what you call camping, isn't it!"

"Kids, stay away from those little tents over there – people have to live in them."

"Dad, do people really sleep *in* there? But how to do they fit in?"

An ice-cream van tinkles into the field. It sits, sulking, for a few minutes as the occupants of the tents and caravans resolutely ignore it, then silently slips away.

From Themelthorpe, we make an unpropitious choice of byway – our route is clearly a favourite with off-road motorcyclists. The two parallel tyre-ruts become progressively muddier, until we sink to our ankles with each step. We press ourselves close in to the grime-spattered hedge, hoping to find firmer ground amongst the hawthorn roots.

"You're not as muddy as me," Stephanie sounds almost accusatory.

"That's because you went first and wiped most of the mud off the hedge."

I try to brush the gritty paste from my hands, but merely succeed in transferring it from one hand to the other. When we next pass a patch of dock, I dab at my arms and legs with the dark leaves. My efforts stain the sludge chlorophyll-green, but remove very little of it.

Reaching West Beckham, we find figs for sale at the roadside: £1 for three.

"Are you supposed to peel them?"

Neither of us knows. We take one fig apiece, sampling a mouthful with skin and a mouthful peeled: the latter is less bitter, but undoubtedly messier.

We are slowly drawing nearer to Sheringham, and can judge where the coastline lies from the line along which fluffy cumulus give abrupt way to lower, hazy clouds. We eventually reach the town in the late afternoon, in time for Stephanie to return home by train. I will stay for two nights in the Youth Hostel and enjoy a day of rest at the seaside.

Beacon Hill (County Top of Norfolk), Wattisham Airfield (County Top of East Suffolk) and Great Wood (County Top of West Suffolk)

Sheringham to Haverhill. 118 miles, 1,530 metres ascent.
Monday 21st – Saturday 26th August

I breakfast upon the third fig, then find a bench on the sea front, from where I can watch the cormorants disperse as crowds gather on the beach. I tug off my boots, tie the laces together and sling them over my shoulder, then walk out over the bare, wet sand. The surface is hard, but there is an almost imperceptible feeling of yielding as the sands shift to accommodate each footfall. This is the first time I have walked barefoot since the shores of Cow Green Reservoir, almost three months ago.

I stand for a few moments in the shallows, letting the waves brush red and green sea-lettuce around my ankles. Then I turn and walk back up the beach to sit on the pebbled slope beside the slipway. The stones have smooth dust-grey surfaces, marbled by smears of translucent flint. I turn a pebble in the palm of my hand, longing to take it with me. But I have resolved to carry no more than is absolutely essential: since I injured my ankle, I have even discarded my spare clothing. I lay the pebble gently back on the beach.

Turning my back on Sheringham and the sea, I climb through woodland to Beacon Hill, the highest point in Norfolk, and indeed the only part of the county garlanded by a hundred-metre contour line on the Ordnance Survey map. Beacon Hill also goes by the name of Roman Camp, although this is thought to be a Victorian flight of fancy, the earthworks on the summit dating to the time of the Napoleonic Wars, when a signal station was constructed atop the hill.

The coastal high ground is a topographical anomaly: a nine-mile ridge of glacial moraine, moulded by the glaciers that dredged the North Sea basin more than 11,000 years ago. On the next stage of my journey I will walk almost top-to-bottom across East Anglia before I reach my next County Top, confirming William Cobbett's observation that "From the Wen [i.e. London] to Norwich… there is nothing in Essex, Suffolk or this county that can be called a hill."[59]

---

59 William Cobbett, *Norfolk and Suffolk Journal,* (1821).

I turn south. The remnants of wood-banks and ditches testify to the age of the broad-leaved woodland extending southwards from Beacon Hill towards the Fellbrigg estate. I chide myself for spending too long in admiration of the contorted pollarded beeches lining the Lion's Mouth lane: I could while away many hours exploring the woodland, but there are four pages of map to cross today.

Once I have left the woods, the route holds less interest. Apart from a flint-bedded footway alongside the Bure Valley Railway, I follow roads for most of the remaining miles to Norwich. Construction of the Norwich Northern Distributor Road has opened a gash in the arable land to the north of the city, and forces me onto the miserable verge of the busy B1150. A vacuous silence explodes as traffic reaches the smooth, virgin tarmac of a preposterously-proportioned roundabout, which will eventually allow the B1150 to cross the new road. Silent eternities slip by before cars complete their sweeping semi-circles.

I arrive in Norwich through an area of businesses proclaiming themselves to be 'body modification parlours' and shops proffering skull-shaped sofas. Thurstan, who once studied in the city, assures me that such establishments are not uncommon here, but I am unsure whether to believe him. Continuing straight through the city, I camp at Whittlingham Broad, though I will need to return to the railway station tomorrow morning to meet Matthew, who has either sufficiently recovered from, or forgotten, his experiences in Wales to agree to join me again for single-day walks.

I sleep deeply, but I am woken at 5am. Thunder? A dream? Or the cyan-blue aeroplanes spiralling upwards from Norwich airport? Once more, everything is sodden – I can wring water from my rolled-up tent. The sun soon burns through the high-pressure haze, but a dark stain seeps up the fringes of the sky like a tide-mark, threatening heavy rain.

Matthew's journey to Norwich has been less eventful than his travel to Carmarthen, and we are walking before the start of the working day (although having been awake for so long it feels as though it is much later). We pause to explore Norwich's Romano-British predecessor, named Venta Icenorum by the Romans who wrested these lands from the Iceni following Boudicca's unsuccessful uprising of 60-61AD. Little remains of the Roman town apart from the circuit of defensive walls, probably constructed in the third century AD. Far more emotive is the war memorial standing outside the nearby church of Caistor St Edmund. The eight men of the parish who fell in the First World War, and the single casualty of the Second, are commemorated individually on a panel adjacent to the memorial.

We reach Diss with barely enough time for Matthew to check the departure board before leaping aboard a train. I shuffle a short distance further to Scole, where I have made contact with a campsite to confirm that they are willing to host a backpacker.

"I expect you've only got a tiny tent, so we'll do you a tiny price," the proprietor says when checking me in.

The 'tiny price' is £13. I don't like to say that this is more than twice as much as I've been charged in many places; nor do I enquire what the regular price would be.

I am alone again the next day. Dam Lane is empathetic: quiet, sunken and sullen. It leads me to the village of Mellis Green, where large white cattle graze on the green, immured by a seemingly inadequate single strand of wire.

A short distance past Gislingham, a notice tells me that my path is closed at the railway crossing ahead. Faced with a lengthy diversion, and seeking consolation in chocolate, I reach over my shoulder to unzip the top pouch of my rucksack, where I have a bag of chocolate buttons stowed for easy access. I tug the corner of the plastic packet. Something tears. A cascade of chocolate buttons tumbles down the back of my neck and into the grass at my feet. Wearily, I heft off my pack and begin the laborious task of button-collecting: concerns about littering aside, the ground is not muddy and I do not want to waste the chocolate.

Having pitched my tent in a patch of woodland south of Stowmarket, I try to fit my stove onto a new gas cylinder, to brew tea. Liquefied gas fizzes out of the valve. The screw-thread must be damaged on either the cylinder or the stove – I suspect the latter, since it has been getting increasingly fiddly to attach the stove to gas bottles over recent days. The prospect of cold food – and cold tea – stretches before me, until such time as I can acquire a new stove – on a Bank Holiday weekend, in a part of the country where I expect to find few outdoor shops. But, my parents are due to visit me on my birthday, now only a couple of days away: I send my mother a text message with a last-minute suggestion for a birthday present.

I drift off to sleep within a soft cloud of melancholy – a cloud which settles more heavily the next day, when I must reconcile myself to my first failure. I had known since planning my walk that I would be unable to reach the absolute summit of East Suffolk, since it lies within the bounds of Wattisham Airfield, to which there is no public access. Most County-Top-hunters are content to visit the highest point on the airfield perimeter; standard practice seems to be to walk round the perimeter fence. Thick brambles prevent me from getting even this close, but I trespass round the edges of fields until I get as near as I possibly can – without lacerating my limbs – to a man-made mound just inside the fence. In almost any other county, my failure to stand atop this mound would surely have been a severe disappointment, but here, I feel strangely dispassionate, since the concept of East Suffolk seems a rather artificial construct.

Nearing the end of my day's walk, I reach a sign welcoming new arrivals to Brighthouse Farm. A tawny deerhound has other ideas: barking and snarling, it drives me out of the campsite and back onto the road. We are engaged in a stand-off when a car towing a trailer tent pulls into the farm. I jog back down the driveway, keeping the trailer tent as a shield between myself and the dog. The car driver is a regular visitor to the site, on good terms with both the dog and its owner, the latter presently nowhere to be found. Three or four groups of new arrivals are roaming the site looking for the owner, who is eventually located cleaning the toilet block. He shows me to a pitch beneath trees on the edge of a field with a wide outlook towards Shimpling Street.

As the daylight fades, I realise that my pitch is not as idyllic as I had first thought. The trees are infested with bugs which hop all over my tent and pepper me with tiny red bites. The protrusion of my pelvis on the left side of my back is swollen and sore. It feels infected, but I lack the gymnastic ability to see whether this is the case. It is too painful to lie on my back, and on hard ground I find it too uncomfortable to sleep well lying on my side. Over the next few days, I experiment with a rolled-up jacket in the small of my back, which takes the pressure off my sore – which is soon definitely septic – though by tilting my rucksack forwards it makes walking much more tiring.

In addition to the tree-dwelling bugs, a colony of spiders arrive in my tent during the night to help me celebrate my thirty-first birthday. Mark, a more welcome walking companion, will also be joining me later in the day, and I hope that his company will raise my spirits from my recent melancholy. We have arranged that Mark will meet me at the radio mast close to the West Suffolk County Top, then will walk with me as far as Haverhill. There is no visible sign of him when I arrive, so I send a text message to inform him of my location. Seconds later, my phone buzzes as his reply comes in, to say that he too has arrived: we have been waiting on opposite sides of a small spinney.

Before resuming the journey, we need to find the highest point. The radio mast appears to occupy a slight rise relative to the surrounding fields and woodlands, but there are two other contenders for the County Top. One is the site of a former trig point and the other is a 128-metre spot height close to a farm road only a short distance away.

Later in the morning, we plunge from wheat-fields onto a narrow path winding through hawthorn and blackthorn. The dense thorns are evocative of a fairy-tale enchanted thicket, but instead of emerging at a castle to discover that a thousand years have elapsed, we reach a pink gingerbread house after a more prosaic ten minutes, then continue on until the stark modernity of Haverhill proves that we have not escaped from East Anglia into a fairy-tale realm.

From Haverhill Bus Station, the outlook towards the town centre is familiar – but I turn around to see a new leisure complex, containing cinema, sports centre, fast food outlets and restaurants. The contrast between the two feels almost as though photographs of different eras have been spliced together.

The staff of Haverhill Travelodge have anticipated my arrival: a sign on the door requests that guests "Please remove muddy boots before entering." I have time to check in and wash myself and my clothes before my parents arrive. It is, of course, good to see them, but it is even better that my mother has answered my appeal and brought a new stove: no more cold porridge.

Great Chishill (County Top of Cambridgeshire), Chrishall Common (County Top of Essex) and Dunstable Downs (County Top of Bedfordshire)

Haverhill to Dunstable. 70 miles, 1,290 metres ascent.
Sunday 27th – Wednesday 30th August

Ashen clouds cover the sky. I know these thin cloud-pillows will soon burn off, but my parents, transplanted from wet Lancashire, don't realise how hot the day will become.

"Have you got plenty of water?" I ask, knowing that they often carry little or no fluid – or coffee only.

"Lots?" my mother looks startled by the question, but I manage to convince them to carry a litre and a half between them and hope that this will be sufficient.

The roundabout outside the Travelodge evidently lies on the Suffolk-Essex border, for we pass a 'Welcome to Essex' sign lurking in the vegetation. We stride along well-trodden paths, pausing whenever my father's ears catch an interesting bird call: buzzard, green woodpecker, greater spotted woodpecker, an unidentifiable warbler. Most of the wheat and barley has now been gathered in, and combine harvesters are guzzling through the remaining crops, clouds of chaff billowing behind them. Tractors follow like forlorn dogs.

We join the Harcamlow Way, familiar from a half-forgotten autumn in which I walked the complete figure-of-eight in four long sections. New waymarkers have been erected in the intervening decade, but they are positioned for walkers heading in the opposite direction to us, so provide little assistance with navigation. We break for lunch near Saffron Walden, then cut up the map: I take the western half, and my parents take the eastern half, to allow them to return to Haverhill.

The heat builds as the afternoon wears on. In Elmdon, I find a water tap at the village hall and am grateful for the excuse to rest after refilling my flask. I continue to Great Chishill, where I camp at Lynchetts Farm in a quiet field with open views north over Cambridgeshire. I can pick out the distant tower of Addenbrooke's Hospital, the spire of King's College Chapel and the chimney of Barrington Cement Works. As darkness falls, the sky melts into horizontal bands of cinnabar, mazarine and indigo, and the setting sun gently impales itself upon the silhouette of a telegraph pole.

I eventually retreat into my tent, hoping for a sunrise to match the sunset, but the next day dawns misty – weather which connotes winter, not August anticyclones. Although the clouds soon clear, and the temperature soars back to the highs of recent days, the cool start means another damp tent.

The couple who run the campsite at Lynchetts Farm also farm the land where the County Top of Cambridgeshire lies. Though the relevant field is planted with flax, I can skirt the edge of it to reach the highest point without damaging the crop. The County Top of Essex is only a couple of miles away, nestling in a corner of an irregularly-shaped woodland. In fact, Great Chishill was once part of Essex, only being transferred to Cambridgeshire in 1895; I would be interested to learn where the highest point of Cambridgeshire could be found prior to this date. I smile to myself as I remember an occasion on which I led a walk to both Great Chishill and Chrishall Common, suggesting, with my tongue in my cheek, that as we were to scale the summits of two counties, attendees should bring rope, ice axe and crampons – then received a number of enquiries from would-be walkers expressing genuine concern that they did not possess the necessary equipment.

The arable landscape has changed overnight. Dry, earthy browns have replaced the pale yellow of wheat: most of the fields have now been ploughed. This makes it harder to identify and follow paths: I stumble over irregular furrows which have churned up footprints, burying paths in the rich loam. In a few fields I am guided by bedraggled spinach, which must have colonised the rights of way and has somehow survived the ploughing – but more often I scan for a fingerpost in the far hedgerow, then clump across the ploughed earth towards it as best I can. I am grateful that the ground is dry; in the perpetually damp memory of my previous East-Anglian walks, my footsteps were always heavy with cloying mud. I have never really seen this landscape in summer before, and grudgingly concede that it is beautiful in its own way.

My next campsite is a short distance north of Baldock. I have been told to pitch my tent anywhere, and that someone will tour the campsite "in the late afternoon" to take payment. It is not until an hour after dusk, by which time I have long since retired to my tent to read,

Where's the path? East Anglian ploughed land, 28th August 2017.

that I hear a single-cylinder engine puttering round the field.

"Hello! Anyone there?"

I poke my head out of the tent. A man and a woman, whose combined age I judge to be at least a century and a half, are sitting astride a contraption that appears to be a relative of a golf buggy.

"Are you two fifteen-year-olds?" the lady calls over to me.

"No, there's definitely just one of me." Fifteen-year-olds may not be fully-grown, but I think it would be difficult to fit two of them in this tiny tent.

The couple seem a little disappointed. "Are you sure? How old are you?"

I have to think for a moment before I recall that it is only two days since my birthday. "Thirty-one. So you could add two fifteen-year-olds together to get me."

I pay for my pitch, and the couple resume their search for their missing fifteen-year-olds.

Next day, Matthew is back for more. From Baldock Station, we follow the Icknield Way: easier said than done, because although it is nominally a waymarked trail, it is best described as braided. At each junction as many as four waymarkers make conflicting suggestions about possible directions for onward travel – often in disagreement with the long-distance trail diamonds depicted on my map. I believe this is at least partly in consequence of the historical ambiguity of the Icknield Way, which, at any given time, occupied whichever ground was least muddy, and could extend up to a mile in width. References to the trackway first appear in written records of the early tenth century, although it is believed to be of pre-historic origin, the appellation possibly referring to the Iceni who lent their name to Venta Icenorum.

I am grateful not to be completely reliant on the ambiguous signage, having walked most of today's route before, during the 'Varsity March', an eighty-mile continuous walk that my student walking club undertook as a grand finale to each academic year. Too sensible to attempt the Varsity March in its entirety, Matthew has in many years filled a supporting role, so much of our conversation relates to the Varsity March in some way: this or that landmark is a checkpoint in the route description; this is where so-and-so dropped out; this is the point where time was always wasted deciding whether to go left or right, forgetting that the paths join up less than a mile further on.

"We cross the road ahead at the place called the Invisible Picnic Tables," I quote a Varsity March checkpoint.

"How do you know the picnic tables are invisible?" Matthew queries.

"Because you can't see them." To me, this is (oxymoronically) obvious.

"Well how do you know they're there?"

"Because they're marked on the Ordnance Survey map."

"Sometimes," Matthew ventures, "I think the Varsity March enters a rather surreal state during the night."

Near Mortgrove Farm (another checkpoint), we leave the Icknield Way and the Varsity March route. Matthew steers us down from the chalk hills into Luton, and towards an upmarket shopping centre, where he remembers a café by the name of Robby's.

"Ten years ago, this was the Arndale Centre, but I think it may have been refurbished."

The change of environment is so abrupt as to be almost incredible, almost frightening. We step from a sparsely-populated conventional shopping street into a pulsating mass of tote bags, plastic carriers, smartphones, denim-clad legs, faces, purses and pushchairs. Only the inertia of my rucksack keeps me from turning and running back through the automatic doors. Weaving unsteadily through throngs of shoppers, we push through the crowds to the far end of the mall.

"We should probably have walked round the outside of the building," Matthew narrowly misses a small child.

Robby's is still in business, on the less fashionable (hence quieter) upper floor – a proper tea shop, serving good, strong tea, with a dated interior and a waitress who calls each of us 'my love'. Something goes awry at the till when Matthew tries to pay, and rolls of receipt paper blossom from the waitress' arms.

I linger a little too long in Matthew's company. This is the last time he will join me before I reach Land's End, but I still have two hours further to walk before I reach my accommodation on the fringes of Dunstable. I follow the A505, through Bury Park: though just as busy as the Arndale Centre, the brightly-clad crowds divest themselves of any sense of oppressiveness in the bright sunshine and open air. Matthew had recommended this area for its excellent fabric shops, but I am entranced and enticed by the grocers, from which rainbows of fresh fruit and vegetables cascade onto the pavement.

The Holiday Inn where I will be staying for two nights dispenses free newspapers: extremely useful for sock-drying. I collect as many as I think I can risk without attracting undue attention from the reception staff.

My parents visit me during my rest day – as with Matthew, this will be the last time I see them during my journey; I have only 500 more miles to walk. Though this is officially a day off, we decide to tick off one more County Top. In soft rain, we skirt Kensworth Chalk Pit to reach Dunstable Downs Gateway visitor centre. The official County Top of Bedfordshire is a trig point at the entrance to the visitor centre car park, but a new embankment running alongside the driveway is definitely higher.

Introspection: Sky

When I lived in East Anglia, I often felt bewildered and disorientated by the limitless, uniform horizon, or subdued by the leaden skies, and could never come to understand the thrall in which the fenland landscape held writers such as W. G. Sebald, Graham Swift or Philip Pullman. At other times, I had the unbearable sense of being trapped within a novel by Thomas Hardy, which rather removed any sense of enjoyment from reading his books.

Inwardly, I agree with the writer Frank Showell Styles, who complains that "I cannot bear the overbearing sky / That crushes down these sad and slavish lands, "[60] bringing to mind an image resembling Atlas hefting not the globe but the skies upon his shoulders, or perhaps the story told in the Aboriginal Noongar dreaming that the sky once lay heavily upon the ground, and was only separated from it by being propped on sticks up by enterprising magpies (goruk). This Noongar dreaming was related by William Buckley, a convict who escaped a penal colony in 1803, was later found by and adopted into an Aboriginal tribe with whom he lived for thirty-two years, before eventually making contact with European settlers. A highly fictionalised account of Buckley's life forms the narrative arc of Alan Garner's book Strandloper[61] *and links my response to the East Anglian horizons back to the rolling countryside of Cheshire that I walked through many months previously.*

Though Garner's re-telling of the story has been dismissed as "the usual anthropological nonsense, "[62] it nonetheless paints a compelling picture of the Aboriginal relationship with land and landscape, myth and mythography. We see William Buckley transformed into the shaman Murrangurk, and taking on the rituals of story-telling and dream-track walking essential to his adoptive tribe. To

---

60 Frank Showell Styles, 'From the Plains', *Speak to the Hills: An Anthology of 20th Century British and Irish Mountain Poetry,* Hamish Brown and Martyn Berry (eds.) (Aberdeen: Aberdeen University Press, 1985), p.13.

61 Alan Gardner, *Strandloper* (London: Harvill Press, 1996).

62 Jenny Turner, 'Lost in the bush' *The Guardian,* 24 May 1996, p.A10.

Sunset over Cambridgeshire, 27th August 2017.

Buckley/Murrangurk, the walker is literally vital to the land, just as the land is vital to the walker: "And if we don't thole [suffer], land dies. It needs walking, and it's us must walk it. Do you not see? We're all one, and have been since I don't know when, since Beginning."

My County Tops walk was perhaps something of a personal dream-track or songline; a journey that I found it necessary to complete in order to re-inforce my own understanding of the world and my relationship with the landscape, and to perpetuate my own personal myths. I am under no illusion that the continued existence of the British Isles owes anything to my madcap plan to walk between an arbitrary selection of hills. However, there is a sense in which the County Tops will continue to hold some sort of significance only as long as we celebrate them as such. Similarly, defunct geographical designations, such as Westmorland or Radnorshire, are meaningful only while we choose to acknowledge them. My walk needed walking – and I needed to walk it.

The Apathy of Trees

Hertfordshire – Buckinghamshire – Oxfordshire –
Middlesex – London – Kent – Surrey

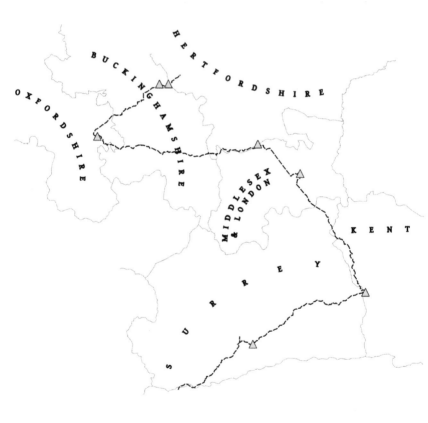

Pavis Wood (County Top of Hertfordshire), Wendover Woods (County Top of Buckinghamshire) and Bald Hill (County Top of Oxfordshire)

Dunstable to Black Jack's Mill. 56 miles, 1,520 metres ascent.
Thursday 31st August – Saturday 2nd September

I leave Dunstable in the direction of Whipsnade, to visit its Tree Cathedral, planted by Edmond Blyth in memory of friends lost in the First World War. A variety of species of tree form the approximate outline of a medieval cathedral: lime for the nave, silver birch and yew for the chancel, horse chestnut and tulip tree for the transepts.

The day's walk seems too easy – almost disquietingly so, and I have a nagging sense that I have mislaid a heavy item of equipment from my rucksack, though I check through my belongings carefully when I next pitch my tent, and do not miss anything. In defiance of the showery forecast, I stride along the Chiltern escarpment beneath pellucid skies. As my route wends through broad-leaved woodland I realise that the brilliance of chlorophyll-stained sunlight filtering through sycamore leaves is one of the things that I will miss most when I return home.

My path spills onto a sweeping expanse of gravel on Pitstone Common. Two women are walking in the opposite direction.

"Are we on the right track?" one of them asks.

Before I have chance to open my mouth, the second woman replies. "I think we're on the right track. We set off on the right track, and we haven't left it."

"Where did you come from?" the first woman asks.

Once again, the second woman answers on my behalf. "Scotland." The exchange is ludicrous: I am being engaged in a conversation, yet at the same time being made to feel no more than a spare part.

"Actually, I did come from Scotland," I decide to participate, "but not this morning; I only came from Dunstable this morning." And I am walking to Land's End, I mentally continue, but not this afternoon: first I must cross London, then reach the south coast.

I can make further progress in numerical terms, being able to cross another two County Tops off my list today. The first, Pavis Wood, the highest point of Hertfordshire, is an unimposing bend on a minor road. Only a few miles further west, a small stone monument marks the summit of the Chilterns and the County Top of Buckinghamshire on Haddington Hill. I have been told that the latter is hard to find, but my experience certainly doesn't bear this out, since I come across the highest point quite by accident before I have even started to consciously look. I have also heard rumours that the monument has been relocated at some point and that the exact high point is now uncertain; the nearby car park certainly feels higher.

Sycamore light, Pavis Wood, 31st August 2017.

I ascend the Ridgeway trail out of Wendover towards Coombe Hill. Heavy showers are grumbling over the plains to the north, looking like petulant toddlers taking their first unsteady steps in Wellington boots. I camp in beech woodland just before the Ridgeway crosses the Chequers estate. Deer bound away between the holly bushes before I can identify their species, but later a runtish muntjac returns to nose about my tent.

The next day is different in two respects. Firstly, although walking for similar lengths of time and distance, I am heavy-limbed and weary. My minimal rations are making themselves felt only two days after my rest day, presumably as I no longer have the energy reserves that I did at the outset of my walk.

Secondly, today's County Top – Bald Hill, the highest point in Oxfordshire – is much more difficult to locate than either of the previous day's highpoints. The hill itself, labelled on my map as Cowleaze Wood, is an effortless ascent, but then I find myself wandering aimlessly about a woodland, searching for high ground described by a previous visitor as being "twenty metres south west of an intersection of paths by a telegraph pole." Not able to see the telegraph pole for the trees, I resort to GPS to check my position.

Unable to see the telegraph pole for the trees: Bald Hill, County Top of Oxfordshire, 1st September 2017.

A deep red sunrise burns through the beech canopy. Red sky in the morning: is a change of weather on the way? I emerge from the woodland into fog-soaked fields, with sun smiling fuzzily through the dewy air. A pale fallow deer stands silhouetted atop a rise, then, in the flicker of an eye, it vanishes.

I have only a few short miles of footpath this morning, to take me as far as High Wycombe, and then the rest of the day will be along roads. The paths in this part of the Chilterns seem oblivious to the topography, ploughing up steep banks of hills, only to descend on the far side. It is quite difficult to construct sensible routes, and impossible to avoid unnecessary loss of height.

The ground becomes more and more overgrown with nettles and blackthorn as I approach the M25, until I reach an area that is thick with litter, much of it fly-tipped. I cannot avoid treading on the smaller items of rubbish – plastic bottles and bags, cans, newspapers, food packaging – at times I am almost wading. A vinegary smell of decay emanates from mouldering semi-organic mounds and the soggy remnants of sofas and soft furnishings.

The litter peters out when I turn off the road onto a canal towpath, which takes me the last few hundred yards to my bed and breakfast at Black Jack's Mill. There is a choice of two doorbells. I press one, and receive no response. I try the other: still no response. I nudge the front door ajar and call out a greeting: nothing. A taxi driver arrives to collect a passenger. I now feel justified in entering, and eventually find the proprietor in the kitchen. When the taxi's passenger has been tracked down, she shows me to my room.

"The door sometimes sticks a bit. We're looking into it."

I unpack my rucksack and collect the paraphernalia that I will need for a shower; the shared washroom is just across the landing from my room. I tug the doorknob. It turns slightly, but doesn't release the door catch. This is more than 'sticking a bit' – I am effectively locked in. Fortunately my penknife, incorporating a cross-headed screwdriver, is incarcerated with me.

Bushey Heath (County Top of Middlesex), Hampstead Heath (County Top of London), Betsom's Hill (County Top of Kent) and Leith Hill (County Top of Surrey)

Black Jack's Mill to Holmbury St Mary. 76 miles, 1,950 metres ascent.
Sunday 3rd – Thursday 7th September

There is something arresting about the bird's call – the same captivating effect as a woodpecker's laugh, but a harsher, jay-like rasp, and not one that I recognise. Then I see it: a parakeet. This is my first glimpse of one of the nearly 9,000 breeding pairs of ring-necked parakeets living in the UK. The colouring of the bird is similar to that of the green woodpecker, but it possesses nothing of the elegance of the woodpecker in flight. It flaps heavily, putting on a display of arduousness, then scrabbles its way into a tree as though it were scarcely seconds from a crash landing.

I have left the countryside behind me now, and am walking through an anonymous, affluent suburb. If it weren't for the London Transport logos emblazoned on bus stops, I could be in any city in the country. Sections of the London Loop path provide opportunities to get off the pavement, to thread my way through patches of litter-strewn scrub, or along grubby guinnels at the backs of houses.

I pass foul duckweed-smothered pools of stagnant water on Harrow Weald Common, and slip through leaf-litter which is as much plastic and cardboard as it is leaves. The trees have an air of apathetic detachment. I can't quite call to mind the precise word. Resignation? Weariness? Disregard? It is as though the trees know that we are trying to kill them, but at the same time recognise that we will poison ourselves with our accumulations of toxic trash long before they themselves succumb.

I lose the London Loop somewhere in the woods, but find instead a tunnel beneath rhododendron. There is less litter here, the ground underfoot is undisturbed, and the arch of the bushes is low over my head, so that I am forced to walk at a stoop. The sense of almost illicit freedom in following this road less taken compels me onwards, though I do not know where, if anywhere, it will lead. The driveway of an upmarket hotel cuts through my rhododendron tunnel. I crunch across the gravel and plunge back into the bushes on the other side, in full view of expensively-dressed guests admiring a luxury soft-top, and wonder whether their self-importance has deigned to acknowledge the scruffy walker trespassing across their field of vision.

When the rhododendron tunnel comes to an end, I re-emerge from the scrub into Bushey Heath, where the County Top of Middlesex occupies a traffic island in the centre of a busy road. I cross halfway, stand on the island for a while, then return to the same side of the road.

For the next nine miles, I lose all sense of time as I walk the dead-straight line of the A5, the old Watling Street, an arrow piercing the heart of the capital. The afternoon is humid, sultry, stultifying. Oppressive clouds boil overhead. It feels as though it should be raining, but something about the heat of the city seems to be repelling the raindrops. I am out of my element: I cannot read the weather forecast in the sky, nor can I smell the air for the traffic and the litter. When it does start to drizzle, in the late afternoon, the raindrops are sour, with

Probably the most urban of the County Tops: Bushey Heath, County Top of Middlesex, 3rd September 2017.

a wet-dog aroma, not the clean cut-grass scent I am accustomed to. The topography is smothered by the urban sprawl, forcing me to navigate by relying on the features I normally mentally sweep away – power lines, radio masts – to distinguish one road from another.

At Cricklewood, I leave Watling Street and turn east towards Hampstead Heath and the County Top of London. This County Top is another uninteresting stretch of road, but in compensation there are hazy views over the city. I follow a cycle route across the Heath, then make for the home of Laurence's cousin. Chris and his partner Hannah have been away on holiday and are due to return home in the middle of the night, but their friend Michael, who has been house-sitting, is there to let me in. The evening is a surreal experience, as I sit chatting to a complete stranger, in a flat where neither of us lives.

"I've got more stuff than you," Michael comments, "and I'm only away from home for a week, not six months."

Chris and Hannah tiptoe into their own home shortly before 1.00am, though I feign sleep so that they will not worry that they have disturbed the visitor sleeping on the floor of their living room. They confront their breakfast blearily, as they reconcile themselves to the world of work and the "dishcloth grey" (Chris' description) English sky, while I fail to deflate their air mattress. Their residential road funnels me towards King's Cross, where queues are wrapping themselves around the courtyard of the British Library, awaiting the opening of the doors at 9.30am. Although I had hoped to purchase postcards from the library, my large rucksack precludes me from entering even the gift shop – only now do I come to realise how many of London's doors are closed to me. But, given the prominently-displayed reminders that "Reporting anything unusual won't hurt you!" I will consider myself lucky if I can traverse the capital without being reported as 'unusual' for my over-sized rucksack, tattered clothes and the headscarf that I wear to keep the hair out of my eyes and prevent heatstroke.

I walk past St Paul's Cathedral, to cross the Thames on the Millennium Bridge. On the south bank I follow the river downstream alongside the cumin-scented water, through an atlas of docklands: Greenland Dock, Russia Dock, Surrey Dock. This isn't the direct route to Bromley, my destination for the evening, but I have a sudden desire to find the Greenwich Meridian. The day is muggy again, mak-

Saint Paul's Cathedral, 4th Septenber 2017.

ing walking tiring, and it takes me much longer to reach Greenwich than I had anticipated. I long for air where I can breathe freely.

The Greenwich Meridian runs through the old Royal Observatory, but the Meridian Line is fenced off, with a £9.50 ticket charge – and a prohibition on people with large rucksacks. Having spent so many months roaming freely over moors and hills, I can barely comprehend that a line of longitude has an admission charge. I stride out into the park and use my compass to steer myself until I am due south of the Observatory. This is my Meridian.

Next morning, walking south out of London at rush hour, I have the same sense of swimming against the current that I experienced on the West Highland Way. Navigating with a paper Ordnance Survey map, I am reminded of the stereotyped image of a walker struggling with an unwieldy map in a howling gale – only the gale is one of harried commuters. Happily free of the worry of whether I will get to work on time, I can walk at my own pace, away from the world of offices and suits and towards the equable quiet of Hayes Common.

The common is scrubby, grubby, overgrown, but the avian chatter announces a variety of bird species, not just pigeons, and even the slimy urban leaf-litter is preferable to walking on hard concrete or tarmac. This is both a breathing space and a barrier, separating leafy commuter villages from suburban sprawl.

The woods disgorge me into a changed world. Place names now relate to discrete settlements, not vaguely-delineated housing estates. The view to the south west from Biggin Hill looks more like a painting than reality – the curve of the wooded valley is too gentle, the colours too perfect, and the showers lend a slight, soft nap to the air.

My friend Ian is waiting at Hawley's Corner. He has brought joy, in the form of a fiddle. My longing for hill country is betrayed when the first melodies to come to my fingers are Scottish: I play *The Gentle Light That Wakes Me* and *The Farley Bridge* standing in the rain by the side of the A233, and for a few brief seconds am transported back to the Highlands. When, before my departure on this walk, my colleagues asked me what I would miss most about my home-life, I answered "my fiddle." Though in truth I find that I miss Laurence far more than any material possession or home comfort, I have a vague fear – vague because I am trying not to acknowledge it – that I will forget how to play the fiddle as the months go by without my touching

217

an instrument. The loan of Ian's fiddle, therefore, is more than the simple kind gesture of a friend: it reassures me that I can still play, and I hope that this will give me the courage to pick up my own fiddle as soon as I return home.

Ian accompanies me to Betsom's Hill, the Kentish County Top. We locate the official grid reference of the highest point, on a lane leading to Little Betsom's Farm. The adjacent, artificial higher ground of an old hill fort doesn't count – logic which contradicts the designation of Pinchbeck Marsh and possibly Arbury Hill. More to the point, a wooden gate is daubed with the letters

THE DOG IS VERY BIG

so we are content to visit only the official County Top.

I have only fourteen miles to walk the next day, so loiter in Redhill until the shops open and I can replace my boots, having worn through the soles on the hard, urban surfaces of recent days. A pair of leather walking shoes catch my eye, but I feel a sting of pain in my ankle on my first exploratory circuit of the shop: a reminder that the injury hasn't recovered at all. Instead, I settle for some cheap trainers, which, with luck, will suffice until I reach the next town with an outdoor shop.

I have chosen to follow the Greensand Way for much of the day, in the hope that the long-distance path will be well signposted. It is, but many of the posts stand awry, or have toppled completely, enigmatically disguising the very directions which they were intended to provide.

Leith Hill is one of the few County Tops in the south of the British Isles that I have visited previously. My first visit was earlier in the year, when I paid a belated Christmas visit to my sister, who lives on the Surrey-Berkshire border. I took advantage of some free time to explore the North Downs and covered more than thirty miles on foot in a single morning. It rained uncontrollably, and I was soon muddier than I had been in a long time, but I felt a greedy enjoyment of the sensation of the rainwater upon my skin, the wind in my face and the physical ache in my limbs. I wondered then, as I do now, why I find it necessary to push myself so hard physically in order to find such exhilaration.

That day, I visited both Leith Hill and Holmbury Hill. As I approached the summit of Holmbury Hill, I was overtaken by a pack of runners, clad in Lycra and mud.

"It looks like today's got potential to get a bit muddy."

This jibe was clearly wearing thin.

"If you say that one more time, you'll be running the rest of the way on your own."

Today, though still muddy, the ground is drier. As I draw nearer to Holmbury St Mary I am obliged to concentrate hard on the navigation to ensure that I find the Youth Hostel nestling within the woods. There are many more paths on the ground than are marked on my map, but by luck more than judgement I arrive in the right place. The hostel is quiet, most other guests being people rendered temporarily homeless rather than the usual crowd of holidaymakers: workers needing a temporary base from which they can commute into London; a family in transition between lives in the UK and abroad. I am fortunate to be the only person in the female dormitory, and infer that there has been some trouble with snoring in the male dormitory from cautious questions to the warden: "Is, er, Gerald still here?"

On my rest day in Holmbury St Mary I venture little more than a mile from the hostel, to acquire fresh fruit and vegetables from the village shop in Peaslake, and otherwise spend the day reading and crocheting socks until I run out of wool. I find it easy to remember the crochet pattern for socks, and a tent peg makes an ideal crochet hook – the main difficulty lies in making two socks of approximately the same size. When I break for tea, another hosteller engages me in conversation in the kitchen.

"I hadn't realised what good exercise walking is."

"Yes," I concur, "you can go at your own pace, and stop for a break whenever it suits you, so it's accessible to most people." This is an observation that I often find myself making; I suspect that I have developed this stance as a means to deflect attention from the extreme nature of my own walking.

"Mind you," the tone of the other hosteller changes, "I went rambling once. It was such hard work – the gradients, and the altitude."

He seems to consider walking and rambling to be two completely different pastimes – and, contrary to most people who hold this view, regards rambling as by far the more arduous. I dare not admit the length of the journey that has brought me to Holmbury St Mary.

Introspection: Trees

While I have been writing this chapter, my mind has been knitting my thread of ideas into a very different pattern from that formed by my words, so that flowing through the linear narrative of my walk I have an imaginary braided current. The source of this current is Whipsnade Tree Cathedral, where I felt the dignity of mature birch and chestnut distil the muted tranquillity of a medieval cathedral into the chalk of the Bedfordshire Downs. Later, as I walked through Greater London, I also found the trees placid, benign and calming, quite unlike the tortured agony of the storm-swept birches in the far north of Scotland.

In London I also walked past a second, more conventional cathedral: St Paul's. Though this cathedral stands in a comparatively unsylvan area of the city, my mind was already ahead with the current. For the cathedral is linked by its patron saint to St Paul's Girls' School, which lies about five miles further west, in Hammersmith. There, in the early twentieth century, a decade or so before the Whipsnade cathedral was planted, the composer Gustav Holst wrote his well-known St Paul's Suite. In the suite's finale, the gentle melody of Greensleeves soars above a furious jig known as the Dargason. The effect is the same as when, in crowded semi-urban or urban landscapes, the trees sing a calming counter-melody to the frantic scrabble of our busy lives.

Though many will derive inner peace from the religion of these two cathedrals, for me, the power of the trees is just as compelling.

The Revenge of Slugs

West Sussex – East Sussex – Hampshire – Berkshire –
Wiltshire – Dorset – Somerset – Devon – Cornwall

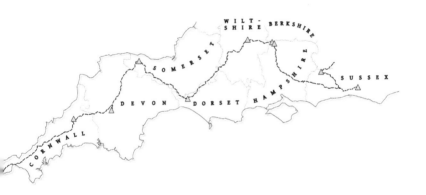

Black Down (County Top of West Sussex) and Ditchling Beacon (County Top of East Sussex)
Holmbury St Mary to Winchester. 126 miles, 3,950 metres ascent.
Friday 8th – Wednesday 13th September

"Looks like you're going to get wet today," the warden comments as he sees me off.

"It can't be as bad as Wales."

But it can. In the cavernous darkness beneath the woodland canopy, I need a torch just to see the ground. Light drizzle is supplanted by heavy rain, with intermittent bursts so intense that the cascading water feels almost solid – easily commensurate with the worst of the weather I experienced in Wales. I don't have time to put my waterproof jacket on before the first downpour reaches me, so am wearing only a thin 'shower-proof' layer over my t-shirt. The rain is soon pouring straight through. I un-tuck my t-shirt to prevent the water running down the inside of my trousers.

Despite the weather, Black Down is a beautiful hill. I have become accustomed – or perhaps resigned – to the dank, muddy woods of Surrey, so I feel a sense of elation as I climb onto heathland, where heather and birch proclaim the acidic sandstone beneath, as well as serving as a reminder that this area was once cleared by 'heathens' for use as grazing land. The trig point is sheltering from the weather, concealed slyly amongst the trees. A few yards away, a viewpoint at the Temple of the Four Winds looks out towards the line of the South Downs and Ditchling Beacon, my next County Top.

I camp in woodland on Ebernoe Common: grazed by cattle, it is not an ideal location, but I am too wet and too tired to continue. By the time I crawl into my tent I can wring the water out from my clothing, even my underwear. I have been wearing my old boots and carrying my new trainers, to prevent the new shoes becoming unnecessarily sodden, but the boots are now soaked through and I resolve to discard them at the next opportunity, irrespective of the weather.

By dawn, there are slugs everywhere. Fat, greenish-grey, orange-rimmed sausages of slime have invaded my belongings and are slicking over the inside and outside of the tent. Everything that I left in

An unwelcome visitor to the tent.

the porch because it was too wet to bring into the tent has been colonised by slugs and smeared with slime-trails. A wrinkle in the sleeve of my waterproof jacket alerts me to the slug inside before I slip my arm in.

Disinclined to bring anything from the porch into the inner tent, I alter my usual morning routine, eating breakfast before I dress, then clambering out of the tent to embark upon systematic slug removal. I pick off the visible molluscs, then whirl items of clothing and equipment around my head to try to centrifuge out any stubborn adherents.

It takes a good ninety minutes to de-slug everything; I finally set off walking at 7.30am. I am grateful that the warm sun has returned, as I can trail damp clothing from the back of my rucksack to allow it to dry. I have started early with the intention of walking all the way to the Youth Hostel at Truleigh Hill, where I have booked a camping pitch for tomorrow evening – a hard day today will mean an easy day tomorrow; a relatively quick there-and-back jaunt to Ditchling Beacon, without the need to carry my tent and sleeping bag.

I stop for a late-morning break and pitch my tent to dry. When I remove my boots to air my feet an unsavoury gelatinous mess inside my right boot suggests that my slug removal had not been wholly successful.

In Steyning I deposit my wet, slug-smeared boots in a public bin, then slip my feet into my new, still-dry, trainers. But the rain has not finished with me yet. Five minutes later the sky darkens and heavy raindrops begin to fall, as a reprise of yesterday's weather begins.

It rains through the hours of darkness, but the next day begins bright with buoyant sunlight. Though I have not far to go, I set out early to make the most of the fair weather. Low mist is twining upwards from the plains to the north, and to the south I can see out to the wind farms in the English Channel. The path rises and falls as it follows the chalk escarpment: so much so that I think an easier route might be to descend from the Downs, walk along their northern edge, then climb back up at Ditchling Beacon – but this would feel wrong, almost deceitful.

Windswept hawthorns, South Downs, 10th September 2017.

I reach Ditchling Beacon by late morning. The County Top is a topographical palimpsest: the remains of an iron-age hill fort became first the site of a warning beacon, to be lit in times of invasion, and latterly a recreational landmark, traversed by the South Downs Way. There is a chill on the back edge of the breeze, so I shelter in the narrow wind-shadow of the trig point to rest. It is not until I begin my return journey that I realise how strong the wind has become; walking west is much more arduous than walking east. By the time I approach the dry valley known as the Devil's Dyke, the wind has reached gale force. I hunch my shoulders and jostle my way through the turbulent air.

Whether in consequence of my reduced speed, or the fact that I am no longer facing into the sun, the Downs are more revealing now that I am walking west: my eyes can easily trace the undulations of the crest of the ridge. The morning's mist having dispersed, the low ground to the north is now disappearing into clouds of rain. A rust-coloured kestrel hovers ahead of me, drops halfway to the ground, hovers again, then swoops down for a kill.

Back in the Youth Hostel, I sit in the common room, crocheting, listening to the howl of the wind and trying not to fret about how my tent is faring in the hostel garden. One group of guests is on a training and getting-to-know-you weekend, prior to a trek abroad. When the group have returned from their day's training, one of their number – a young man with flat cap and fashionable stubble – decides that a post-exertion warm-down is required and initiates a yoga session in the centre of the common room. Participation for those in the trekking group is compulsory, and other guests are coerced into joining in by virtue of the fact that it is now impossible to move about the Youth Hostel. I am left with the impression that the young man is making things up as he goes along, particularly when he begins to make sucking noises to illustrate the importance of correct breathing.

"Breathe in [suck]. Put one foot behind the other. Now raise your arms above your head." Several of the group begin to wobble unsteadily.

"Breathe out [suck] and bring your shin down as close as you can to your back toe." This instruction is followed by an undercurrent of muttering about which toe is the back one.

One of the trekking group looks to be well into his seventies, and

I feel some concern that serious injury may result from him being asked to touch his toes or kick his own behind.

The weather continues to rage through the night and the next day: perfect for singing. A ferocious westerly is blowing parallel to the ridge, tearing away all sound except for its own muffled roar and the flute-like melodies of tubular metal gates. My own voice returns to me after a devious windswept path, and I am conscious of a delay between the words leaving my mouth and reaching my ears. I have a sense of disconnection from my own voice – of singing and listening to myself sing being separate acts. I belt out lines from the First World War poem inscribed on a wayside granite block close to Steyning, which I passed the day before yesterday: "I can't forget the lane that leads from Steyning to the Ring…"[61]

I haven't experienced wind like this since my ascent of Ben More Assynt in Sutherland – and I will be heading into the wind all day. In Scotland, I was aware of the dangers of the weather. Here, I am (perhaps unwisely) able to relax into it, to feel the joy of the wind in my face. The return of my hill-freedom-happiness accentuates its recent absence, and I feel more elated than I have done since I left Wales.

Reaching the village of Amberley, I come across a café just as dark, menacing clouds rear their heads over the western hills, so I dive inside. This is easily the most exorbitant café I have visited during my walk – the least expensive sandwich on the menu costs £9.95 – but, as some malevolent weather-god pelts the earth with fistfuls of rain like iron nails, I reflect that I would be willing to pay almost any price to avoid another drenching. The shower is sharp, thundery, but relatively fast-moving, and leaves the air clear and the colours of the land around me bright and keen.

More showers are roaming around when I leave the café, but I somehow avoid the worst of them and only get briefly splattered by the fringes of the rainclouds. It is quite a strange experience to pass so close to a thunderstorm but to avoid the soaking.

---

63 John Stanley Purvis, '*I Can't Forget the Lane That Goes from Steyning to the Ring*' (1916), see http://steyningmuseum.org.uk/purvis.htm.

I spend the night at Gumber Bothy, a bunkhouse and camping field run by the National Trust, which lies a short distance off the South Downs Way, south of Glatting Beacon. Hilaire Belloc wrote in poetic praise of Gumber and the surrounding landscape: his phrase "lift up your hearts in Gumber"[62] makes me think of the word as an action noun, like 'admiration', rather than the name of a place.

The year is beginning to fade: the sun peers over the ridge later and later with each passing dawn. Even before sunrise, I can sense the beauty of the morning. The clear-skied glory and the brilliant colours left by yesterday's rain have not yet leached away – but my phone buzzes with messages from friends, alerting me to forecast gales for the coming night.

The undulations of the South Downs mean that I am doing upwards of 700 metres of ascent per day, on a ridge which doesn't vary much outside 100 to 240 metres in height. The highest point of today's walk is the summit of Butser Hill: at 271 metres, this is the second-highest point within the South Downs National Park after Black Down. I ascend past groups of people with large rucksacks, trekking poles and South Downs Way guidebooks, recognisable from their distinctive red covers; these must be walkers completing their first day out from Winchester.

I find a hedgerow near Tegdown Hill where I can insinuate myself beneath a protective holly bush, though my tent is more exposed to the wind than I would like. The hedge also contains a mixture of mature ash and coppiced beech, but the tough, evergreen leaves of the holly form the greater part of the leaf-litter, which pricks holes in the groundsheet of my tent.

The forecast storm feels gentle in comparison to the strength of the wind on Truleigh Hill. However, I sleep fitfully, waking several times to find that my air mattress has shrunk to less than a quarter of its fully-inflated depth, presumably having been punctured by the holly which has damaged my groundsheet.

The South Downs Way becomes increasingly slippery after I pass the Old Winchester hill fort, and I slither my way down into the valley. By Exton I am worn out with the effort of trying to brace my drunkenly unsteady self against the mud. Seemingly beyond my

---

64 Hilaire Belloc, *Sonnets and Verse* (London: Duckworth, 1923).

control, my legs march me to the Meonstoke village shop for refreshment and rest. I am recuperating on a bench outside the shop when a local man comes out.

"Want one of these to go with your sandwiches?" He holds up a dog biscuit. I assume he's joking – surely I don't look that hungry? – and politely decline the offer.

The next shoppers to emerge are an older couple. Their accents suggest Canadians and their apparel suggests walkers on the South Downs Way. A shop assistant follows them outside and offers to "put up a brolly," a proposal which is met with looks of incomprehension, until the term 'brolly' is translated. I chat to the couple about conditions underfoot: if the path to the west is as muddy as it was at Old Winchester, I would be tempted to walk along roads for the remainder of the day, but the couple reassure me about the next section of the route.

Arriving in Winchester, I find that my accommodation has a washing machine, so lose little time in loading all of my clothes into it. Looking over my plans for the final section of my walk, I discover that the Ministry of Defence timetable for live firing on Dartmoor has just been published. The Okehampton range, which contains High Willhays, County Top of Devon, will be closed from 26th to 29th September: I have scheduled High Willhays for the 27th. I calculate that if I miss my planned rest day in Sherborne, and increase my daily mileage over the following week, I will be able to reach Dartmoor by Monday 25th September – but even the prospect of doing so is exhausting.

Pilot Hill (County Top of Hampshire), Walbury Hill (County Top of Berkshire,), Milk Hill (County Top of Wiltshire) and Lewesdon Hill (County Top of Dorset)

Winchester to Wellington. 152 miles, 3,640 metres ascent.
Thursday 14th – Thursday 21st September

Re-waterproofing my waterproofs; trying (and failing) to find the hole in my air mattress; telephoning campsites and motels to re-arrange my bookings in the hope that I can get to Dartmoor two days ahead of schedule – I have so many jobs to do that no time remains for either sight-seeing or relaxing. There is a silver lining to my enforced change of plan: I will be able to explore more of the south-west tip of England after I cross Dartmoor. If I can work out how to get there on foot, I decide that I will use the spare time to visit the Eden Project on my way to Land's End.

In the evening, I meet friends Alex and Katie and their son Matthew for a meal, and they deliver my next – and final! – set of maps.

I rise at 6.00am the next day, ready to make an early start. It is a perfect morning to be out early: cold and crisp, with limpid blue skies, although the chill in the air is a reminder that I will soon be finding it much colder to stay out overnight. It is a reminder, too, of my home village, where the onset of autumn causes pockets of cold air to form alongside the beck, then to press outwards into the woodlands and up the valley sides. This is the time of year when night-time running is most exhilarating: being suddenly doused with ice-sharpened air is uniquely refreshing and leaves you with the liberating sensation of having run through a wall.

A pleasant pathway through roadside woodland leads me out of Winchester. Skirting Moody's Down firing range, then crossing the A35 and the River Test, I arrive at Katie's parents' house in the village of Longparish. Jeremy gives me a tour of the garden, then Maggie serves tea and freshly-baked cake. There are two choices: a carrot cake, which was deemed a failure, and a coffee cake to compensate. I have a slice of each – both are delicious, elbowing the chocolate brownie at Loggerheads Country Park into third place.

Cake eaten, all six of us set off along the Test Way together.

Jeremy is extremely knowledgeable about the parish, is eager to show off local points of interest – including the second-largest anaerobic digester in the United Kingdom – and talks extensively about the history of rights of way in the area. An enthusiastic long-distance walker and runner, he also regales us with his tales of his experiences in the UK and abroad.

"I had to go for an interview at Bangor University. I thought I'd camp, so I drove up into the hills and camped when I found a flat patch of ground. Turns out I'd camped in a bus stop." I find an unexpected symmetry between Jeremy's tale and my night spent in the same university's Botanical Gardens.

Maggie turns back towards the washing up after only a mile; Katie (expecting their second child) a little later; and the others accompany me as far as St Mary Bourne. After their departure, I follow the Brenda Parker Way – named in memory of a keen walker from Andover – towards and through Binley, until I find a flat patch of woodland (which is definitely not a bus stop) in which to camp.

I have no difficulty recognising the figure standing outside Faccombe Church, although Rob and I have seen little of each other since we attended primary school. Rob now lives in Newbury, so has come to join me for what is, for him, a local section of my walk. We have much to talk about as we ascend Pilot Hill, the County Top of Hampshire, then follow a path called the Wayfarer's Walk westwards along the ridge.

Purely by chance, two friends whom I haven't seen in many years have chosen today to visit me. Helen – not the same Helen who visited me in the Highlands – with whom I lost contact more than a decade ago, is waiting on Walbury Hill. The summits of Pilot Hill and Walbury Hill are ostensibly uniform in character – trig points standing a little way off the main path – though not content with being merely a County Top, Walbury Hill is site of the area's largest Iron Age hillfort and holds the additional distinction of being the highest chalk hill in England. Having found a pair of glasses lying beside the Pilot Hill trig point, Rob bestows upon it the honour of being (probably) the highest chalk hill in sunglasses.

Possibly the highest chalk hill in sunglasses: Pilot Hill, County Top of Hampshire, 16th September 2017.

The rain returns. In the blink of an eye, Helen is wearing her waterproof trousers, while Rob and I hop around, each trying to balance on one foot whilst sliding the second into a tube of uncooperative plastic fabric. Re-attired, we continue along the ridge, passing Inkpen Hill, then descend to Wilton for a picnic beside the village pond. Laurence arrives, having driven down from Yorkshire that morning, then returns Helen and Rob back to their respective starting points, while I walk on alone towards our overnight accommodation in East Kennet.

"I knew that Helen had married since we last saw her," Laurence says, when we meet again at our B&B, "but it wasn't until Rob mentioned growing up in Lancashire that I realised he wasn't her husband."

Milk Hill, the County Top of Wiltshire, lies almost due south of East Kennet, on the continuation of the line of hills that I had been following with Rob and Helen. In honour of the name, the sky is a milky mist, and clouds caress the ridge. The summit itself is indistinct and uninspiring – a field of beans, without even a trig point – but the prospect back towards the ridge as I descend on its southern side gives more of an impression of the hill. The gentle slopes and mist-muted colours make the landscape appear stretched, like the fragile, supple skin which forms when bread-dough is torn.

Laurence has plans to visit Stonehenge before returning home, while I make do with the acrobatic squirrels of Urchfont. One squirrel is sitting atop a telegraph pole; when I approach, it nimbly runs along the wire, leaps into a gutter, then scrambles away over the rooftop. A second descends a pitched roof as though oblivious to the angle.

I buy drinking water in Market Lavington before grinding my way up onto Salisbury Plain. The skies begin to clear from the north east – surely this is the wrong direction? – so that as I finally reach the rim of the Plain I have views back to Milk Hill, now gratifyingly distant. I follow the Imber Range Perimeter Path anticlockwise, to camp in woodland near Coulston Hill. Laurence has generously swapped my punctured air mattress for his own; though his is longer, and therefore heavier, than mine, this change of equipment does mean that I can sleep through the night without the need to rouse myself and re-inflate my bed.

I am not the only nocturnal visitor to these woods. The morning light strobes the conical outlines of children's dens alongside more professional-looking dugouts sheltered by low walls of branches, presumably of army origin.

For most of the morning I continue around the rim of Salisbury Plain, then descend to Warminster to buy food and water. I am due to meet Mirva in Gillingham tomorrow morning, so my objective for the day is to find somewhere to camp within a two-hour walk from the town. I have identified a plausible patch of woodland on my map. A well-trodden path leads from the right of way into the trees. I duck under a 'Trespassers Will Be Prosecuted' sign and enter.

I blink, trying to rush my eyes into adjusting to the semi-darkness beneath the woodland canopy. Only a few yards away, and moving in my direction, is an elderly gentleman wearing a pink baseball cap, accompanied by a Jack Russell. I have little choice but to continue walking confidently towards him, aware that there is a chance that he, too, is trespassing.

"Hello," I say. "Are you going to prosecute me?" This is perhaps not the best choice of greeting, but no other words present themselves.

"Quite possibly," he replies, his tone inscrutable, then asks what I'm doing in his woods.

I explain that I am on a long-distance walk and am looking for somewhere to camp for the night, "So I was wondering whether I might camp in this woodland? Or whether you'd prefer me to walk on?"

"Of course you can."

With the feeling of relief comes knowledge of just how nervous I had been prior to hearing these few, generous, words. My mind continues to relax as my host talks about the woodland, showing me the different species of tree. "These are ash. There's some disease. Some of ours have it, and some don't. When I was young, these hazel trees were cut back every year, on a rota. You can see which ones have been coppiced. Now there isn't the demand for firewood, so we just cut what we need ourselves."

He also asks about my journey. "Bit off course, aren't you?" he remarks, when I tell him that I'm travelling from John O'Groats to Land's End, leading me into an explanation of my pursuit of the County Tops.

"I take my hat off to you," he says, raising his baseball cap.

"What are – ow! – these?" Mirva exclaims.

"They're nettles. It's probably best to walk round them."

"And what are the prickly ones?"

"Thistles."

"And the ones that stick scratchy things to your legs?"

"I think that's burdock. Don't you have *any* prickly vegetation in Finland?"

Mirva ponders the question. "There's something that grows round the castles in fairy tales, but I can't work out how to translate the name into English."

"We usually have brambles or briars in fairy stories," I reply.

"I actually wish we had brambles in Finland," Mirva decides. "I miss the blackberries."

Mirva, an academic based at a university in Finnish Lapland, has been attending a conference in London, and has thus been able to join me for today's walk. I have been trying to steer us from Gillingham to Sherborne by the most direct route possible, staying close to the railway line. Unfortunately, the paths I have chosen seem to be infrequently used and are rather overgrown. Mirva has walked extensively in the UK, but usually in Wales, or the Highlands of Scotland; I suspect this may be her first visit to the countryside of southern England, and I am not presenting its most welcoming aspect.

Since I am staying the next night in a town, I have booked accommodation at a small guest-house. Breakfast is supposed to be served from 6.30am. At 7.00am, the breakfast room is like the *Marie Celeste*: tables are set, tubs of cereal stand on the sideboard, and yet there is no sign of a living soul. I flick the light switch in the hope of attracting attention and sit down to read.

No members of staff have appeared by 7.30am, and I am anxious to be walking: in lieu of today's planned rest day, I have more than 25 miles to walk, and must reach the village of Thornecombe by 5.30pm in order to purchase water before the community shop shuts. In a cupboard beneath the sideboard, I find a stack of bowls. I retrieve the kettle from my room, along with a sachet of instant coffee and my own supply of powdered milk, then help myself to an indulgently large serving of muesli. Setting my room key upon the breakfast table, I walk out of the deserted guest-house at 8.00am.

A succession of flooded and muddy bridleways bring me to the foot of Lewesdon Hill, the County Top of Dorset. My trainers are already in a state of advanced disrepair, and my sodden-sore feet are abused further as I climb along a track bedded with jagged flints. Lewesdon Hill is my planned objective for tomorrow night and any further progress will bring me to the day after tomorrow. I rewind my thoughts and run through this one again, but having expunged a rest day from my schedule has confounded my concept of time: I abandon all attempts at comprehension, and focus instead on plodding onwards.

After Lewesdon Hill I climb Pilsdon Pen, thought to be the County Top until a survey in 1995 revealed Lewesdon to be the higher of the pair by two metres; indeed, the notice board at the bottom of the short, steep path leading to Pilsdon's summit proclaims it "traditionally the highest hill in Dorset." The contrast between the open heathland of

Pilsdon and the wooded Lewesdon is striking. The site of the hill fort on Pilsdon feels expansive, permissive, suggestive of freedom – for me, it evokes memories of Pendle Hill, in my native Lancashire, for the way the rest of the world gradually sinks from view as you ascend.

To reach Thornecombe, I need to cross the River Synderford. Descending towards the river, I am halfway across a field when a sixth sense tells me something is wrong. I turn. A Friesian cow is rushing full tilt down the hill towards me. Though cut by a serrated, metallic terror, my mind remains alert enough to register surprise: dairy cows are so used to being handled that they seldom cause trouble to walkers. I stamp my feet, wave my arms, scream "No!" and she stops dead, bucking and kicking her hind legs. Now I walk backwards down the hill with a wary eye on the cow and the herd behind her. The same cow makes two further attempts to rush me. It is hard to ignore the fear which engulfs me, and to stand my ground, yet I know that to run could be fatal. My composure evaporates when I am nearly at the gate, and I cannot prevent myself from sprinting the final few yards. With a metal barrier now between myself and the herd, my mind tentatively reconnects with my physical self. I find myself shaking, and drained of energy.

A steep climb up into Thornecombe, and the village has a water tap – I need not have worried about my arrival time. I head into the community shop anyway, where I am warmly welcomed by a group of local ladies relaxing over a post-keep-fit cup of tea. When they ask where I've walked from today, my reply of 'Sherborne' is echoed back in a chorus of incredulity and my toasted teacake is augmented with lashings of butter and jam. The keep-fit ladies also proudly inform me that I have just conquered the second-steepest climb in Dorset – the steepest apparently being a street in Shaftesbury named Gold Hill.

I walk out of the shop into a newly-damp world, and pitch my tent beneath the spreading arms of a beech in nearby woodland. My campsite is sheltered, but the slope is too steep. To prevent everything from sliding off down the hill, I create an artificial ledge by stuffing my rucksack beneath my air mattress; this works provided I don't wriggle. There is not enough room to sit upright, even hunched, which makes cooking something of a challenge.

My beech sanctuary provides some protection from the rain, but the tent is still sodden in the morning, and the weather is miserable. So are my feet, in desperate need of respite from wet socks and abrasive tarmac. Perhaps in response to the weather *For those in peril on the sea* echoes round inside my head. I fall into step with the music and march towards Chard at Church-of-England speed.

The fine views of Somerset promised from Castle Plain have been supplanted by simmering, silver clouds. Off road, I slip and squelch through woodland sludge, trying to decipher which muddy trench is the right of way; on the road, rust-tinged signposts toll the weary distance still to walk. Eight miles. Six miles. Five and a half miles. Taunton is teasingly nearer than Wellington (my objective for the night), but still too far. I miss a turning on a bridleway from Forches Corner, led astray by a winding ribbon of fallen pine needles, and suddenly realise that I am not descending, as I should be, but following the edge of the woodland. My soft pine path disgorges me onto a steep, flinty forestry track, which I tumble down on hairpin bends, my feet screaming at the uneven surface, until I find myself back on the bridleway.

With only three miles remaining to Wellington, the weather begins to clear. The path I choose to take me to a point where I can cross the M5 plunges blindly into a field of sweetcorn, the plants towering well above my head. I resort to navigating by GPS; although a magnetic bearing would work equally well, the GPS allows me to gauge my progress as the cursor blinks dolefully across the screen towards the motorway bridge. Upon reaching the town, I collect a new – and hopefully final – set of footwear, which has been delivered into the foster-care of a petrol station. These are low-cut fabric walking shoes, although rubber boots might be more appropriate to both location and atmospheric conditions.

Dunkery Beacon (County Top of Somerset) and High Willhays (County Top of Devon)

Wellington to Okehampton. 80 miles, 3,160 metres ascent.
Friday 22nd – Tuesday 26th September

I wallow in depths of despondency. I will never get there. I will never get anywhere. Today's walk is too far. I'm bone-tired, and my feet have withdrawn their cooperation. Although dry, the new shoes are very stiff and would benefit from being broken in; not having that luxury, the shoes are breaking my feet in instead.

On the outskirts of Wellington, I waste a good twenty minutes trying to locate a bridge over the River Tone, eventually finding a slender metal arch, concealed by vegetation. I curse myself for not moving faster, for not having set out earlier. Once across the river, I try to think in small stages – from this stile to the next signpost – but it seems impossible that these tiny distances can ever constitute meaningful progress.

A narrow trail round the shores of the whimsically-named Wimbleball Reservoir leads me to rest and revival: a cheese-and-chutney sandwich and a pot of tea in the Duck Café. The savoury food is extremely welcome. I have been subsisting on predominantly sweet provisions for so long that I can barely face eating. No more malt loaf, cereal bars, or dried fruit, please: I am only tempted by the prospect of plain, rough, bread.

It is drizzling again as I leave the café. This is the trailing edge of a weather front that should by now be sweeping across Wales and north-west England. I had half hoped (not with any real expectation) that it might miss me. But, as the rain starts to drive in, I am at last climbing high, towards the purple moors. The changing colour and texture of the mud, from a very ordinary brown to brick-red, slick and sticky, apprises me that I am walking into a new geological area. A rainbow hangs low in the sky to my north east: tawny, bright colours, with a paler supernumerary arc beneath. Dark skies to the south west contradict the rainbow's promise of the end of the deluge and liberate me from any concern about pitching my tent before the weather deteriorates. Instead, I begin to worry about whether I will reach Wheddon Cross before nightfall.

Eventually traipsing into Wheddon Cross, I fill my water bottles at the petrol station and briefly consider sleeping on the veranda of the Moorland Hall, deciding against it on the probability of getting even wetter if the angle of the prevailing wind changed. I press on, following Tom's Path in the direction of Dunkery Beacon. A barn owl silently folding its way through the night startles at my presence and veers away, momentarily losing its serene rhythm. I sense its fear; the same fear I feel when my bicycle skitters too close to the kerb, the fleeting sensation of falling before I regain control and right myself. Not for the first time, a question forms in my mind: why do I hear only tawny owls, but see only barn owls?

Moss-covered limbs of lifeless rhododendron have woven a deep mat around the trunks of the trees. I wonder if the rhododendron has been deliberately cut and killed, but never cleared. I locate an approximately flat patch of rhododendron-free earth upon which to pitch my tent, realising as I do so that the ground is not as level as I had first thought – it is going to be another nocturnal battle against gravity.

It seems to have stopped raining by morning, but everything is very wet, and what I can see of the sky looks muted and greyish. Blood begins to stream from my nose as I am packing up the tent, so the first half-hour of the walk is spent with my head down and my nose pinched between finger and thumb. When I emerge from the top of the path at Dunkery Gate and raise my gaze from my chest, I realise that the day's grey hues are a result of thick, sobbing fog. An easy track sweeps to the summit of Dunkery Beacon, which is marked by a squat, troll-like cairn, so I am unconcerned at the prospect of navigating in low visibility. Now only two County Tops remain to be climbed.

As I descend towards Exford via tumuli on Rowbarrows, my solitude is disturbed. Groups of teenagers coalesce out of the fog at regular intervals, their large rucksacks labelling them as participants on Duke of Edinburgh's Award expeditions. I rest in the Exford bus shelter, and watch as one such group strides confidently off along the B3224 in the direction of Wheddon Cross. Ten minutes later they're back at the crossroads looking bemused and sheepish. Maps are consulted, rotated, consulted again, before the group opt for the minor road towards Edgcott.

An exposed, high road across Exmoor leads me to North Molton.

*Summit of Dunkery Beacon, County Top of Somerset,
23rd September 2017.*

Though I am constrained to tarmac, the open moorland around me
buoys my spirits after yesterday's despondency. Most of the heather
has already faded to a coppery brown, and the sight arouses a genial
longing for my Yorkshire home, although I am aware that the resemblance is superficial in some respects. The mud is a different colour,
and there are hedges here, high on the moors – I suspect that beech
would struggle to grow at this altitude in Yorkshire.

From North Molton, I choose a footpath alongside the River Mole,
but find it so wet and muddy that I soon regret my decision to leave
the tarmac. The riverside marsh is so extensive that I cannot simply
sidestep it, and I frequently sink to my ankles. When I arrive at my
campsite in South Molton, I try to rinse the mud off my shoes – and
inevitably fill them with water. The interlude of dry feet is over.

The overnight gate-crashers are of the usual species, but with a
new character trait: the slugs have changed colour. When the mud
was the colour of coffee or chocolate, the slugs were bright orange.
Now, when the mud is red, the slugs are greyish-brown, as though
they feel the need to stand out, the antithesis of chameleons.

The next day is another day of road walking, across a map flecked with chevrons. Each crossroads has a name, which is often marked on my Ordnance Survey map and always written on the vertical of the signpost with the silhouette of a St John's Cross in place of the word 'cross'. Jose's Cross seems to be the subject of local controversy; the 's' in Jose has been covered by a sticker bearing the letter 'c'. Signposted distances are less useful: the distance to King's Nympton seems to vary more in accordance with the space between the two words than the distance I've walked in its general direction. Later, Bondleigh plunges from two miles to half a mile distant in the space of about 400 yards.

The church in Chulmleigh, with its overly-tall tower topped by four conical ears, has the appearance of a startled rabbit. The church bells are being rung as I arrive in the village, but without any discernible sense of rhythm or harmony; it sounds as though the bells are being tumble-dried, or there are three teams of bell-ringers in aggressive competition. When the cacophony stops abruptly at 10.45am, I have the strong impression of sudden deafness. Rain is forecast for the afternoon, so I have a long mid-morning rest on a bench in the centre of the village and spread my tent out to air.

"That looks interesting." The observation is made in a distinctly Queen's English accent.

"I'm just trying to dry out," I reply, keen to reassure the passer-by that I don't intend to camp here.

"What is it?" he asks, sounding a little like a child who has just received a gift of uncertain nature. I reflect that I have pitched the tent upside down (the inside being wetter than the outside), so maybe it isn't at all obvious that it's a tent.

My stop proves well timed. As I descend to cross the Little River Dort, the rain sets in again and doesn't really let up for the rest of the afternoon. Soon, my waterproofs begin to leak and water soaks down my trousers into my socks and shoes. The fronts of my shins are beginning to ache, I think in consequence of my unrelenting road-walking, and my feet increasingly feel like flippers, flapping around uselessly.

Once again, daybreak reveals radii of slugs converging on my tent.

After plodding along roads to Okehampton, I linger in the town, willing the day to get going, but wary of exploring too thoroughly while I wait, as I will have a whole day to spend here tomorrow. By late morning, I conclude that the sun isn't going to rise today, and begin the steep ascent out of the town towards the grim, grey clouds concealing Dartmoor.

The date is September 25th: I have reached Dartmoor one day in advance of the MOD live firing. Although the moors are open to walkers today, soldiers are climbing ant-like up the ridge of Rowtor, while a machine gun emplacement fires (what I hope are) blanks down towards them. I stand and watch as the tiny, dark green figures swarm up to the summit of the tor and 'capture' it. There are several other walkers, too, on the ridge between Yes Tor and High Willhays. One solitary woman looks to be equipped for the Andes rather than Dartmoor, wearing gaiters, a down jacket and a red knitted hat with ear flaps, tassel and a cord under the chin.

Tors rise around me: needles of fissured granite that, for reasons that are only partially understood, have withstood the weathering processes that swept the surrounding bedrock into a smoothly undulating plain. Dartmoor's iconic tors are close cousins of those I saw in the Cairngorms many months ago.

By the time I have rounded West Mill Tor the cloud has lifted from the summits and pale patches of sky are deepening towards a rich blue, vindicating my late start. I visit Yes Tor first, then High Willhays, my penultimate County Top. I had planned to retrace my steps past West Mill Tor, but on a sudden impulse I strike off the path and plunge down the hillside along Red-a-Ven Brook. At once I have the joys of soft ground beneath my feet and the spray of water up the backs of my legs. The bracken on the higher moors is the colour of caramel: Dartmoor must already be experiencing frosts. I have walked through an entire year in the life of the bracken.

Reaching Meldon Reservoir, I sit for over an hour, drying my tent, reading a newspaper purchased earlier in the day and savouring the autumn colours that are beginning to smoulder now that the seeping rain has finally ceased. The decision to dry my tent proves wise; when I reach my accommodation at Betty Cottles Inn, my room is tiny – the floor area is exactly twice the size of the small single bed. I rinse my clothes in the bath, but struggle to get them dry.

In the morning, my clothes are still damp, so I put on a sleeveless dress (a recent useful acquisition from a charity shop), with a long-sleeved thermal base-layer beneath to hide the fact that I'm not wearing a bra. The combination looks a little odd – but the only other option available to me would be waterproofs with nothing underneath. I walk the two miles back into Okehampton to spend my rest day there.

The Tourist Information Centre provides me with the map I will need to find the Eden Project, but not the one that would help me re-join my planned route, because "We don't do Cornwall." I am also given a lesson in the correct Devonian, Cornish and Australian (apparently they have a place of the same name) pronunciations of Launceston, none of which I can really get my northern tongue around. A cupboard beneath a display unit is unlocked, a leaflet is extracted and then presented to me with a reverential air: "You can have one of these. They're very rare." My endangered species of leaflet is a route description for the Two Castles Trail, a 24 mile walk linking Okehampton and Launceston castles: perfect for tomorrow's walk.

Autumn colours, Meldon Viaduct, Dartmoor, 25th September 2017.

Brown Willy (County Top of Cornwall)

Okehampton to Land's End. 118 miles, 3,330 metres ascent.
Wednesday 27th September – Tuesday 3rd October

My resolve to follow the Two Castles Trail evaporates almost before
I step out of the Inn. The trail tacks up and down the edge of Dartmoor
– or, as the leaflet puts it, "meanders through rolling countryside" –
while a cycle route glides effortlessly along a disused railway line:
there is no contest. Close to the village of Stourton, there is a peculiar
section where for 230 metres the cycle route is a right of way only
when bounding gates are unlocked: apparently this occurs during August, on Bank Holidays and otherwise at the landowner's discretion.
I am relieved to find the gates open.

The moors above Bearlake Dam are seething with hounds, while
mounted fox-hunters jog languidly over the heather. I do not find the
hunt upsetting, as many do; rather it angers me that people should
flaunt their enjoyment of tearing a living creature apart. The crimson-
clad hunt leader is closest to me. It is evident from his tirade of ex-
pletives – "Come on Rodney. Move, you f*****g horse!" – that his
contempt for living creatures is not limited to foxes.

I ease my way back onto the Two Castles Trail and follow it to
Lewtrenchard, where I rest on a churchyard bench. A sign on the wall
of the church directs visitors to the graves of the Reverend Sabine
Baring-Gould and his wife, Grace. The surname would be euphonious
for one of the Magi, although it also possesses a teasing familiarity,
which lingers until a leaflet inside the church informs me that, in addition to being vicar of the parish in the early twentieth century, Baring-Gould penned the hymns *Onward, Christian Soldiers* and *Now
The Day Is Over.*

Back on the bench, I am approached by a local man.

"Are you walking the Two Castles Trail? What did you make of
the path in the field up there?" He gesticulates towards the slope
above the churchyard.

"I'm going the other way," I apologise. "Why? Is there a surprise
waiting for me?"

He just smiles. I have a suspicion that whatever is to be found 'in
the field up there' is more likely to be mud and/or frisky bullocks, than

someone dispensing free chocolate, so decide to circumvent it. I step out of the churchyard and resume my walk, a patchwork medley of *Onward, Christian Soldiers* and *We Three Kings* cycling through my head. Later, when I do encounter a field of cattle, I discover that I have lost my nerve after the Dorset Dairy Cow Débâcle, and find myself scampering through slurry, running for safety in a field of elderly donkeys. The safety is relative: the donkeys gang up on me and hound me out of their field, but they move with a merciful, arthritic slowness.

From Launceston, I am tossed along the fog-filled valley by the barking of farm dogs, each escorting me off his territory and into that of the next dog. Almost every place name begins with 'Tre': Tredidon, Tredundle, Trebursye, Trecongdon, Treniffle. Words that appear ludicrous in isolation are somehow rendered acceptable toponyms by the addition of a 'Tre-' prefix, which denotes a settlement or homestead. Launceston, once the county capital, is conspicuous for its dissent: the Cornish spelling of the name, *Lannstevan*, feels almost Welsh, and I am wont to write it as *Llansteffan*.

'Brown Willy' is an Anglicisation of the Cornish *Bronn Wennili*, hill of swallows. In Scandinavian legend, swallows are the birds of consolation, named for their cries of *svale*! as they soared above the crucified Christ. This hill of swallows is my hill of consolation: though I know I must soon return to civilisation, the morning's fog is lifting and this final County Top of my three-thousand-mile journey brings also my last night of wild camping, and a last, nourishing breath of moorland freedom. I descend from the summit feeling at once quiet triumph and resigned sadness, a song lyric floating above the dissonant chords striking my mind: "Come down from the mountain, you have been gone too long…"[63]

Belting rain fills the night air. I have camped in the outline of old mine workings on Trehudreth Moor, so the shell of the building around me provides some shelter. By dawn, the moor is waterlogged. Jets of water squirt up from every step. I am navigating from the map purchased in Okehampton Tourist Information Centre – it is not the most recent edition, and the A30 appears to have been upgraded since its publication. A footpath comes to a dead end by the dual

---

65 Fleet Foxes, 'Ragged Wood', *Fleet Foxes,* (2008).

Brown Willy, County Top of Cornwall, 28th September 2017.

carriageway, beside a sign:

THE A30 IS UNSUITABLE FOR PEDESTRIANS

I think the moor is also unsuitable for pedestrians – unless amphibious – but this will be my last experience of moorland for weeks, if not months, so I would not leave it a step sooner than I need to.

In Bodmin, I stock up on food supplies and purchase a newspaper, which I flick through over a cup of coffee, although its real purpose is to absorb the water which nightly soaks up through the floor of my tent.

That afternoon I walk through swampy, moss-covered deciduous woodland. I don't know if the flooding between the trees is normal, or due to last night's heavy rain; I am glad that I will not need to camp here, as I have booked a camping pitch at the Youth Hostel at the Eden Project. When I eventually reach it, I find the Youth Hostel somewhat bizarre: the rooms are termed 'snoozeboxes', which is a euphemism for portacabins, and the communal area is a large marquee. The camping field is far from flat, but I have it to myself, so there is no competition for the toilets or showers.

I spend the final rest day of my walk at the Eden Project. The clouds collapse under their watery burdens, disgorging a harsh rain which limits my appreciation of the outdoor garden areas. I spend as long as I can in the bio-domes: the rainforest bio-dome is over-humid and I am quickly discovered by the resident ants when I perch on a bench – but the Mediterranean bio-dome is a more comfortable temperature for me to sit and crochet. I initially assume that the birdsong is piped, like the atmospheric rainforest sound effects playing in the neighbouring dome, but then I realise that the acoustics of the dome itself are amplifying the song of robins perched high on the metal girders of the dome's frame. A fragment from Wordsworth's *Prelude* comes to mind, evoking a melodic ancestry to the geodesic modernity of the Eden bio-domes.

> *The invisible bird*
> *Sang to itself that there I could have made*
> *My dwelling-place, and lived for ever there*
> *To hear such music.*[64]

The next day's walk is governed by the need to reach my campsite before my map dissolves. I try to memorise chunks of the route, so that I don't have to consult the map too frequently. Each time I tug it out from the pocket of my waterproof coat, it looks twice as soggy as previously. I wrap it in a plastic carrier bag and stuff some tissue into my pocket in an attempt to absorb some of the water. According to the weather forecast, it is not raining at the moment, but will do later. I could believe that, if I could somehow contrive to get underneath the cloud, it might not be raining, but the mordant cloud extends down to the ground.

The hardest navigation of the day is escaping from the Eden Project. There are cycle-route signs, but they are all labelled with places that I know I don't want to go to (Bodmin: been there already) or can't find on my map (Wheal Martin). By the time I work out that I'm on the wrong track, it's too late (or rather, I've gone too far downhill) for me to want to retrace my steps, so I have to work out how best to curve round and reorient myself.

The 'Tre' prefixes have been replaced by 'Wheal', which is a

---

66 William Wordsworth, *Two-Part Prelude* (London, 1799).

Cornish word meaning 'place of work'. Usually the second word is a name: Wheal Rose, Wheal Jane, Wheal Alfred – but I also see a sign to Wheal Busy. Wheal Rose campsite gives me my last night under canvas free of charge, provided I name-drop the campsite at every opportunity. It's a lovely site, set in an area dotted with old chimneys from tin mines, although there are some unusual plumbing arrangements in the ladies' washroom.

The morning brings liberation, as I realise how much of my equipment I can throw away: one of my two water bottles; my tent repair kit; a nearly-empty gas cylinder. I could actually throw away the tent and sleeping bag, but, though the tent is badly damaged, and the sleeping bag has lost much of its down, they will still be serviceable – once they have been thoroughly dried.

I'm so tired that I am grateful for the lighter load. My exhaustion must be visible to others: when I stop to purchase food in Camborne, an elderly lady offers me a sandwich and a packet of crisps, with the words, "I don't want to offend you, love, but I saw you on my way in, and bought these, and wondered if you'd like them." I try to decline the offer as politely as I can, wondering if I have just been mistaken for a homeless person.

I can sense that I am walking along a peninsula, even though I catch only occasional glimpses of the sea on either side. It is the same feeling that I get when walking up Borrowdale, in the Lake District: that the land – or sea – is pressing in on both sides. I had vaguely anticipated that the tapering peninsula would act as a funnel, and that I would suddenly start to encounter bands of other long-distance walkers converging on Land's End. But I meet almost no-one.

I don't know quite what I had expected of Cornwall, but it certainly wasn't this mixture of heathland around old mines, and saturated woodland of stunted oaks and birches, hemming in the towns, with seemingly very little space left for agricultural fields.

The place names on the map grow more and more ludicrous. Yesterday, I walked close to Goon Gumpas; today, I pass Splattenridden and Praze-an-Beeble. I decide that the Ordnance Survey have mapped only the coastline and major settlements (which have normal, respectable names, like Redruth and St Ives) and then passed the map to Roald Dahl, or perhaps Lewis Carroll, to fill in the blanks.

I reach the outskirts of Penzance by mid-afternoon. Before

heading to the Youth Hostel, I have shopping to do: clean underwear, soap and shampoo from a supermarket, then trousers, a shirt and jumper from charity shops in the town centre. I rent a towel from the Youth Hostel, and by half past five am cleaner and better-smelling than I have been since June. It feels wrong to be enjoying the cleanliness and new clothes when I have not actually completed my walk, but there is so much happiness to be found in a seventy-five-pence bottle of shampoo.

On my final day of walking, I set out at first light, and watch as a burning orange glow rises out of Penzance bay, then fades as the sun ascends behind low clouds. I walk first in the wrong direction, to Newlyn, the place where sea level was measured and defined in the 1970s. The Ordnance Datum benchmark is inside the tidal observatory in the lighthouse at the end of the south pier, and is not publicly accessible, so I walk along the harbour front, then visit the nearest fundamental benchmark at Tolcarne. Only about 800 metres horizontally from the Newlyn Datum, it is already 95 metres above sea level.

The walk from Newlyn to Land's End is a recapitulation of the themes of my walk. The inland footpaths are muddy, overgrown and poorly marked – or bear signs requesting that walkers follow the way-marked route, but then no waymarkers. I encounter fields of cows which take a dislike to me, paths that don't exist, paths that exist ephemerally and abandon me in fields of cows... I climb over stone walls and broken gates, and plough my way through stands of towering sweetcorn. Then for the final short distance from Sennen Cove I freewheel along the gloriously smooth tarmac of National Cycle Route 3.

Mirroring my visit to John O'Groats, the visitor attractions of Land's End are winding down for the end of the tourist season. The gift shops are noticeably low on stock, although it is possible to purchase a Land's End Donut, or visit the Shaun the Sheep Experience. I prefer instead to look out across the Atlantic, to the waves breaking around the lighthouse.

Turning back inland, I complete my pilgrimage beside the Land's End signpost. Visitors can choose to add the distance to their own home town beneath the arm reading 'John O'Groats 874'. I notice with some pride that I have walked further than the signposted distance to New York – a mere 3,147 miles. I collect a stack of letters

The end at last! 3rd October 2017.

and numbers from the kiosk beside the signpost. When my turn comes
to have my photograph taken, I spell out

VIA COUNTY TOPS 3400[67]

"Where's that?" the official photographer asks. "Is it in the UK?"

The end.

---

67 It was not until I returned home and did some adding up that I realised I had
walked more than 100 miles further than this.

Epilogue

Yorkshire
Sunday 31st December

Night-running. Racing myself through the darkness, exhilarated by the speed at which I can move through the night air, unencumbered by a heavy rucksack or hiking boots. Nearly three months have elapsed since I returned home, and I still feel as though I am only just beginning to taste the freedom of being able to run.

Reflected moonlight outlines the banks of late-December snow where it has drifted under the hedgerows and not yet melted, but the track is rough and gritty beneath my feet. Night-running transcends space and time, invoking a distorted law of general relativity, so that the faster I run, the more my gravity pulls stars from the heavens. My mind whirls with half-remembered lines from a poem by Hamish Brown: *"Freedom is a glance / At the wheeling stars and we / Find that sight by choice, not chance."*[66] To me, these words serve as a reminder that freedom can sometimes be as simple as choosing to view our lives from a different perspective, whether by exploring the minutiae of our immediate surroundings, or losing ourselves in the immensity of the night skies.

By the time I reach our cottage the darkness above me is heavy with twinkling lights. I have chosen to end my wandering, but I can still choose freedom.

Besides these alternations in pace and perspective, there have been many other changes to become accustomed to. As the south west peninsula funnelled me down towards Land's End, I found myself wondering how I would manage to re-integrate into society. Would I settle down, content in having achieved a lifetime's ambition? Or

---

68 Hamish Brown, 'Choice', *Speak to the Hills: An Anthology of 20th Century British and Irish Mountain Poetry,* Hamish Brown and Martyn Berry (eds.) (Aberdeen: Aberdeen University Press, 1985) p.7.

would I find myself impossibly restless, with even more sense of un-belonging than I had felt before my walk?

Now, as the year of my County Tops walk draws to a close, I re-alise that reality is more complex than a binary choice. The need to earn a living means that I no longer have the freedom to walk mile after mile, day after day – but neither do I have an itinerary, a list telling me which county or hill I need to make for next. I am not trav-elling through changing landscapes – but I can watch winter weaving its intricate web through the village that I choose to call 'home'. And so I feel that I am, finally, becoming re-acclimatised to life indoors, reconciling myself to sleeping in the same place each night, in a warm, dry, slug-free bed, where the sounds to lull me to sleep are the creaking of the roof timbers and the tick of an analogue clock, rather than the soft velvet calls of tawny owls. As Hamish Brown's poetry reminds us, freedom has many guises.

This is the time of year when the media occupies itself with retro-spective analyses of the events of the preceding twelve months. This year, I feel an odd sense of disconnection, having been out of touch with current affairs during much of my long walk. Rather than being recapitulations, the digests of the year's news help me to pick up the threads of stories which I have partially or wholly overlooked.

At the same time, they bring a fresh sense of isolation: I can learn but a little of what others have done during my absence, and find it impossible to communicate the enormity of my walk, even to those who have shared a part of it with me.

We are all shaped by our experiences in life. Some events con-tribute to a gradual metamorphosis of our character or world-view, while others feel like thresholds that vanish once we have crossed them, bringing more abrupt and irrevocable changes. Experiences shared can bring us closer to those that we share them with, while others serve to separate us from people who will never see what we have seen, feel what we have felt, know what we have known. There is a passage by John Steinbeck which I love because it conveys this idea in language which echoes Hamish Brown's star-poetry:

*I cannot go back to my town and my fields for I have seen great
beauty and I must stay behind… I am different and my friends
would not know me… And because I would be different my
friends would reject me and hate me. I have seen the stars.*[69]

Steinbeck is also making the point that even insignificant events can
lead to significant changes, for he later reveals that the character
speaking above is unable to return home simply because he has seen
a merry-go-round. I feel that I understand this sentiment perfectly:
my County Tops walk has been a tapestry of formative experiences,
some transient, some trivial, which together have opened a fresh gulf
between me and the rest of the world.

I feel this gulf most acutely when asked such simplistic questions
as: What was it like? What was the best bit? It would be utterly hope-
less to attempt to condense seven months and 3,500 miles into a convenient sound-bite, or to pinpoint a single location as being the 'best
bit', whatever that might mean. I can talk of the Loch Pattack sunset
and the rain in Pontneddfechan. I can misrepresent my walk through
photographs taken only in fair weather or photogenic surroundings.
But – even through the pages of this diary – I cannot convey just how
demanding, and how rewarding, it was.

Then there are the people who persist in asking: *Why?*

My walk has been meaningless, purposeless, for anyone but me.
I have done it for me, and me alone. There is no higher meaning to
be found in my pursuit of the County Tops. But, if we proceed with
thoughts in this vein, then life itself is meaningless – and therein lies
its beauty. In our incentivised society, we have a tendency to associate
actions with rewards, to seek to justify, to falsely imbue life with
meaning, rather than letting life imbue us with wonder: we're all looking for answers where no answers can be found.[70] Yet we inhabit the
extraordinary everyday world; a world of exquisite meaningless de-
lights, "could we but look with seeing eyes."[71] Jim Perrin encapsulates this perfectly, describing his reaction to the world as a beautiful,
painful ache:

---

69 John Steinbeck, *The Wayward Bus* (New York, 1947).
70 Laura Marling, 'When Were You Happy (and How Long Has that Been)?'
    Once I Was an Eagle (Virgin, 2013).
71 Christina Rossetti, *Later Life: A Double Sonnet of Sonnets,* (1881).

*I am at a loss to find meaning in the rainbow shimmer that
follows a hare through the dew or the pulsing colour of bluebells
or the whistle of wind through a raven's pinions. I can feel them
only as simple wonder, the ache of which stops my heart.*[72]

This year has, for me, been both extraordinary and everyday. I have
done nothing more than walk, that most ordinary of activities. Yet my
walk has granted me an exalted, absolute freedom, and led me
through an extraordinary spectrum of landscapes and perspectives,
from Highland winter to West Country autumn. I know that I will
never forget the solitude of walking alone on high moors, the sweet,
buttery scent of gorse, the taste of liquorice mixed with snow. For a
whole seven months, I have been able to do exactly what I have always wanted to do: to walk, to climb and to explore the landscape
around me. Returning to civilisation, a stationary abode and regular
employment, I am aware of how privileged I am to have experienced
such freedom.

As I conclude my writing, there is one more thing that I must do.
I have a new ribbon to sew onto my patchwork map.

---

72 Jim Perrin, *Travels with the Flea: And Other Eccentric Journeys,* 2nd ed.
(Glasgow: The Inpinn, 2003).

Acknowledgements

To all those named in the text, who provided company and moral or logistical support along the way, I extend my heartfelt thanks.

I would also like to thank the following people in particular:

Helen, Becky, Ray, Laura, Naomi, Mirva, Rob, Helen, Thurstan and Caroline, for your companionship and cheerful conversation; Jan, Chris and Carrie, Chris and Hannah, for providing safe places to sleep; Anne, Diana and Martin, Jeremy and Maggie, for your hospitality – and cake; Anne and Paul, Val and Nigel, Maggie and John, Katie and Alex, Richard and Elizabeth, for delivering maps and supplies; Anne and Richard, Ann and Andrew, Hannah and Ed, Alan, Sharon, Adele, Michael, David, Jess and Andy, for finding time to visit me; Ian, for the loan of your fiddle; Alasdair, for the use of your playing cards; Rebecca and Mike, for advice on keeping warm; Mark, for translating political events into language comprehensible to a nonparticipant; my colleagues, for putting up with a stream of increasingly unhinged postcards; Richard, for information about his father, Ted; Matthew and Stephanie, for forgiving me for what I put you through; Val, for diligent proof-reading and lessons in grammar (I accept full responsibility for any remaining grammatical errors); and above all, Laurence, for encouragement at every step of the way, from concept to completion.

Overview of route.

Appendix 1: Walking by Numbers

Defining the County Tops

There are many different lists of County Tops,[73] depending upon whether you consider current or historic (in England, this broadly means pre-1974) counties, unitary authorities, London boroughs, and other administrative areas. The Association of British Counties[74] can be a useful source of information regarding the possible interpretations of the word 'county'. I chose to walk between the historic counties, principally because these are the counties I believe in (and I had no particular desire to climb to the County Top of Milton Keynes Unitary Authority).

I allowed myself to omit a County Top if either (i) it lies on an island, and could not therefore be reached on foot, or (ii) climbing it would be likely to result in my death (for example because of extreme adverse weather, or military firing). However, I was relieved to find that no hills fell into the latter category.

For County Tops within England and Wales, I based my list of hills upon Edward Moss' 1951 article[75] in the *Rucksack Club Journal*; for summits within Scotland, I used Jonny Muir's excellent guidebook.[76] In both cases, the Database of British and Irish Hills (available online[77]) proved a valuable source of grid references.

73 Long Distance Walkers' Association, 'Hillwalkers' Register 3: The County Tops of England, Wales and Ireland', accessed 26 December 2017, https://www.ldwa.org.uk/hillwalkers/register3.php.

74 Association of British Counties. 'The problem of "county confusion" – and how to resolve it.' http://county-wise.org.uk/counties/county-confusion/.

75 Edward Moss, 'The County Tops of England and Wales', *Rucksack Club Journal* XI, no. 4 (1951), pp.319-27.

76 Jonny Muir, *The UK's County Tops: 82 Walks to reach the top of 91 Historic Counties* (Milnthorpe: Cicerone, 2011).

77 'Database of British and Irish Hills', n.d., http://www.hills-database.co.uk/.

HIGHPOINTS

Summary of the walk

Total distance: 3,573 miles
Total ascent: 119,396 metres

Mean daily distance (excluding rest days): 19.1 miles
Mean daily ascent (excluding rest days): 638 metres

Maximum daily distance: 30 miles
(Thursday 15th June, Elloughton Dale to Normanby Top)
Maximum daily ascent: 1,460 metres
(Friday 2nd June, Grasmere to Moasdale)

Number of walking days: 187
Number of rest days: 24
Total: 211

Accommodation:
Camping: 124
Hostels: 29
Bothies/bird hides: 4
With friends: 7
Travelodges/B&Bs/other indoor accommodation: 47

Number of pairs of boots/shoes worn out: 7

A note on units

The daily mileages and ascents given within the text and the itinerary table (Appendix 3) are rounded to the nearest mile and ten metres, respectively; for this reason the total mileage and ascent given by my itinerary do not tally exactly with the figures quoted above, which are calculated more exactly. The locations of County Tops are given as six-figure grid references (using the UK National Grid), and their heights are given to the nearest whole metre.

I make no apology for the fact that I use both metric and imperial units when giving distances, and simply chose whichever system of units felt more appropriate at the time. I have, however, endeavoured to use only metres for the heights of hills.

Appendix 2: Equipment

Rucksack

Rucksack (60 litres)	1.4kg
Waterproof bags to line rucksack	300g

Sleeping

Tent	900g
Sleeping bag	800g
Inflatable mattress (¾ length)	300g
*Bivvy bag	300g

Cooking

Stove	90g
Cooking pot	120g
†Fuel cannister (x 2)	460g
Matches	50g
Mug	100g
Spoon	10g
Pen knife (with can opener)	80g
Matches	50g
†Water bottles (2 x 1-litre bottles, one empty)	1kg
†Food	2kg
Water purification tablets	50g

Clothing

Underwear	Worn
Thin socks	
Thick socks	
*Thin long-sleeved baselayer	
T-shirt	
Leggings	
Fleece	
Boots	
Spare underwear	50g
Spare thin socks (x 2 pairs)	100g
Spare thick socks (x 2 pairs)	200g
Spare t-shirt	140g
Spare leggings	200g
Waterproof jacket	580g
Waterproof trousers	300g
*Balaclava	100g
*Mittens	200g
Fingerless gloves	100g

Other

Mobile phone (+ charging plug)	500g
†Maps	400g
†Book to read	500g
Camera	400g
Notebook & pen	Combined weight: 800g
Wallet	
Compass	
Whistle	
Torch	
First aid supplies (plasters, painkillers, non-adherent dressing pad, safety pin, scissors)	
*Midge head-net	
Toothbrush & toothpaste	
*Trowel	400g
*Ice Axe	1kg
*Crampons	1kg

Indicative total weight: 14.9kg

* indicates items not carried for the duration of the walk.
† indicates items of variable weight.

Worn-out boots (set 1 of 7).

Appendix 3: Itinerary

Day	Date	Route (with county tops noted in italics)	Distance (miles)	Ascent (metres)
1	Tues 7th March	John O'Groats to Hastigrow	15	290
2	Wed 8th March	Hastigrow to Loch More	20	270
3	Thurs 9th March	Loch More to Small Mount *Morven (County Top of Caithness, ND 005 285, 706m)*	20	1,020
4	Fri 10th March	Small Mount to Loch Badanloch	20	340
5	Sat 11th March	Loch Badanloch to Bun nan Tri-allt	15	500
6	Sun 12th March	Bun nan Tri-allt to Lairg	14	70
7	Mon 13th March	Rest day in Lairg		
8	Tues 14th March	Lairg to Glen Cassley	21	400
9	Wed 15th March	Round trip from Glen Cassley *Ben More Assynt (County Top of Sutherland, NC 318 201, 998m)*	10	950
10	Thurs 16th March	Glen Cassley to Culrain	22	330
11	Fri 17th March	Culrain to Srath Mòr	20	710
12	Sat 18th March	Srath Mòr to Conon Bridge	15	240
13	Sun 19th March	Rest day in Conon Bridge		
14	Mon 20th March	Conon Bridge to Cannich	24	630
15	Tues 21st March	Cannich to Glen Affric	19	630
16	Wed 22nd March	Round trip from Glen Affric *Càrn Eighe (County Top of Ross and Cromarty, NH 124 262, 1,183m)*	13	1,300

Day	Date	Route (with county tops noted in italics)	Distance (miles)	Ascent (metres)
17	Thurs 23rd March	Glen Affric to Loch na Beine Baine	19	750
18	Fri 24th March	Loch na Beine Baine to Fort Augustus	12	430
19	Sat 25th March	Rest day in Fort Augustus		
20	Sun 26th March	Fort Augustus to Glen Markie	20	1,030
21	Mon 27th March	Glen Markie to Slochd Summit	22	480
22	Tues 28th March	Slochd Summit to the Haughs of Cromdale *Carn Glas-choire (County Top of* *Nairnshire, NH 892 292, 659m)*	22	600
23	Wed 29th March	The Haughs of Cromdale to Tomintoul *Carn a'Ghille Chearr (County Top of* *Morayshire, NJ 140 298, 710m)*	14	760
24	Thurs 30th March	Rest day in Tomintoul		
25	Fri 31st March	Tomintoul to West Milton Burn	21	580
26	Sat 1st April	West Milton Burn to Glen Tanar	15	330
27	Sun 2nd April	Glen Tanar to Glen Esk *Mount Battock (County Top of* *Kincardineshire,* *NO 550 845, 778m)*	18	1,070
28	Mon 3rd April	Glen Esk to Glen Doll	18	1,050
29	Tues 4th April	Glen Doll to Braemar *Glas Maol (County Top of Angus,* *NO 167 766, 1068m)*	18	900
30	Wed 5th April	Rest day in Braemar		
31	Thurs 6th April	Braemar to Luibeg Bridge *Ben Macdui (County Top of* *Aberdeenshire & Banffshire,* *NN 989 989, 1,309m)*	18	1,160

APPENDIX: ITINERARY

Day	Date	Route (with county tops noted in italics)	Distance (miles)	Ascent (metres)
32	Fri 7th April	Luibeg Bridge to Insh	22	670
33	Sat 8th April	Insh to Loch Pattack	27	590
34	Sun 9th April	Loch Pattack to Loch Ossian	14	390
35	Mon 10th April	Loch Ossian to Glen Nevis	19	420
36	Tues 11th April	Round trip from Glen Nevis *Ben Nevis (County Top of Inverness-shire, NN 167 713, 1,345m)*	8	1,330
37	Wed 12th April	Rest day in Glen Nevis		
38	Thurs 13th April	Glen Nevis to Glen Coe	20	950
39	Fri 14th April	Round trip from Glen Coe *Bidean nam Bian (County Top of Argyllshire, NN 143 542, 1,149m)*	12	1,370
40	Sat 15th April	Glen Coe to Loch Laidon	20	670
41	Sun 16th April	Loch Laidon to Allt Baile a'Mhuilinn	21	610
42	Mon 17th April	Alt Baile a'Mhuilinn to Killin *Ben Lawers (County Top of Perthshire, NN 636 414, 1,214m)*	17	1,260
43	Tues 18th April	Rest day in Killin		
44	Wed 19th April	Killin to Strath Dubh Uisge	22	640
45	Thurs 20th April	Strath Dubh Uisge to Inversnaid *Ben Vorlich (County Top of Dunbartonshire, NN 295 125, 943m)*	16	1,120
46	Fri 21st April	Inversaid to Balmaha *Ben Lomond (County Top of Stirlingshire, NN 367 029, 974m)*	17	1,280
47	Sat 22nd April	Balmaha to Dumbarton	18	610
48	Sun 23rd April	Dumbarton to Muirshiel	19	630

Day	Date	Route (with county tops noted in italics)	Distance (miles)	Ascent (metres)
49	Mon 24th April	Muirshiel to Locher Water *Hill of Stake (County Top of* *Renfrewshire, NS274 630, 522m)*	15	540
50	Tues 25th April	Locher Water to Glasgow	18	250
51	Wed 26th April	Glasgow to the Campsie Fells	19	780
52	Thurs 27th April	Campsie Fells to Stirling	19	550
53	Fri 28th April	Rest day in Stirling		
54	Sat 29th April	Stirling to Maiden's Well *Ben Cleuch (County Top of* *Clackmannanshire,* *NN 903 006, 721m)*	19	1,020
55	Sun 30th April	Maiden's Well to Kinross *Innerdouny Hill (County Top of* *Kinross-shire, NO 032 073, 497m)*	17	500
56	Mon 1st May	Kinross to Loch Gelly *West Lomond (County Top of* *Fife, NO 197 066, 522m)*	24	650
57	Tues 2nd May	Loch Gelly to Newbridge	16	260
58	Wed 3rd May	Round trip from Newbridge *Cairnpapple Hill (County Top of* *West Lothian, NS 988 711, 312m)*	20	360
59	Thurs 4th May	Newbridge to the Pentland Hills	14	620
60	Fri 5th May	Not-quite-a-rest-day in Penicuik	9	160
61	Sat 6th May	Penicuik to Hartside Hill *Blackhope Scar (County Top of* *Midlothian, NT 315 483, 651m)*	22	780
62	Sun 7th May	Hartside Hill to Dye Water *Meikle Says Law (County Top of* *Berwickshire & East Lothian,* *NT 581 616, 532m and* *NT 581 617, 535m)*	20	690
63	Mon 8th May	Dye Water to Sweethope Hill	16	390

Day	Date	Route (with county tops noted in italics)	Distance (miles)	Ascent (metres)
64	Tues 9th May	Sweethope Hill to Kirk Yetholm	13	320
65	Wed 10th May	Round trip from Kirk Yetholm *Cairn Hill West Top (County Top of Roxburghshire, NT 896 193, 743m) and The Cheviot, (County Top of Northumberland, NT 909 205, 815m)*	20	1,380
66	Thurs 11th May	Kirk Yetholm to Jedburgh	15	600
67	Fri 12th May	Rest day in Jedburgh		
68	Sat 13th May	Jedburgh to Borthwickbrae	21	720
69	Sun 14th May	Borthwickbrae to Gameshope Burn *White Coomb (County Top of Dumfriesshire, NT 163 151, 821m)*	25	1,390
70	Mon 15th May	Gameshope Burn to Kingledors Burn *Broad Law (County Top of Selkirkshire and Peeblesshire, NT 146 235, 840m)*	15	760
71	Tues 16th May	Kingledors Burn to Abington *Culter Fell (County Top of Lanarkshire, NT 053 291, 748m)*	20	1,170
72	Wed 17th May	Abington to Cloud Hill	21	1,350
73	Thurs 18th May	Cloud Hill to Coran of Portmark	21	530
74	Fri 19th May	Coran of Portmark to Glen Trool *Kirriereoch Hill (County Top of Ayrshire, NX 419 871, 782m) and The Merrick, (County Top of Kirkcudbrightshire, NX 428 855, 843m)*	19	1,230
75	Sat 20th May	Round trip from Glen Trool *Craigairie Fell (County Top of Wigtownshire, NX 236 737, 321m)*	26	640
76	Sun 21st May	Glen Trool to Clatteringshaws Loch	14	520
77	Mon 22nd May	Clatteringshaws Loch to Walton Park	24	610

267

Day	Date	Route (with county tops noted in italics)	Distance (miles)	Ascent (metres)
78	Tues 23rd May	Walton Park to Dumfries	17	290
79	Wed 24th May	Rest day in Dumfries		
80	Thurs 25th May	Dumfries to Gretna Green	26	240
81	Fri 26th May	Gretna Green to Armathwaite	20	360
82	Sat 27th May	Armathwaite to Burnhope Seat *Burnhope Seat (County Top of* *County Durham, NY 788 375, 746m)*	23	1,180
83	Sun 28th May	Burnhope Seat to Cow Green Reservoir *Mickle Fell (County Top of North Riding* *of Yorkshire, NY 806 245, 790m)*	18	630
84	Mon 29th May	Cow Green Reservoir to Dufton	9	260
85	Tues 30th May	Dufton to Shap	15	460
86	Wed 31st May	Shap to Patterdale	14	960
87	Thurs 1st June	Patterdale to Grasmere *Helvellyn (County Top of* *Westmorland, NY 342 151, 950m)*	10	980
88	Fri 2nd June	Grasmere to Moasdale *Scafell Pike (County Top of* *Cumberland, NY 216 072, 978m)*	12	1,460
89	Sat 3rd June	Moasdale to Blawith *Old Man of Coniston (County Top of* *Lancashire, SD 272 978, 803m)*	14	1,000
90	Sun 4th June	Blawith to Whitbarrow Scar	16	800
91	Mon 5th June	Whitbarrow Scar to Killington Lake	13	480
92	Tues 6th June	Killington Lake to Flinter Gill	11	510
93	Wed 7th June	Flinter Gill to Langstrothdale *Whernside (County Top of West* *Riding of Yorkshire,* *SD 738 814, 736m)*	20	1,050

APPENDIX: ITINERARY

Day	Date	Route (with county tops noted in italics)	Distance (miles)	Ascent (metres)
94	Thurs 8th June	Langstrothdale to Scar House Reservoir	16	550
95	Fri 9th June	Scar House Reservoir to Home	22	430
96-97	Sat 10th & Sun 11th June	Rest days at home		
98	Mon 12th June	Home to York	26	250
99	Tues 13th June	York to Pocklington *Bishop Wilton Wold (County Top of the East Riding of Yorkshire, SE 822 570, 248m)*	25	360
100	Wed 14th June	Pocklington to Elloughton Dale	22	460
101	Thurs 15th June	Elloughton Dale to Normanby Top *Normanby Top (County Top of Lincolnshire, Parts of Lindsey, TF 121 965, 168m)*	30	600
102	Fri 16th June	Normanby Top to Gainsborough	27	260
103	Sat 17th June	Rest day in Gainsborough		
104	Sun 18th June	Gaisborough to Clumber Park	22	300
105	Mon 19th June	Clumber Park to Tibshelf *Newtonwood Lane (County Top of Nottinghamshire, SK 456 606, 205m)*	17	310
106	Tues 20th June	Tibshelf to Stanage Edge	26	900
107	Wed 21st June	Stanage Edge to Crowden	19	710
108	Thurs 22nd June	Round trip from Crowden *Black Hill (County Top of Cheshire, SE 077 046, 582m)*	9	470
109	Fri 23rd June	Crowden to Hope *Kinder Scout (County Top of Derbyshire, SK 085 876, 636m)*	18	930
110	Sat 24th June	Rest day in Hope		

Day	Date	Route (with county tops noted in italics)	Distance (miles)	Ascent (metres)
111	Sun 25th June	Hope to the Roaches *Cheeks Hill (County Top of* *Staffordshire, SK 026 699, 520m)*	19	800
112	Mon 26th June	The Roaches to Sandbach	18	400
113	Tues 27th June	Sandbach to Raw Head	21	360
114	Wed 28th June	Raw Head to Hope	21	490
115	Thurs 29th June	Hope to Moel Famau *Moel Famau (County Top of* *Flintshire, SJ 161 627, 555m)*	15	770
116	Fri 30th June	Moel Famau to Llyn Brenig	16	620
117	Sat 1st July	Llyn Brenig to Betws-y-Coed	18	480
118	Sun 2nd July	Rest day in Betws-y-Coed		
119	Mon 3rd July	Betws-y-Coed to Gyrn	17	1,330
120	Tues 4th July	Gyrn to Llyn Cefni	18	450
121	Wed 5th July	Llyn Cefni to Holyhead *Holyhead Mountain (County Top of* *Anglesey, SH 219 829, 220m)*	20	490
122	Thurs 6th July	Holyhead to Bangor	26	410
123	Fri 7th July	Bangor to Nant Gwynant *Snowdon (Yr Wyddfa)* *(County Top of Caernarfonshire,* *SH 610 544, 1,085m)*	19	1,440
124	Sat 8th July	Nant Gwynant to Afon Taihirion	16	1.090
125	Sun 9th July	Afon Taihirion to Cadair Berwyn *Moel Sych (County Top of* *Montgomeryshire, SJ 066 319, 827m)* *and Cadair Berwyn (County Top of* *Denbighshire, SJ 072 324, 832m)*	23	1,000
126	Mon 10th July	Cadair Berwyn to Bala	12	200

APPENDIX: ITINERARY

Day	Date	Route (with county tops noted in italics)	Distance (miles)	Ascent (metres)
127	Tues 11th July	Rest day in Bala		
128	Wed 12th July	Bala to Mallwyd *Aran Fawddwy (County Top of Merionethshire, SH 863 224, 905m)*	19	1,200
129	Thurs 13th July	Mallwyd to Pumlumon Fawr *Pumlumon Fawr (County Top of Cardiganshire, SN 790 869, 752m)*	24	1,320
130	Fri 14th July	Pumlumon Fawr to Cors Caron	19	480
131	Sat 15th July	Cors Caron to Llanybydder	21	340
132	Sun 16th July	Llanybydder to Dre-Fach Felindre	16	620
133	Mon 17th July	Dre-Fach Felindre to Foel Cwmcerwyn *Foel Cwmcerwyn (County Top of Pembrokeshire, SN 094 312, 536m)*	18	760
134	Tues 18th July	Foel Cwmcerwyn to Carmarthen	25	720
135	Wed 19th July	Rest day in Carmarthen		
136	Thurs 20th July	Carmarthen to Ponarddulais	21	900
137	Fri 21st July	Ponarddulais to Carn Caca	18	580
138	Sat 22nd July	Carn Caca to Nedd Fechan *Craig y Llyn (County Top of Glamorgan, SN 907 032, 600m)*	20	940
139	Sun 23rd July	Nedd Fechan to Sarn Helen *Fan Foel (County Top of Carmarthenshire, SN 821 223, 781m)*	23	1,180
140	Mon 24th July	Sarn Helen to Danywenallt *Pen y Fan (County Top of Brecknockshire, SO 012 216, 886m)*	19	1,370
141	Tues 25th July	Danywenallt to Llanthony *Chwarel y Fan (County Top of Monmouthshire, SO 258 294, 679m)*	21	1,060
142	Wed 26th July	Llanthony to Glasbury *Black Mountain (County Top of Herefordshire, SO 256 350, 703m)*	14	560

Day	Date	Route (with county tops noted in italics)	Distance (miles)	Ascent (metres)
143	Thurs 27th July	Rest day in Glabury		
144	Fri 28th July	Glasbury to Great Rhos *Great Rhos (County Top of Radnorshire, SO 182 639, 660m)*	22	1,060
145	Sat 29th July	Great Rhos to Aymestry	17	540
146	Sun 30th July	Aymestry to Brown Clee Hill *Brown Clee Hill (County Top of Shropshire, SO 594 867, 540m)*	21	930
147	Mon 31st July	Brown Clee Hill to Woodbury Hill	23	800
148	Tues 1st Aug	Woodbury Hill to Great Malvern *Worcestershire Beacon (County Top of Worcestershire, SO 769 452, 425m)*	18	980
149	Wed 2nd Aug	Great Malvern to Cleeve Hill *Cleeve Hill (County Top of Gloucestershire, SO 997 246, 330m)*	24	460
150	Thurs 3rd Aug	Cleeve Hill to Broadway	22	590
151	Fri 4th Aug	Broadway to Alveston *Ebrington Hill (County Top of Warwickshire, SP 188 426, 261m)*	21	410
152	Sat 5th Aug	Rest day in Alveston		
153	Sun 6th Aug	Alveston to Napton-on-the-Hill	19	320
154	Mon 7th Aug	Napton-on-the-Hill to Rugby *Arbury Hill (County Top of Northamptonshire, SP 540 588, 225m) and Big Hill, Staverton Clump (County Top of Northamptonshire, SP 549 612, 225m)*	21	360
155	Tues 8th Aug	Rugby to Leicester Forest East	23	320
156	Wed 9th Aug	Leicester Forest East to Birstall *Bardon Hill (County Top of Leicestershire, SK 460 132, 278m)*	23	530

Day	Date	Route (with county tops noted in italics)	Distance (miles)	Ascent (metres)
157	Thurs 10th Aug	Birstall to Whissendine *Cold Overton Park (County Top of Rutland, SK 827 085, 197m)*	24	440
158	Fri 11th Aug	Whissendine to Callan's Lane Wood *Viking Way (County Top of Lincolnshire, Parts of Kesteven, SK 890 237, 151m)*	22	310
159	Sat 12th Aug	Callan's Lane Wood to Spalding *Pinchbeck Marsh (County Top of Lincolnshire, Parts of Holland, TF 279 286, 8m)*	21	110
160	Sun 13th Aug	Spalding to Stamford	20	150
161	Mon 14th Aug	Stamford to Bedford Purlieus *Racecourse Road (County Top of Northamptonshire, Soke of Peterborough, TF 035 042, 81m)*	8	130
162	Tues 15th Aug	Bedford Purlieus to Molesworth	19	220
163	Wed 16th Aug	Molesworth to Houghton Mill *Boring Field (County Top of Huntingdonshire, TL 049 713, 81m)*	23	220
164	Thurs 17th Aug	Houghton Mill to Ely *Haddenham village (County Top of Cambridgeshire, Isle of Ely, TL 467 752, 39m)*	20	150
165	Fri 18th Aug	Ely to Everett's Farm	25	150
166	Sat 19th Aug	Everett's Farm to Swanton Morley	22	240
167	Sun 20th Aug	Swanton Morley to Sheringham	23	270
168	Mon 21st Aug	Rest day in Sheringham		
169	Tues 22nd Aug	Sheringham to Norwich *Beacon Hill (County Top of Norfolk, TG 184 414, 105m)*	29	340
170	Wed 23rd Aug	Norwich to Scole	28	340

Day	Date	Route (with county tops noted in italics)	Distance (miles)	Ascent (metres)
171	Thurs 24th Aug	Scole to Ringshall	23	280
172	Fri 25th Aug	Ringshall to Brighthouse Farm *Wattisham Airfield (County Top of East Suffolk, TM 024 502, 91m)*	19	270
173	Sat 26th Aug	Brighthouse Farm to Haverhill *Great Wood (County Top of West Suffolk, TL 785 559, 128m)*	19	300
174	Sun 27th Aug	Haverhill to Great Chishill	19	370
175	Mon 28th Aug	Great Chishill to Baldock *Great Chishill (County Top of Cambridgeshire, TL 427 386, 146m) and Chishill Common (County Top of Essex, TL 443 362, 147m)*	22	300
176	Tues 29th Aug	Baldock to Dunstable	22	410
177	Wed 30th Aug	Not-quite-a-rest day in Dunstable *Dunstable Downs (County Top of Bedfordshire, TL 009 194, 243m)*	7	210
178	Thurs 31st Aug	Dunstable to Chequers *Pavis Wood (County Top of Hertford-shire, SP 914 091, 244m) and Wendover Woods (County Top of Buckinghamshire, SP 891 091, 267m)*	19	620
179	Fri 1st Sept	Chequers to Dell's Wood *Bald Hill (County Top of Oxfordshire, SU 729 958, 257m)*	17	570
180	Sat 2nd Sept	Dell's Wood to Black Jack's Mill	20	330
181	Sun 3rd Sept	Black Jack's Mill to Central London *Bushey Heath (County Top of Mid-dlesex, TQ 151 939, 154m) and Hampstead Heath (County Top of London, TQ 263 865, 134m)*	23	450
182	Mon 4th Sept	Central London to Bromley	15	470
183	Tues 5th Sept	Bromley to Redhill *Betsom's Hill (County Top of Kent, TQ 436 564, 251m)*	24	730

Day	Date	Route (with county tops noted in italics)	Distance (miles)	Ascent (metres)
184	Wed 6th Sept	Redhill to Holmbury St Mary *Leith Hill (County Top of Surrey, TQ 139 432, 295m)*	14	500
185	Thurs 7th Sept	Rest day in Holmbury St Mary		
186	Fri 8th Sept	Holmbury St Mary to Ebernoe Common *Black Down (County Top of West Sussex, SU 920 296, 280m)*	24	550
187	Sat 9th Sept	Ebernoe Common to Truleigh Hill	23	540
188	Sun 10th Sept	Round trip from Truleigh Hill *Ditchling Beacon (County Top of East Sussex, TQ 332 131, 248m)*	17	720
189	Mon 11th Sept	Truleigh Hill to Glatting Beacon	20	700
190	Tues 12th Sept	Glatting Beacon to Tegdown Hill	22	1,000
191	Wed 13th Sept	Tegdown Hill to Winchester	20	440
192	Thurs 14th Sept	Rest day in Winchester		
193	Fri 15th Sept	Winchester to Binley	20	460
194	Sat 16th Sept	Binley to East Kennet *Pilot Hill (County Top of Hampshire, SU 398 602, 286m) and Walbury Hill (County Top of Berkshire, SU 374 616, 297m)*	27	630
195	Sun 17th Sept	East Kennet to Coulston Hill *Milk Hill (County Top of Wiltshire, SU 104 643, 294m)*	18	440
196	Mon 18th Sept	Coulston Hill to Mere	19	370
197	Tues 19th Sept	Mere to Sherborne	20	370
198	Wed 20th Sept	Sherborne to Thorncombe *Lewesdon Hill (County Top of Dorset, ST 438 012, 279m)*	25	770
199	Thurs 21st Sept	Thorncombe to Wellington	23	600

Day	Date	Route (with county tops noted in italics)	Distance (miles)	Ascent (metres)
200	Fri 22nd Sept	Wellington to Wheddon Cross	26	980
201	Sat 23rd Sept	Wheddon Cross to South Molton *Dunkery Beacon (County Top of Somerset, SS 892 416, 519m)*	18	740
202	Sun 24th Sept	South Molton to Sampford Courtenay	23	780
203	Mon 25th Sept	Sampford Courtenay to Betty Cottles Inn *High Willhays (County Top of Devon, SX 580 892, 621m)*	13	660
204	Tues 26th Sept	Rest day in Okehampton		
205	Wed 27th Sept	Betty Cottles Inn to Launceston	20	610
206	Thurs 28th Sept	Launceston to Trehudreth Downs *Brown Willy (County Top of Cornwall, SX 159 800, 420m)*	21	670
207	Fri 29th Sept	Tredhudreth Downs to the Eden Project	17	490
208	Sat 30th Sept	Rest day at the Eden Project		
209	Sun 1st Oct	The Eden Project to Wheal Rose	26	770
210	Mon 2nd Oct	Wheal Rose to Penzance	21	470
211	Tues 3rd Oct	Penzance to Land's End	13	320

Bibliography

Adams, Anna, 'Walking Downhill, High Cup Nick' in *Speak to the Hills: An Anthology of 20th Century British and Irish Mountain Poetry*, edited by Hamish Brown and Martyn Berry, p.251. (Aberdeen: Aberdeen University Press 1985).

Akhmatova, Anna, *I Asked the Cuckoo* (1919).

Anderson, Benedict, *Imagined Communities: Reflections on the Origin and Spread of Nationalism* (London: Verso (1983).

Anderson, Peter, and George Anderson, *Guide to the Highlands and Islands of Scotland: Including Orkney and Zetland* (Edinburgh: A. & C. Black 1827).

Association of British Counties, 'The problem of "county confusion" – and how to resolve it' http://county-wise.org.uk/counties/county-confusion/.

Bathurst, David, *Walking the County High Points of England* (Chichester, West Sussex: Summersdale, 2012).

Belloc, Hilaire, *Sonnets and Verse* (London: Duckworth, 1923).

Brown, Hamish, 'Choice', *Speak to the Hills: An Anthology of 20th Century British and Irish Mountain Poetry*, edited by Hamish Brown and Martyn Berry (Aberdeen: Aberdeen University Press, 1985), p.7.

Clarke, Mark, *High point* (Sheffield: Vertebrate, 2014).

Cobbett, William, *From Ryall, in Worcestershire, to Burghclere, in Hampshire* (1826).
   Norfolk and Suffolk Journal (1821).
   Ride, from Malmsbury, in Wiltshire, through Gloucestershire, Herefordshire, and Worcestershire (1826).

Conrad, Joseph, *Under Western Eyes* (London: Methuen, 1911).

'County Highs', *Country Walking*, no. 259 (February 2009), pp.26-37.

Cropper, Margaret, 'Up There', in *Collected Poems* (Kendal, Cumbria: Titus Wilson, 1958).

Database of British and Irish Hills, http://www.hills-database.co.uk/.

Day-Lewis, Cecil, *Noah and the Waters* (London: L. & V. Woolf, 1936).

Dunbar, John (ed.) *Sir William Burrell's Northern Tour*, (1758). Sources in Local History (No. 6) (East Linton: Tuckwell Press, 1997).

Eckersley, John E., *Echoes or Eckoes? (*York: John E. Eckersley, 2000).

Eliot, T. S., *Little Gidding* (London: Faber & Faber, 1942).

Fleet Foxes, 'Ragged Wood' Fleet Foxes (2008).

Fletcher, Colin, *The Thousand Mile Summer* (New York: Vintage, 1987).

Garner, Alan, *Strandloper* (London: Harvill Press, 1996).

Gingell, Dave.,'The Valley' in *Speak to the Hills: An Anthology of 20th Century British and Irish Mountain Poetry*, Hamish Brown and Martyn Berry (eds.) (Aberdeen: Aberdeen University Press, 1985), p.3.

Ginsberg, Allen, 'Wales Visitation' *New Yorker,* 11 May 1968.

Grass, Günter, *Dog Years* (New York: Harcourt, 1965).

Griffin, A. H., *Long Days in the Hills* (London: Robert Hale & Company, 1974).

Henderson, D. M., and J. H. Dickson (eds.) *A Naturalist in the Highlands: James Robertson, His Life and Travels in Scotland, 1767-1771* (Edinburgh: Scottish Academic Press, 1994).

Housman, Alfred Edward, *A Shropshire Lad* (London: K. Paul, Trench, Trübner, 1896).

Huc, Évariste Régis, *Travels in Tartary, Tibet and China: During the Years 1844-5-6.* Translated by William Hazlitt, Vol. 1. (London: National Illustrated Library, 1857).

Long Distance Walkers' Association, 'Hillwalkers' Register 3: The County Tops of England, Wales and Ireland', https://www.ldwa.org.uk/hillwalkers/register3.php.

MacCulloch, John, *The Highlands and Western Isles of Scotland... in Letters to Sir Walter Scott* (London: Longman, Hurst, Rees, Orme, Brown and Green, 1824).

Maconie, Stuart, *Never Mind the Quantocks* (Newton Abbot: David & Charles, 2012).

Marling, Laura, 'When Were You Happy (and How Long Has That Been)?' *Once I Was an Eagle* (Virgin, 2013).

Michal, M. L., 'From Skye, Early Autumn', in *Speak to the Hills: An Anthology of 20th Century British and Irish Mountain Poetry*, Hamish Brown and Martyn Berry (eds.) (Aberdeen: Aberdeen University Press, 1985), p.493

Mitchell, Ian, *Scotland's Mountains before the Mountaineers*, 2nd edition (Edinburgh: Luath, 2013).

Moss, Edward, 'The County Tops of England and Wales' *Rucksack Club Journal* XI, no. 4 (1951), pp.319-27.

Muir, Jonny, *The UK's County Tops: 82 Walks to Reach the Top of 91 Historic Counties* (Milnthorpe: Cicerone, 2011).

Nuttall, John, and Anne Nuttall, *The Mountains of England and Wales,* Vol. 1: Wales (Milnthorpe: Cicerone, 1989).
The Mountains of England and Wales, Vol. 2: England. (Milnthorpe: Cicerone, 1990).

Perrin, Jim. *On and off the Rocks* (London: Victor Gollancz, 1986).
Travels with the Flea: And Other Eccentric Journeys. 2nd edition (Glasgow: The InPinn, 2003).

Purvis, John Stanley, *'I Can't Forget the Lane That Goes from Steyning to the Ring'* (1916). See: http://steyningmuseum.org.uk/purvis.htm.

Robbins, Royal, 'Foreword', in *Mirrors in the Cliffs*, Jim Perrin (ed.) (London: Diadem, 1983), pp.13-15.

Ross, Charles, *Travellers' Guide to Loch Lomond* (Paisley, 1792).

Rossetti, Christina, *Later Life: A Double Sonnet of Sonnets*, (1881).

Round Tower Churches Society, http://www.roundtowers.org.uk.

Rousseau, Jean-Jacques, *Discourse on the Origin and Basis of Inequality among Men*, (1754).

Showell Styles, Frank,'From the Plains' in *Speak to the Hills: An Anthology of 20th Century British and Irish Mountain Poetry*, Hamish Brown and Martyn Berry (eds.) (Aberdeen: Aberdeen University Press, 1985), p.13. 'The Way Is the Way' *The Journal of the Midland Association of Mountaineers* IV, no. 4 (1966), pp.19-21.

Sidgwick, Arthur, *Walking Essays* (London: Edward Arnold, 1912).

Southey, Robert, *Thalaba the Destroyer* (London: Longman, 1801).

St John, Bridget, 'To B without a Hitch' *Ask Me No Questions* (Dandelion, 1967).

Steinbeck, John, *The Wayward Bus* (New York: Viking, 1947).

Striding Edge, 'Wrapped between Borders' *Borrowdale Johnny*, (2007).

Symonds, Hugh, *Running High: the first continuous traverse of the 303 mountains of Britain and Ireland* (Kirkby Stephen, Cumbria: Hayloft, 2004).

Thomas, Edward, *Beautiful Wales* (London: A. & C. Black, 1905).

Thoreau, Henry David, 'Walking' *Atlantic Monthly* IX, no. LVI (1862), pp. 657-74.

Turner, Jenny, 'Lost in the bush' *The Guardian*, 24 May 1996, p.A10.

Wainwright, Alfred, *The Southern Fells* (Kendal: *Westmorland Gazette*, 1960).

Waugh, Evelyn, *Brideshead Revisited*, (1945).

Wilson, Graham, *Tops of the North. Volume 1: Three Shire Head to Carlisle* (Disley, Cheshire: Millrace, 2008).
Tops of the North. Volume 2: Carlisle and the Cheviot to the Cat & Fiddle (Disley, Cheshire: Millrace, 2009).

Wordsworth, William, *Two-Part Prelude* (London, 1799).

ABOUT THE AUTHOR

Victoria Morris is an experienced mountaineer and long-distance walker. She has completed rounds of the Munros and Lakeland fells, as well as climbing notable peaks in the Arctic, Alps and Andes.

Born and brought up in the north west of England, Victoria now lives in North Yorkshire with her husband. She is a Chartered Librarian, a Fellow of the Royal Geographical Society, and in her spare time plays fiddle in a ceilidh band.